Library of
Davidson College

Peasants, Entrepreneurs, and Social Change

About the Book and Author

Following the 1952 revolution in Bolivia, both state and international aid agencies channeled capital and technology to regional elites for the development of large-scale cash-crop agriculture in the lowland frontier. In this book, the author examines the contradictory path taken by capitalist development in the region over the last thirty years, with a special emphasis on the role played by rural settlers.

Focusing on the establishment of frontier communities in the west-central Santa Cruz department, Dr. Gill analyzes how the cultivation of sugarcane and the growth of commerce led to changes in the composition of communities and to a reorganization of social and productive relationships. Expansion of the regional economy was accompanied by extensive migration into the region, and people from diverse geographical, economic, and cultural backgrounds were incorporated into an expanding web of commercial relationships as seasonal laborers, subsistence cultivators, and small-scale entrepreneurs. Their attempts to limit the effects of the boom-bust nature of the economy while taking advantage of new economic opportunities shaped the character of the new frontier society.

Lesley Gill received her Ph.D. in anthropology from Columbia University. She was a visiting fellow at the University of East Anglia in 1984-1985 and is currently affiliated with the Facultad Latinoamericana de Ciencias Sociales in La Paz, Bolivia.

Peasants, Entrepreneurs, and Social Change

Frontier Development in Lowland Bolivia

Lesley Gill

Westview Press / Boulder and London

303.4
G475p

Westview Special Studies on Latin America and the Caribbean

This Westview softcover edition is printed on acid-free paper and bound in softcovers that carry the highest rating of the National Association of State Textbook Administrators, in consultation with the Association of American Publishers and the Book Manufacturers' Institute.

All rights reserved. No part of this publication may be reproduced or transmitted in any form or by any means, electronic or mechanical, including photocopy, recording, or any information storage and retrieval system, without permission in writing from the publisher.

Copyright © 1987 by Westview Press, Inc.

Published in 1987 in the United States of America by Westview Press, Inc.; Frederick A. Praeger, Publisher; 5500 Central Avenue, Boulder, Colorado 80301

Library of Congress Cataloging-in-Publication Data
Gill, Lesley.
  Peasants, entrepreneurs, and social change.
  (Westview special studies on Latin America and
the Caribbean)
  Bibliography: p.
  Includes index.
  1. Agriculture--Economic aspects--Bolivia--Santa
Cruz (Dept.) 2. Santa Cruz (Dept.)--Commerce.
3. Sugarcane industry--Bolivia--Santa Cruz (Dept.)
4. Land settlement--Bolivia--Santa Cruz (Dept.)
5. Peasantry--Bolivia--Santa Cruz (Dept.)
6. Agriculture, Cooperative--Bolivia--Santa Cruz
(Dept.) 7. Social change--Bolivia--Santa Cruz
(Dept.) I. Title. II. Series.
HD1870.S25G54 1987   303.4'0984'3   86-28207
ISBN 0-8133-7339-5

Composition for this book was provided by the author.
This book was produced without formal editing by the publisher.

Printed and bound in the United States of America

 The paper used in this publication meets the requirements of the American National Standard for Permanence of Paper for Printed Library Materials Z39.48-1984.

6   5   4   3   2   1

Contents

List of Illustrations xi
Acknowledgments xiii

INTRODUCTION 1

    Frontier Expansion and Settlement 2
    Perspectives on Social Change 5
    Labor Organization and Peasant
      Production 8
    Method and Chapter Organization 13

1   FROM LATIFUNDIA TO AGRICULTURAL
    ENTERPRISE 19

    Early Settlement and Commercial
      Activity 24
    The Rubber Boom and the German Import-
      Export Houses 26
    The Chaco War and the National
      Revolution 29
    The United States and the Opening
      of the Oriente 36

2   THE EXPANSION OF CAPITALIST
    AGRICULTURE 47

    The Growth of Capitalist Agriculture
      in the 1960s 48
    Agricultural Credit in the 1970s 51
    Laying Private Claim to the Frontier 57
    Cash-Crop Production and Labor
      Acquisition 65

3	FRONTIER SETTLEMENT AND PROLETARIANIZATION	73

The Settlement Process and Land Acquisition ... 74
Immigration and Socioeconomic Differentiation ... 85
Decline of the Syndicates ... 90
Frontier Settlement in a Broader Context ... 94

4	PROLETARIANIZATION AND THE PEASANT HOUSEHOLD	99

Labor Costs for Peasants and Capitalist Producers ... 100
Wage Labor and Subsistence on the Frontier ... 104

5	SETTLERS BECOME ENTREPRENEURS	121

Sugarcane Production and Commerce ... 122
The Emergence of Small-Scale Agriculturalists ... 131

6	AGRICULTURAL COOPERATIVES AND RURAL DEVELOPMENT	147

The Formation of Community-Based Agricultural Cooperatives ... 148
Mechanization ... 155
Community Differentiation and Cane Grower Dominance ... 158
The Cooperative and the Poor Peasants ... 167
CCAM and Social Change ... 169

7	THE AGRO-INDUSTRIAL BOURGEOISIE, ECONOMIC CRISIS, AND THE COCAINE TRADE	173

Growth and Crisis in the Santa Cruz Agro-Industries ... 174
The Development of the Cocaine Trade in Santa Cruz ... 183

8	ECONOMIC CRISIS AND SOCIAL CHANGE IN THE 1980S	195

The Fall of the Military and the Rise
  of the UDP 196
Democratization and Economic Crisis 201

CONCLUSION 215

The Agrarian Reform in Northern Santa
  Cruz 217
Capitalist Development and Social
  Differentiation 218

Bibliography 225
Index 237

Illustrations

TABLES

1.1 U.S. Expenditures on Agricultural Development: Santa Cruz, 1953-1961 39

2.1 FRA-1 and FRA-2 Credit Disbursements, 1973-1978 54

2.2 Distribution of Commercial Bank Agricultural Loans by Department, 1973-1978 55

2.3 Annual Distribution of Credit by Purpose of Loan BAB, 1970-1978 56

2.4 Distribution of Properties Affected by the Agrarian Reform in Obispo Santiesteban Province, 1953-1975 59

2.5 The Sale of Land Grants over 2,000 Hectares in Obispo Santiesteban Province, 1971-1979 60

2.6 Land Accumulation in the Mineros Region of Obispo Santiesteban Province 64

4.1 Corn Production Costs, 1980-1981 101

6.1 Sources of CCAM Financial Assistance 153

FIGURES

1.1   Map of Bolivia 20

1.2   Department of Santa Cruz 21

1.3   Northern Santa Cruz 22

3.1   Syndicate Land 77

4.1   Accumulation of Syndicate Land 112

6.1   Organizational Structure of the
      Cooperative 152

PHOTOS

Settler Harvesting Rice 82

Woman Washing Clothes in Nuevo Mundo 103

Sugarcane Harvesters Loading Cane onto
a Truck 108

Rice Stored in a Field 126

River Crossing in Northern Santa Cruz 129

Cooperative Leaders 161

Acknowledgments

During the course of my research in Bolivia, I benefited from the support and encouragement of many people. My greatest debt is to the peasants of northern Santa Cruz, particularly those from the communities of Nuevo Mundo, Rio Viejo, and Paichanetu as well as the Central de Cooperativas Agropecuarias Mineros (CCAM). These men and women opened their homes to me, and they gave me hours of their time, despite the tasks demanded of them, to recount their experiences, their hopes and their frustrations. To them and especially to a few close friends--Iber Barriga, Adan Algaranaz, Regina Montero de Algaranaz, Sergio Quintela, Susano Terceros, Ramona de Mendoza, and Carlos Mendoza--I offer my warmest thanks. This book is dedicated to them.

I am also thankful to several people for their help and encouragement at different times and in different places. Phil Blair, Edith Klein, Lucas de Conik, Dudley Conneely, and Mary Revollo de Conneely were gracious hosts in Bolivia and always willing to help. I owe much, personally and intellectually, to my friends Susan Lowes, Ann Zulawski, Maria Lagos, Donna Plotkin, and Marc Edelman for providing support, ideas, and criticism over the last ten years. In addition, I have also benefited from the excellent advice and guidance of several scholars. Xavier Albo offered useful suggestions and a much-appreciated sense of humor. June Nash prodded me to finish, and without her support and involvement in my work, I could never have carried this project through to the end. Herb Klein's knowledge of Bolivia enriched my graduate studies at Columbia

University, and Lambros Comitas and George Bond played important roles in my training as an anthropologist. Vanalyn Green provided important editorial assistance, and Jose Bayro helped with the maps. Finally, I am grateful to my parents, Joan and Herbert Gill, for their patience and support and to Rodrigo Munoz-Reyes, who shared with me the joy of discovering northern Santa Cruz.

It would have been impossible for me to undertake research in Bolivia without financial assistance from the Inter-American Foundation, Columbia University, and the I.I.E. Fulbright Fellowship Program. These institutions all made contributions to support my doctoral dissertation that is the basis of this book, and their generous assistance is gratefully acknowledged. I am particularly grateful to Kevin Healy of the Inter-American Foundation for his interest in my research and his encouragement while I was in Santa Cruz.

In addition, I benefited from a Leverhulme USA/Commonwealth Visiting Fellowship in the School of Economic and Social Studies at the University of East Anglia (Norwich, England). Through this assistance, I had time to work on the manuscript and explore new ideas. The experience was not only academically valuable, but also personally rewarding. John and Marie Corbin, Rosemary Crompton, Kay Sanderson, Malcolm Moseley, Rhys Jenkins, Ruth Pearson, Juan Sanchez, and especially Lucila Haynes enriched my stay in Norwich and without them I would have written a much weaker study. I will always remember their care and their friendship.

The study, then, has been a collective effort that has involved many people. They are all responsible for the insights it might yield, and I thank them once again for their patience, support, and guidance.

Lesley Gill

Introduction

This book is a study of peasants and entrepreneurs in the frontier of eastern Bolivia. It examines the contradictory path that capitalist development took and the role rural settlers played in this process. It is specifically about the frontier communities in west-central Santa Cruz department and the evolution of peasant political consciousness over a thirty year period of economic expansion and contraction. When sugarcane cultivation was introduced and commerce was stimulated, a drastic reorganization of social and economic relationships occurred. Families were forced to respond to capitalist development with a combination of subsistence strategies that usually involved both wage earning and subsistence cultivation. More broadly, then, this book is an account of people caught in the throes of profound social transformation.

Following the 1952 revolution both the state and international-aid agencies channeled capital and technology to regional elites for the development of large-scale cash-crop agriculture. This support was the basis for the subsequent growth of a powerful regional bourgeoisie. The expansion of the regional economy also initiated a migratory process; people from diverse geographical, economic, and cultural backgrounds were incorporated into an expanding web of commercial relationships as seasonal laborers, subsistence cultivators, and small-scale capitalist entrepreneurs. The attempts of these people both to limit the effects of capitalist development on their daily lives and to take advantage of new economic opportunities shaped the character of the new frontier society. Their struggles are the central focus of this book.

FRONTIER EXPANSION AND SETTLEMENT

The penetration of capitalism into the tropical lowlands of Bolivia and other Latin American countries has never been a smooth process. It is frequently characterized by violent conflicts, as contending groups struggle to control land, labor, and capital (Foweraker: 1981; Schmink: 1982; Wood and Schmink: 1979; Duncan Baretta & Markoff: 1978). Social relationships are rearranged, and culturally diverse groups are often drawn into new patterns of production and social interaction (Shoemaker: 1981; Davis: 1977; Whitten: 1981). The contours of the new frontier societies are shaped by preexisting forms of social and political organization as well as the geographical, ecological, and demographic characteristics of a given area. International forces that affect the demand for agricultural commodities also play an important role in determining the nature and quality of social relationships (Weinstein: 1983).
There is a large body of literature that explores the highland and valley migrants' development of the Bolivian frontier, but these studies do not analyze the relationships of power and inequality that linked impoverished migrants to large-scale cash-crop producers and merchants (Fifer: 1967 and 1982; Zeballos: 1975; Crist and Nissley: 1973; Stearman 1985; Reye: 1970; Maxwell: 1980; Heath, Eramus & Buechler: 1969; Wessel: 1968; Henkel: 1984). Instead, the authors discuss the movement of populations from one geographic region to another and compare and contrast government-sponsored "directed" colonization projects with "spontaneous" settlements. Although such work provides insights into both the settlement process, migration, and formation of new communities, the latter is treated as a separate phenomenon, and the political and economic forces that structure

social relationships are ignored. The authors view change as an a-historical phenomenon that occurs as settlers "adapt" or "enculturate" themselves to the new tropical environment. Similarly, analyses that deal with the emergence of large-scale sugarcane, cotton, and beef production fail to specify how peasant families were drawn into the process as wage laborers, subsistence cultivators, and at times, small-scale entrepreneurs (e.g., Heath: 1959b; Fletcher: 1975).

Other research emphasizes the structural inequalities engendered by this type of development. Albo (1979) examines rural development after twenty-five years of agrarian reform and situates the difficulties encountered by settlers, seasonal wage laborers, and indigenous groups squarely within the contradictions arising from capitalist agricultural expansion. He makes the important--but often forgotten--point that large land grants ranging from 500 to 50,000 hectares to private individuals constitute another type of settlement, in contrast with the appropriation of ten- to fifty-hectare parcels by peasant settlers. This distribution policy establishes the basis for the inequalities between peasants and neolatifundists. Wiggens (1976) notes how peasant settlement zones in Chapare and Santa Cruz are frequently overtaken by more powerful commercial interests. Other articles by Green (1977 and 1978) and Riviere d'Arc (1980) discuss state policies towards the agro-industries and their consequences for rural people in the frontier zone. Finally, Clark (1974) outlines the land conflicts in cattle ranching areas, and Riester (1977 and 1979) assesses the situation of lowland indigenous populations and the disruption of their social organization.

This work contributes to our understanding of the process of social change affecting lowland Bolivia--particularly the department of Santa Cruz. The emergence of capitalist production relations, however, and the department's integration into national and international markets remain to be explored in greater depth. Also, the development of new social classes and the role played by rural people in this process must be understood with greater clarity.

This book attempts to answer a number of specific questions: What was the character of capitalist penetration in eastern Bolivia? How have state and international agencies shaped regional development? What has been the impact of thirty years of agrarian reform on the land tenure arrangements, and how have frontier communities developed and changed? In what way have land, labor, and capital been directed to and utilized by large capitalist producers and frontier settlers? What were the different conditions for each group reaching the frontier, and how did these conditions affect their relationships with each other? Also, how did the growth of the cocaine traffic affect the region, and finally what implications does capitalist expansion in this region have for class consciousness and future social change?

Marx's (1977) and Lenin's (1977) discussion of capitalist development and the emergence of free wage labor offers important guidance for understanding the social and economic changes affecting rural Bolivia. Their analyses of Europe and Russia in the late nineteenth and early twentieth centuries, however, cannot be mechanically applied to the social reality of contemporary Bolivia. Although capitalist development has transformed a large number of peasant producers into wage laborers in the department of Santa Cruz, the process has been neither steady nor complete.

My study shows that although agro-industrial expansion and the cocaine traffic enriched a small minority of landowners, military officers, and businesspeople, it did not lead to a unilinear transformation of the rural population from peasant to proletarian. A fluid relationship developed between subsistence cultivation and wage labor, with peasants moving in and out of both roles. Because subsistence agriculture continued to be viable and poor peasants' access to frontier land made labor scarce and expensive, the attempts of the state and the emergent regional bourgeoisie to institute large-scale capitalist agriculture were only partially successful. And, peasant resistance to proletarianization limited accumulation and the transformation of the regional economy.

The expansion of the regional economy also created the conditions for the emergence of an entrepreneurial group of small-scale agriculturalists in Santa Cruz, the members of which were often of peasant origin. Although they shared some of the concerns of the poor peasants, these people were primarily interested in increasing production for the market and improving their position as small-scale capitalist producers. By building on past accumulations and the work of original pioneers, they took advantage of new opportunities for profit and successfully established their own farming and commercial operations based on the exploitation of wage labor. Thus, they benefited from the integration of the frontier into the nation as well as taking advantage of the labor power of others and the emergence of new institutions to further their own ends. But the shaky foundations of these newly constituted, small-scale capitalist enterprises were tested by class conflict at the local level and an economic crisis that engulfed the entire country in the 1980s.

Ultimately, the tenuous nature of capitalist development in Bolivia hindered a total transformation of social relationships, and the regional bourgeoisie was unable to sustain the process of capital accumulation and transform production relationships. The response of poor peasants reflected the way class formation occurred in the region and was the outcome of the structural conditions that shaped frontier settlement and commercial agricultural development in eastern Bolivia.

PERSPECTIVES ON SOCIAL CHANGE

A new concern for social change and the situation of rural people in the so-called Third World developed following World War II. During the postwar expansion of the U.S. economy, many social scientists speculated about the inability of Latin American, Asian, and African nations to improve their standard of living. The dominant theoretical model that emerged in the advanced industrial nations to explain this phenomenon came from neoclassical economics and was called modernization theory. It divided nations into so-called traditional and modern sectors, with change occurring in the former only through the diffusion of new values and technological innovations from the latter.

Anthropological corollaries to this point of view emphasized acculturation and assimilation. In these studies (e.g., Redfield: 1941 and 1947; Tax: 1941; Foster: 1965; Erasmus: 1968; Lewis: 1966), social change or the lack of it was considered to be a functional explanation of a group's cultural characteristics. Culture was the shared images and beliefs of a group of people, and the basis for social transformation rested on the diffusion and adoption of cultural characteristics. Writers separated the culture concept from the social structure and social relationships that are integral to culture—focusing instead on the community as the unit of analysis (Silverman: 1979). The community was reified and treated as a separate social system—peasants remained conceptually outside the mainstream of society, and the notion of dual societies persisted.

Another line of investigation in North American anthropology was an attempt to transcend the sterile discussion about peasant society and conceptualize the links between the local level and the broader social system. This trend began with Steward (1955) and was continued by some of his students, who carried their analyses in new directions. Mintz (1953 and 1956) challenged Redfield's belief that cultural change occurred along a folk-urban continuum and attempted to formulate a definition for rural proletarians. Wolf (1956: 51) proposed that communities be viewed as "the local termini of a web of group relations which extend through intermediate levels from the level of the community to that of the nation." These articles challenged the notion of a homogeneous peasant community and called attention to power relationships beyond community boundaries. Yet as Roseberry (1978) has pointed out, such theories remain rooted in the tradition of community studies, having failed to conceptualize relationships with the more powerful social groups, state-level organizations, and foreign countries. Although Wolf and Mintz situated their communities within the framework of capitalist society, they still accepted the community as the unit of analysis, and their studies lacked a dynamic perspective to explain the development and spread of capitalist production relations.

The anthropological theories and sociology of development that emerged in the advanced industrial nations were shaped by the forces and events that structured social discourse at particular points in history. They often provided convenient and flattering justifications for the power and wealth attained by such countries as the United States at a time when it was emerging as a world power. Although certain anthropological studies suggested alternatives to these points of view, a powerful critique did not alter North American anthropology until the mid-1960s. Not surprisingly, this criticism did not originate in North American academia but from social scientists in Latin America.

Marxist in much of its interpretation, the new approach became known as dependency theory (Frank: 1969; Furtado: 1970; Dos Santos: 1973; Cardoso & Falleto: 1971). There were several conflicting interpretations under the heading of dependency theory, but the main contribution of these writers was that the study of development in Latin America could not be isolated from the growth of North American and European economies. Different sectors of Latin American nations, rather than constituting isolated parts of a dual society, were actually closely integrated because of their historical ties with the world market. Subsequently, other writers--stimulated by the dependency debate--attempted to move beyond an analysis of the circulation of commodities in an international market system. They wanted to understand the nature of production and the social and ideological relationships associated with different patterns of production.

In an approach similar to the early dependency writers--particularly Frank--Wallerstein (1974) argued for the existence of a single world economic system based on numerous forms of labor use and extraction and not limited by national or regional boundaries. Although the concept encountered many of the same difficulties as earlier analyses by focusing attention on circulation rather than production, it shared a similar aim: to understand how countries or regions in the Thrid World were subjugated by advanced industrial centers. The strength of world-systems analyses and the early work of the dependency writers lay in their emphasis on a single, world capitalist system, which helped them avoid the problem of relating parts of society to the whole. It has fallen to other authors to explain more systematically how the expansion of capitalism has drawn people into the production process in specific areas of the world.

LABOR ORGANIZATION AND PEASANT PRODUCTION

With the social unrest of the 1960s, there was an upsurge in Marxist scholarship among Western academics. Old debates were frequently recast in new terminology, but many novel explanations and fresh insights also were offered. Several authors investigated the historical, political, and economic relationships that gave rise to various forms of capitalism in Latin America (e.g, Duncan & Rutledge (eds.): 1977; Gudeman: 1978; Wasserstrom: 1983; Roseberry: 1983). These writers examined how land, labor, and capital have been combined to produce numerous patterns of labor organization.
To analyse the ways in which labor is organized in the process of capitalist development, Wolf (1982:74) has focused on the social relations of production. According to this author, the concept's utility lies in its ability to conceptualize the "social mobilization, deployment, and allocation of labor." Following this approach, my analysis of capitalist development in northern Santa Cruz concentrates

on the social relations of production. As Wolf (1978: 72) explains:

> the term 'social relation of production' designates the nexus, the link, the articulation between two terms: on the one hand the deployment of social labor - men in definite connections and relations with one another (Marx); on the other, the social allocation of the means of production - the resources of nature and the instruments available for their transformation for human use. The relation, the nexus, between these two terms sets up the field of force within which men carry on material production...

Within this perspective, peasant production is not a holdover from a bygone era. Rather, it is part of the entire range of social relations that constitute all of society.

It is necessary to explain what is meant by peasant and peasant production. Peasants are rural cultivators whose surpluses are appropriated by a dominant group that depends on peasant surpluses both to maintain themselves and to distribute among other groups (Wolf: 1966). Because of this domination, production is relegated to subsistence without capital accumulation, and peasants are forced to diversify their productive activities to include wage labor just to meet subsistence requirements (Warman: 1980).

Agriculture is the most important element in peasant production. A large part of each harvest is consumed by the household, but a portion also may be destined for sale during good years. This allows for a combination of use value and exchange value and permits a certain flexibility, which other activities, especially the sale of labor power, do not. In this context, the desire for land does not imply autonomy or self-sufficiency but does, however, reflect a need to control resources and meet subsistence needs. Since agriculture by itself is often not enough to subsist, other productive activities--particularly wage labor--are important pursuits, as well as the unpaid domestic labor of women and

children. Peasant production, therefore, is
characterized by the transference of a surplus to
a dominant group, which leads to the
diversification of productive activities and the
use of unpaid domestic labor (Warman: 1980).
    The income-generating strategies adopted by
peasants in response to broader structural
constraints are mediated through the domestic
unit and determined by the composition of the
peasant household [1]. Multiple strategies are
particularly important to resource-poor
households, where neither agriculture nor wage
labor alone fulfill all the material needs of the
individual members (Schmink: 1984). Although
adult men tend to concentrate on generating a
cash income, the domestic labor of women and
children produces important use values and plays
a crucial role in sustaining the work force in
the absence of higher wages and progressive state
policies (Birdsall & McCreevy: 1983; deJanvry:
1977). By carefully manipulating available
opportunities and exploiting resources, many
impoverished households remain viable even under
conditions of extreme hardship.
    This is not to suggest homogeneity or the
absence of divisions among peasants. Rural
communities in Latin America are highly
differentiated (e.g., Leeds: 1977; Roseberry:
1983; Deere: 1978; Adams: 1964) and have been for
some time (Mallon: 1983; Spalding: 1984). In
Santa Cruz, capitalist development caused people
from a variety of cultural and economic
backgrounds to form new kinds of relationships
with each other. The availability of international markets and fluctuations in world
commodity prices increasingly affected local crop
prices, and the boom-bust rhythms of the export
economy forced peasants to create new methods of
satisfying their most basic subsistence needs.
Work relations based upon reciprocity and
redistribution were undermined or redefined by
newly developing vertical alliances between
dominant and subordinate individuals and groups.
New concepts of ethnicity emerged, as contending
groups gained differential access to resources,
and poor peasants, small-scale agriculturalists,
and a powerful capitalist class manipulated these

notions to either include or exclude people from the rewards that economic growth brought to the region.

Also, the transition made by a number of families--often of peasant origins--from subsistence agriculture to small-scale capitalist production was an important aspect in the transformations that affected frontier settlers. Such families, along with other petty merchants and entrepreneurs, invested in sugarcane cultivation and commercial ventures by employing wage laborers and came to exercise considerable power at the local level. Nevertheless, peasants have not passed into the rural bourgeoisie or the proletariat with sufficient rapidity to posit their elimination (compare Feder: 1977) because of the special factors that characterize capitalist development in Santa Cruz.

In Santa Cruz, competition with capitalist farmers limited the ability of peasant producers to accumulate capital. Following the 1952 revolution, the intervention of the state and international banks and development organizations on the side of large landowners and investors allowed them to expand their operations at the expense of peasants. The greater size and more favorable location of capitalist enterprises permitted these producers to collect a differential rent not accrued to the peasant. Higher labor costs and the distance from market centers imposed more burdensome production expenses onto those peasant households seeking to expand cultivation beyond subsistence levels. Sugarcane quotas limited their access to the market, and dual price structures further curtailed the process of capital formation among peasants and reproduced their impoverishment.

But the growth of a full-fledged rural proletariat also has been slow to materialize. Peasant resistance and the adoption of multiple income-generating strategies protected households to a certain extent from complete proletarianization. The development of jobs outside the agricultural sector has been too slow to absorb a large number of people. The allotment-holding rural cultivator also provides an important subsidy for capitalist agriculture.

Employers can pay lower wages, and the maintenance and reproduction of the labor force remains the responsibility of the domestic unit. Moreover, the continued presence of virgin jungle land makes it possible for peasant households to reestablish themselves in more remote zones, once yields decline and cash-crop expansion forces them out of areas more closely tied to markets and commercial centers (see also LeGrand: 1984). Capitalist producers thus benefit from peasant labor invested in both land clearing, cutting access roads, and even cultivation.

Indeed, the ability of the capitalist enterprise to maintain a completely landless proletariat in Latin America, and particularly northern Santa Cruz, is problematic. The machinery and herbicides necessary for large-scale capitalist agriculture are more expensive than in the industrialized nations of Europe and North America. Agricultural machinery, herbicides, and other industrial products must be imported at great cost, and the international market for agricultural products is structured in favor of the advanced capitalist nations. Volatile world commodity prices can be manipulated and used as a political weapon by more powerful nations, and marketing channels are controlled by multinational corporations, which appropriate a large percentage of the revenues generated by commodity sales in North America and Europe.

Capitalist farmers in an underdeveloped country such as Bolivia produced profitably because they paid much less for land and labor than in developed nations. The state provided them with large extensions of land through the agrarian reform for little more than the cost of the paperwork necessary to gain title to their holdings, and during the peak of the cotton boom, the state helped planters to mobilize a labor force. International aid agencies also extended subsidized credit and technical assistance to large growers during the crucial early phases of agrarian expansion, and military governments granted concessionary loans and shielded debt-ridden growers unable to repay their credit. Throughout the process of capitalist expansion, the peasantry played an indispensable role by providing both their land and their labor at below the cost of subsistence.

Ultimately, however, indebtedness, a world recession, and the unwillingness of many peasants to participate in a process that brought them few benefits led in the late 1970s to a collapse of the economic boom. Cocaine production developed in response to a growing demand in North America and Europe. This new, "nontraditional" agro-export enriched a handful of military commanders and prominent lowland agriculturalists and offered lucrative employment opportunities to poor peasants and others suffering from the contraction of the legal agro-industries. But with the fall of the military and the return of democratic rule in 1982 drug traffickers no longer received state protection, and they relocated their operations. Northern Santa Cruz sank into a profound economic crisis characterized by one of the highest inflation rates in the world.

With the agro-industries in retreat and the military out of power, many peasants began to reassert their rights as subsistence cultivators and insist on higher pay for their labor. This time, the demands were the same for both peasants and proletarians because of the evolution of production relations in the region and the flexible relationship that developed between wage labor and subsistence agriculture. Peasant and capitalist production must not be viewed, therefore, as successive stages in a sequence of events. Subsistence production is neither backward nor a holdover from a previous mode of production. Rigid analytic distinctions between peasants and proletarians ignore the historical process of class formation that has shaped social relationships in Santa Cruz. This study shows that in contemporary eastern Bolivia both peasant production and capitalist agriculture are part of the same production process and are closely related and conditioned by each other.

METHOD AND CHAPTER ORGANIZATION

I conducted fieldwork for this investigation

from August 1980 to December 1982, and from August to October 1984. During the first month, I lived in La Paz, the nation's capital, gathering a wide variety of documentation from published sources and meeting with other social scientists, but because of the repressive political conditions that followed the military coup d'etat in July, I delayed the beginning of my fieldwork in the countryside. In late September, I traveled to Santa Cruz and made arrangements to live in Mineros, a provincial center located eighty kilometers north of the city of Santa Cruz. Through the help of a local cooperative in Mineros, I visited several rural communities in the following weeks and decided upon a site for my own research. The next eighteen months were spent in Mineros and three rural communities--Nuevo Mundo, Rio Viejo, and Paichanetu--attending cooperative meetings, conducting a household survey, and participating in the lives of the local people. Besides the community surveys, a great deal of my data came from the traditional anthropological methods of participant observation and interviewing. Several key individuals in both Mineros and the settlements helped this phase of the project by explaining my presence to other people and unraveling the complexities of local life for me.

As I became familiar with the surrounding region, I started to interview large landowners and sugarcane producers. They maintained homes in Santa Cruz, Montero, and Mineros and responded to my inquiries with a mixture of interest and mistrust. Many of their suspicions were partially relieved by my North American nationality and their present or past participation in U.S.-sponsored development projects or credit schemes. I believe they saw me as a potential conduit to North American organizations, and consequently, several people eagerly discussed their farming operations with me. A much smaller group was less willing to answer my questions. Its members often were linked to the illegal production of cocaine and suspected me of having ties to U.S. drug control operations. Bolivian-U.S. relations were particularly tense at this time because of the cocaine issue; several months earlier a major

drug figure was entrapped selling cocaine to
agents from the U.S. Drug Enforcement
Administration. Although consenting to interviews
in all but one case, this group was hesitant in
its dealings with me and much less forthcoming
with information.

In order to verify interviews and supplement
them with additional information, I consulted a
variety of secondary sources. Land records in the
agrarian reform offices of La Paz and Santa Cruz
and derechos reales were extremely valuable--as
were reports and statistical information gathered
from regional organizations. Such data not only
made it possible for me to check information but
also helped me to understand the broader pattern
of social change in the province and situate
individual landlords and peasants within this
process. Finally, conversations with seasonal
laborers, foremen, and truck drivers contributed
to my understanding of the entrepreneurial
activities of the large producers.

The last months of 1982 were spent
organizing data and drafting an outline of my
research findings. As questions arose in the
course of this analysis, I returned to Mineros
and the communities and contacted landowners in
order to overcome gaps in my information.
Additional conversations with Bolivian social
scientists and agronomists during this period
helped direct my thinking.

Almost two years later, in 1984, I had the
good fortune to return to Santa Cruz. I
encountered many changes: the return to a
democratic government in 1982 led to the
reorganization and reemergence of peasant unions
and popular organizations, and these groups had
become outspoken critics of the status quo. Also,
a severe economic crisis was reversing many of
the trends that I had noted in earlier years. I
spent two months reinterviewing previous
informants, traveling around northern Santa Cruz,
and talking with several leaders of the
reconstituted peasant organizations. It was easy
to see how the economic crisis was affecting
rural people and how they were struggling to deal
with it.

Following a description of the geographical

setting, Chapter One examines the way in which the 1952 national revolution, the agrarian reform, and the influx of U.S. economic assistance set the stage for large-scale agro-industrial development and laid the basis for the growth of a powerful regional bourgeoisie. My analysis focuses on the development strategy adopted by the state and the role of international aid organizations in shaping the emerging agrarian structure during the period from 1952 to 1964.

Chapter Two discusses the expansion of capitalist agriculture under military rule (1964-1978) and the incorporation of the frontier into large-scale cash-crop production. The military encouraged the growth of an agro-export sector in Santa Cruz and rewarded major agro-industrialists for their political support with land grants, concessionary credit, and favorable price policies. As production expanded growers relied increasingly on the highland peasantry for their labor needs, pressuring the state to assist them in mobilizing a labor force.

The third, fourth, and fifth chapters explore the settlement of the frontier by small holders and their integration into the emerging agrarian structure as wage laborers, subsistence cultivators, and small-scale entrepreneurs. The viability of local-level peasant organizations grew more problematic as internal differentiation and the rise of military rule undermined the ability of such groups to act as true representatives of rural people. As some families grew more marginalized, for example, they diversified their productive strategies to include a range of income-generating activities. Also, a group of more prosperous settlers took advantage of both the improvements made by the original pioneers and the opportunities offered by the regional economic boom to establish small-scale capitalist enterprises and commercial ventures. This led to greater class and ethnic conflict.

Chapter Six focuses on the way an internationally financed, agricultural cooperative strengthened--helped to create--a group of small-scale agriculturalists, which took the place of peasant syndicates as the most

important and influential local-level
organization. The cooperative emerged at a time
when military rule precluded independent
syndicate activity and avoided the syndicates'
broader political concerns by concentrating on
more narrowly defined technological issues. The
small-scale agriculturalists benefited from
cooperative services and utilized the new
"cooperative" ideology to justify their pursuit
of profit.

Chapter Seven examines the formation of a
powerful agro-industrial bourgeoisie and the
confirmation of a military-agro-industrial
alliance through the cocaine traffic. The
expansion of the regional economy and military
and international support during the two and a
half decades following the agrarian reform
allowed both the traditional upper class and a
new group of entrepreneurs to invest in
agriculture and urban-based commercial
activities. When their activities were threatened
by a world recession, many turned to the cocaine
traffic, which offered a lucrative alternative to
sugarcane and cotton cultivation. The cocaine
trade was a product of the social relations of
production established in previous decades, and
the involvement of key lowland agro-industrialists and military officers led to the rise of a
repressive military regime in 1980.

Finally, the last chapter explores the
impact of cocaine and the economic crisis on the
rural population. After the cocaine manufacturers
relocated their operations to more remote sites,
Santa Cruz was no longer the center of the drug
trade in Bolivia. But the legitimate agro-
industries continued to decline, and the region
entered a serious economic crisis. Peasant and
worker groups reorganized under the democratic
government and the process of proletarianization
began to reverse itself, as peasants more
forcefully pressed their demands for land, higher
wages, and technical assistance.

NOTES

1. The household or domestic unit refers to a

group of people who live together and share most aspects of consumption. To ensure their material reproduction, they distribute and utilize common resources which include labor (see Schmink: 1984).

1

From Latifundia to Agricultural Enterprise

The department of Santa Cruz is located in the extreme eastern portion of Bolivia. Although it's the largest department in Bolivia, embracing some 370,621 square kilometers, it contains only 15.4 percent of the population (see Figure 1.1). The department is primarily situated on an alluvial plain, with the rugged escarpment of the Andes rising almost 10,000 feet to mark its western limit. Santa Cruz includes temperate valleys in the west and the dry, savannah lands of the Grand Chaco in the south. The area referred to as northern Santa Cruz, or the integrated zone, occupies an intermediate subtropical region of the west central Santa Cruz department. It lies between the wet, tropical forests of the Amazon in the north and the arid Chaco to the south and is comprised of five provinces: Andres Ibanez, Warnes, Ichilo, Sara, and Obispo Santiesteban (see Figures 1.2 & 1.3). A dry winter season, with precipitation averaging less than fifty millimeters, extends from June to September. This period is characterized by strong winds from the south called surazos, which reach velocities up to fifty knots and produce sharp drops in temperature. The arrival of the November-March rainy season, when the majority of rainfall accumulates, brings warm, humid air from the Amazon. Rainfall varies considerably in the northern zone, ranging from 1130 millimeters annually in the city of Santa Cruz de la Sierra to over 2,000 millimeters in new settlement zones in the northwest.

    The Rio Grande and Rio Pirai are the two

Figure 1.1

Map of Bolivia

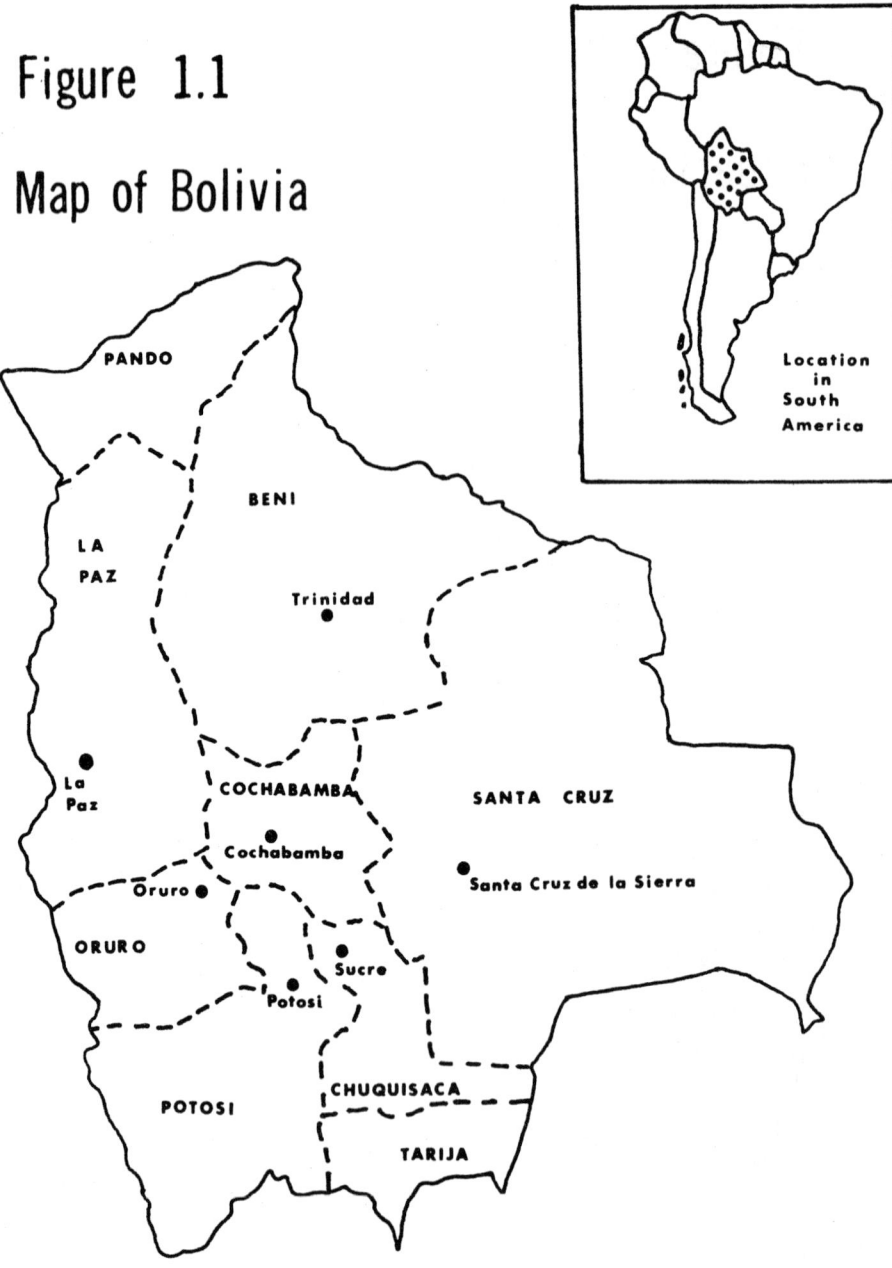

Figure 1.2

Department of Santa Cruz

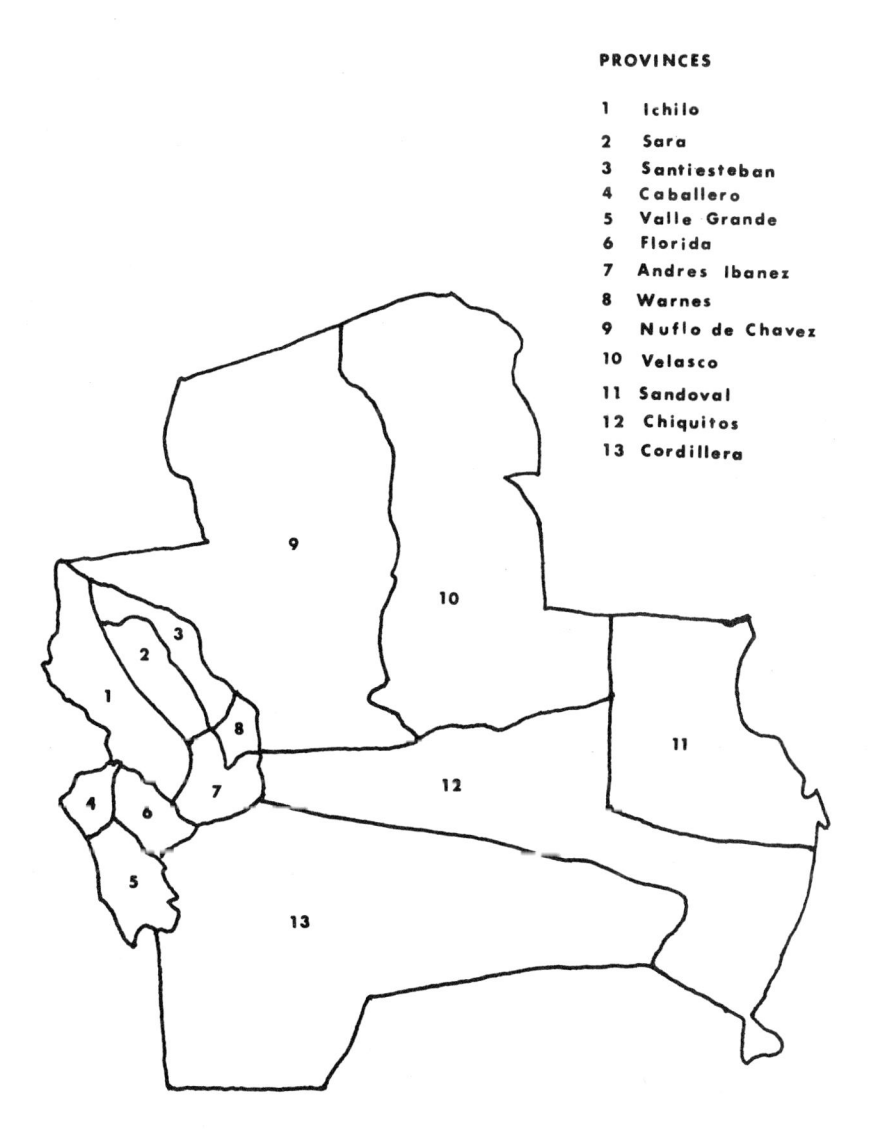

PROVINCES

1 Ichilo
2 Sara
3 Santiesteban
4 Caballero
5 Valle Grande
6 Florida
7 Andres Ibanez
8 Warnes
9 Nuflo de Chavez
10 Velasco
11 Sandoval
12 Chiquitos
13 Cordillera

FIGURE 1.3
NORTHERN SANTA CRUZ

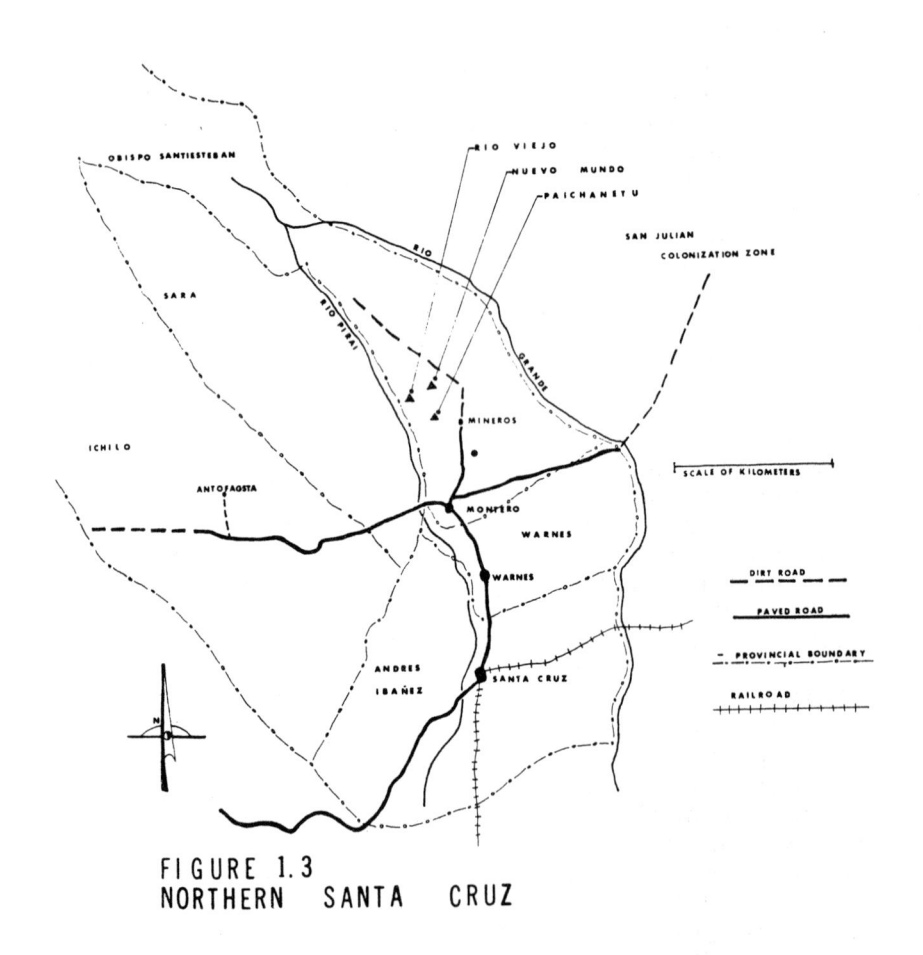

main waterways that traverse the area, although numerous rivers drain the flatlands. The rivers run northward from an altitude of about 1,430 feet at the departmental capital. The region's soil has its origins in these two rivers with textures varying in accordance with the distance earth has been transported. Soils between Santa Cruz and Montero are generally sandy and lighter in texture; those between Montero and Saavedra and extending eastward to the Rio Grande are heavier and more suitable for agricultural exploitation. Deposits laid down by the Pirai are relatively less fertile than those of the Rio Grande.

Two main transportation arteries intersect northern Santa Cruz. The city of Santa Cruz de la Sierra is linked to Montero and the Hardeman colony 160 kilometers to the north by a north-south highway, and an east-west road connects Puerto Grether on the Ichilo river with the Okinawa colony near the Rio Grande. Along the perimeter of these highways one sees only large commercial farms, as peasant families occupy the more remote and inaccessible areas. The region is suitable for a wide range of such agricultural products as cotton, sugarcane, and soybeans, which are all major cash crops. Beef cattle production also is an important economic activity, and corn, rice, cassava, tomatoes, and citrus fruits are grown primarily by small cultivators.

The province of Obispo Santiesteban is the most important sugarcane-producing region in the northern integrated zone as well as an important center for small-scale settlement. Two sugar mills--Guabira and the Union Agroindustrial de Caneros (UNAGRO)--and several rice mills operate in the province. The four rice mills in Mineros handle 60 percent of the provincial rice harvest, and two storage silos--one in San Pedro and the other in Chane Independencia--have a storage capacity of one hundred tons. According to the 1976 census the population consisted of some 78,719 individuals. Montero is the provincial capital with 28,647 inhabitants; Mineros, Villa Busch, Villa Fatima, General Saavedra, San Pedro, and Puesto Fernandez are other urban centers with

1,500 residents or more (INE:1977).
Santa Cruz is a major center of economic and political power. The city of Santa Cruz de la Sierra has a population of 277,791 and is part of the La Paz-Cochabamba-Santa Cruz commercial axis. Since the national revolution, agricultural expansion, petroleum production, and cocaine have given the department a new importance. The department satisfied national demand for rice, sugar, and beef in the 1960s and an 11 percent oil tax levied on all local petroleum production financed a variety of public works. Cocaine interests centered in Santa Cruz provided the financial backing for the July, 1980 coup d'etat of Luis Garcia Meza.

EARLY SETTLEMENT AND COMMERCIAL ACTIVITY

The eastern lowlands were populated by a number of indigenous groups before the first conquistadores set foot on Bolivian soil. The northern region, which the Spaniards subsequently called Grigota, was populated by the Chane, a sedentary, agricultural group later enslaved and displaced by the Guarani. The Spanish encountered the Guarani in 1561, after Nuflo de Chavez and a group of explorers had set out from Paraguay in search of a route to the highland silver deposits. When no satisfactory path was discovered, several settled on the flat, tropical plains of the lowlands, and founded the city of Santa Cruz. They were continually threatened by Indians, however, and at the end of the century, they were forced to move the city to its present location.
A small number of Spaniards gradually gained control over local Indian groups and organized settlements on cleared jungle land for sugar and rice production, cotton growing, and cattle ranching. By 1621, there were twenty-five centers which produced sugar for local consumption and sale in highland markets. A constant shortage of laborers led to the practice of capturing indigenous people in the northern Moxos region and forcing them to work for the nacent agricultural operations and in the homes of the

Spaniards (Sanabria: 1979).

The founding of Jesuit mission stations in the seventeenth century constituted a further shock to local indigenous populations. The Jesuits resettled Indians throughout the lowlands on reducciones, where native cotton and other crops were cultivated. The Jesuits pursued their work for over one hundred years, until their expulsion in the eighteenth century, and they permanently changed the nature of indigenous culture by forcing hunting and gathering peoples to adopt a sedentary lifestyle, Western dress, and Christianity.

There were brief periods during colonial rule and the first decades of the republic when such locally produced goods as sugar, coffee, rice, and hides appeared in highland markets as well as those of Buenos Aires, but transportation was very difficult and slow, since goods were generally shipped by mules over treacherous pathes (Sanabria: 1979). During the republican period, however, the treaties following the War of the Pacific and the advent of the tin boom in the nineteenth century brought this incipient intra-Bolivian trade to an end. The war that erupted in 1879 was the result of the gradual annexation of Bolivia's mineral-rich Atacama territory by Chilean settlers and entrepreneurs. With the defeat of Bolivian troops, the entire coastal territory was lost to Chile. This marked the end of long years of caudillo politics and signaled the beginning of a new, civilian-dominated political system that represented the interests of the emergent tin-mining elite. The civilian government appeared at a time of long-term rises in the price of tin and provided the political stability necessary for economic growth and expansion. The development of the tin industry was contingent upon the construction of a modern communication infrastructure, and rail links to the Pacific coast were built in the last decade of the nineteenth century following the establishment of peace with Chile and indemnification of lands occupied by the railroad (Klein: 1969).

The railroad allowed Bolivia to import cheaper and higher quality foodstuffs to the mining centers of Oruro and Potosi than those goods produced in the remote eastern lowlands. Moreover, a treaty signed between Bolivia and Peru in 1905 guaranteed Peruvian products a market in Bolivia by eliminating import taxes. Such goods competed directly with those produced in Santa Cruz and stifled lowland agriculture. Consequently, Bolivia became completely dependent upon foreign sources for almost all of its internal necessities, and this situation greatly enhanced the importance of the mining sector. The mines generated the foreign exchange necessary to import basic food requirements and squelched Santa Cruz agriculture by preventing the development of a new source of employment for low-paid miners (Klein: 1969).

THE RUBBER BOOM AND THE GERMAN IMPORT-EXPORT HOUSES

The rubber boom (1860-1914), which began in the department of Beni and the extreme northern portions of Santa Cruz department provided some outlet for agricultural products. Rice, for example, was transported to the Beni, where cultivation had declined because of the labor conscription for the rubber forests (Boletin de la Sociedad Geografica e Historica: 1906). The rubber boom also stimulated migration to the northern Amazonian jungle; some 80,000 people left Santa Cruz in search of quick profits. Landlords often forced their workers to accompany them on the long journey, and many people never returned.

The state sought to control the use of long-ignored jungle lands by instituting the Ley de Tierras Baldias. This law represented the first attempt to consolidate nominally populated frontier lands and tax the occupants. It required individuals to purchase their land claims in order to exploit the natural resources and allowed each individual to buy as much as 20,000 hectares for only one peso per hectare.

The brief demand for Santa Cruz products generated by the rubber boom was short-lived. The fall in world prices precipitated a crisis for the Bolivian rubber industry in 1914, and production never regained its former vigor. Also, the conclusion of the Madera-Mamore railroad permitted the importation of such cheaper, foreign agricultural products to the rubber zones as Chinese rice, Cuban sugar, and Brazilian coffee. Santa Cruz sunk into an economic depression, and agricultural production reverted to subsistence.

Formed during the rubber boom, the German import-export houses virtually controlled the commercial activity that existed in Santa Cruz during the first half of the twentieth century. The Casa Zeller, the Casa Schweitzer, and the Casa Elsner were founded by German immigrants from 1898 to 1910. They received large government land concessions and were thus able to control important rubber reserves in the province of Velasco and the Beni department. The houses functioned primarily as import-export institutions, exporting rubber to Europe and importing high-priced manufactured goods to Bolivia, but they also performed a variety of other services. Primary among these was their role as credit lenders. They granted loans to landlords; advanced high-priced imported goods to their own employees in lieu of a salary; and also supplied labor contractors with food and money for rubber gatherers who were then obliged to repay these loans in rubber. Such practices led to considerable debt and dependency among local people, and when the firms curtailed these activities after the decline in rubber and the onset of the Great Depression, the following commentary appeared in a local paper:

> The commercial houses, which purchased our earned assets until now, have suspended all such operations and transactions of this nature. We do not know the details which led the business to such a killing decision. (Ideas 15/9/30)

The houses diversified their activities when the rubber boom collapsed. The Casa Zeller purchased Las Barreras, a large estate near the town of Warnes that employed several hundred workers. The company operated a distillery that converted sugarcane to alcohol and aguardientes for local consumption. The Casa Elsner invested in extensive cattle production in the province of Cordillera and, along with the Casa Zeller, began to exploit numerous timber concessions scattered across northern Santa Cruz. Large mahogany reserves attracted the greatest attention; the timber industry, however, never achieved major significance because of the difficulties presented by transportation. The import-export houses marketed their products via Puerto Suarez, on the Brazilian border, and Yacuiba, on the Argentine frontier. Goods were then taken to coastal ports for shipment to Europe. The situation in 1906 was described as follows:

> The extremely bad roads to Puerto Suarez, exhausted in pasture and forage, a mudhole in the rainy season, without water in the dry season, where the poor traveler leaves his beasts annihilated from hunger and fatigue, dead from the plague, causes enormous transport costs for importer and exporter. Only the most noble articles such as rubber and gold are able to withstand the exorbitant costs of transportation. (Boletin de la Sociedad Geografica e Historica: 1906)

If the commercial houses received lower profits for their exported goods because of high transportation costs, the opposite occurred with the merchandise they imported to Bolivia, and complaints about this situation did not go unheard. In 1919 the prefect of Santa Cruz expressed the feelings of many local residents in his annual report:

> The majority of the import houses are German, remaining few with capital managed by sons of the country. Last year prices rose excessively above the value of the merchandise, to the extreme that people of scarce economic resources were almost unable to acquire the indispensable items that they needed to dress themselves. (Informe anual del Prefecto y Comandante

General de Santa Cruz 1919, quoted in Roca: 1980)

The expansion of agriculture in northern Santa Cruz and the growth of the local economy was constrained by the isolation of the department and a lack of markets. Well aware of these restrictions, local elites sought solutions to their problems in several ways. Prominent landowners organized the Junta Rural del Norte, an organization which represented the interests of the largest hacendados in northern Santa Cruz. Together with the members of a similar organization in Cordillera province, they continuously sent delegations to La Paz to discuss their concerns with the central government. The also founded the Sociedad de Estudios Geograficos e Historicos de Santa Cruz in 1903 to voice their discontent. The society emphasized two principal points, expressed in its magazine: the connection of the departmental capital to the highlands and foreign markets through the construction of a railway, and the protection of national industries in the face of Chilean and Peruvian competition.

Regional demands for a railroad link to the highlands erupted in 1921 in a brief uprising, and a more forceful revolt, which the La Paz press labeled "separatist", followed in 1924 but died out two weeks later. The lack of support from other parts of the country, the weakness of the regional economy, and the power wielded by the highland mining interests all contributed to the rebellion's short duration. The national government remained firm in its commitment to building railroads on the altiplano and steadfastly ignored the eastern lowlands (Roca: 1980).

THE CHACO WAR AND THE NATIONAL REVOLUTION

The Chaco War, which broke out against Paraguay in 1932, marked the beginning of important changes that reshaped Santa Cruz in subsequent decades. Bolivia's crushing defeat brought the entire political and economic system into question. The country lost a major portion of the chaco to Paraguay and thousands of Quechua, Aymara, and Chiriguano Indians, who fought in the war, died. Nationalization of the tin mines became a prominent issue in the years that followed, and equal rights for the Indian population was increasingly discussed. Labor organizers and others influenced by radical thought began to organize Indians and miners and stimulate greater class consciousness (Klein: 1969).

The war also brought direct consequences for Santa Cruz. The necessity to mobilize troops and supplies motivated the government to upgrade the treacherous route connecting Santa Cruz and Cochabamba, and a brief upsurge in agricultural production was generated by the need to feed soldiers fighting on the front. The territorial loss to Paraguay caused further discontent over the department's isolation and refueled demands for a railroad. A desire to promote economic development that was not based exclusively on mining emerged more strongly after the Chaco disaster (Ibarnegaray: 1982).

Such events led to better relations with Brazil and Argentina, as they were interested in Bolivia's gas and petroleum reserves. During the brief government of German Busch (1937-1939), Brazil and Argentina agreed to build railroads from the city of Santa Cruz to Corumba and Yacuiba respectively in exchange for gas and oil sales. In 1948 the first train entered Santa Cruz from Brazil, and in 1954 the Santa Cruz-Yacuiba line was completed.

The railroads established an important base for future development. A 1938 law that recognized departmental participation in hydrocarbon production allowed the department to collect an 11 percent tax on all petroleum and natural gas extracted in Santa Cruz. These earnings eventually became quite substantial once production was intensified in later years, and the law represented a significant victory for the dominant class.

The social discontent aroused by the Chaco War finally erupted in the national revolution of 1952, which ended with the overthrow of the tin oligarchy and the rise of the Movimiento Nacional Revolucionario (MNR) to power. The new government represented a major break with the past and instituted sweeping social reforms that accelerated the process of change in Santa Cruz. At the time of the revolution, the MNR constituted a loosely aligned coalition of miners, peasants, and the petite bourgeoisie united in their opposition to the ruling tin oligarchy. Shifting alignments between these different groups characterized the MNR's twelve-year rule, and the social reforms and policies implemented by the government during this period must be understood as the outcome of numerous conflicts and concessions within this broad-based populist movement.

Under pressure from the powerful mine workers, the MNR consented to the nationalization of the tin mines. The mines had been stagnating since the 1930s because of decapitalization and the exhaustion of high-quality ore, which caused operating costs to rise and profits to fall. After the revolution, the initial disorganization engendered by nationalization caused output to fall further, and world tin prices dropped, throwing the country into a severe foreign exchange crisis.

The government was forced to adopt new strategies to feed its population: Food imports accounted for an astonishing 41 percent of all imports and 21 percent of the country's total food supply (Thorn: 1971). The MNR instituted a series of agricultural import-substitution measures designed to reduce dependency on foreign food supplies, save valuable international exchange, and encourage the expansion of domestic agriculture.

The 1953 agrarian reform created major revisions in the landholding structure and established the conditions for capitalist development. The decree responded to mounting demands of both peasants and the Central Obrera Boliviana (COB) and stated that the land was to be redistributed among the landless and those who had very little land. Property usurped from Indian communities since 1900 was to be returned and the

traditions of the community respected;
agricultural production would be stimulated
through capital investment, credit, and
technological assistance; debt peonage would be
abolished and workers paid a salary; and
migration from the densely populated highlands
and intermontane valleys to the lowland regions
was encouraged.
    The MNR did not initiate the land reform
until a full year and a half after the revolution
and did so only after militant peasants had
already expropriated haciendas in a few key areas
of the country. It was essentially a political
measure designed to win the popular support that
the MNR desperately needed in order to
consolidate its power. Although effectively
abolishing the latifundia in many parts of the
country, the reform made no attempt to reorganize
peasant production, and the majority of entitled
land reform beneficiaries in La Paz and
Cochabamba received little more than the parcels
previously held in usufruct. Prereform inequities
in the size and quality of landholdings persisted, and economic development efforts after
the revolution concentrated on the sparsely
populated oriente which was less affected by the
land redistribution. The MNR also created a new
category called the "agricultural enterprise"
that facilitated the development of capitalist
production relations in Bolivian agriculture. An
agricultural enterprise was distinguished from
the latifundia by capital investment, the use of
modern technology and wage labor, and unlike the
underexploited latifundia, it was not subject to
expropriation.
    Property classification varied among the
different geographical and ecological regions of
the country. In the lowland areas of Santa Cruz
and Beni, an agricultural enterprise reached its
largest extension-- from 500 to 2,500 hectares--
and allowance was made for cattle ranches to
encompass as much as 50,000 hectares. Other
property classifications included a category for
medium agricultural property, extending from
fifty to 500 hectares, and one for a small
agricultural property that was no larger than
fifty hectares.

The basic land tenure pattern found in the main agricultural region of northern Santa Cruz changed little after 1953, and the peasant militancy that so characterized the Cochabamba Valley and parts of the highlands was largely absent in the oriente. Although agitation for urban land reform did occur, pressure for land in the northern zone had never been as acute as in other regions of the country; landowners had always been compelled to make certain concessions to the local population in order to insure the availability of a labor supply. The absence of a strong, organized peasant resistance inhibited a thorough land redistribution. Also, the arrival of vast quantities of foreign capital for infrastructure and agriculture development strengthened the position of many lowland families because it allowed them to convert their properties into agricultural enterprises (Heath: 1959b).

The Bolivian-owned Paz Hermanos import-export house retained numerous properties a full eighteen months following the agrarian reform. The total number of hectares claimed by Paz Hermanos surpassed 14,350 but the firm in 1954 cultivated only 212. It also possessed agricultural machinery valued at $20,582, 136 palm-thatched huts for workers, and an alcohol distillery. These assets were divided among heirs upon the death of the two owners--Roberto Paz in 1954 and Rosendo Paz in 1956. Muyurina, a 502-hectare property was subsequently sold to the U.S.-sponsored Inter-American Agricultural Service (IAS) to establish an agricultural experiment station. Two heirs of the original entrepreneurs embarked on extensive sugarcane cultivation and cattle ranching operations, and by 1980 they were among the largest sugarcane producers in the department.

Like Paz Hermanos, the large German commercial houses were not directly affected by the land reform and took advantage of new opportunities for economic development following the revolution. Most of these houses had their capital in foreign banks and suffered no major confiscation of their assets. Timber and rubber had been extracted from the region through concessions granted by the government, and the firms had made few capital investments on this land. Following the revolution the Casa Elsner and other import-export houses formed the La Paz-based Hansa organization, which subsequently invested in multimillion dollar cattle ranching operations in Beni and became a major importer and distributor of agro-chemicals and machinery. Similarly, the Casa Schweitzer reemerged as the Casa Bernardo in La Paz, and the Casa Zeller relocated to Switzerland.

As part of the MNR's efforts to conciliate the peasantry and retain its political support, the government officially substituted the word indio (Indian) for campesino (country person). This change was the result of two related factors: First, indio had historically implied racial inferiority and signified a conquered population destined to labor in support of a more dominant group. The revolution abolished bonded labor and provided these people with a new freedom unfitting to this notion. Second, the developmentalist ideology that increasingly dominated MNR policy viewed Indian culture as the embodiment of tradition, which--it was believed--would impeded the process of modernization and economic development. It's not surprising that the agrarian reform preferred the more modern category campesino as a means of minimizing the cultural and linguistic differences among the population. But although the terms changed, many of the social distinctions remained the same: In northern Santa Cruz large landowning producers of commercial crops were officially designated agricultores (i.e., non-Indians) even though small producers were campesinos (i.e., Indians) (see Albo: 1979 and Platt: 1982).

The reorganization of work relations after the agrarian reform constituted the principal change for the peasantry. In the highland areas the landlords had previously forced peasants to work several days of each week for the haciendas. Following the reform, peasants recovered those days for themselves--a change that was much more radical than the land redistribution. And in Santa Cruz labor scarcity obliged many landlords to offer a small cash salary, the loan of tools, and the security of housing to attract workers. The availability of vast tracts of jungle land made it possible for families to secure property by working a remote parcel or squatting on the border of a large estate, and lowland landlords had greater difficulty restricting access than their highland counterparts (Heath: 1959a).

The so-called <u>asentado</u> was the most common type of agricultural worker during the years that preceeded the agrarian reform. <u>Asentados</u> worked subsistence plots and provided labor to landlords in exchange for such benefits as housing and minimal cash payments. Granting land to these workers for subsistence cultivation enabled the landlord to increase his cultivable land and expand the agricultural frontier. The <u>apatronados</u> were a smaller group, tied more directly to the hacienda. They primarily consisted of indigenous families who were required to carry out a number of personal services to the landlord (Ibarnegaray: 1982). Finally, several workers from the Guarayo missions of Yotau, Asencion, Urubicha, Yaguaru and the southern province of Cordillera migrated to the northern Santa Cruz estates during the peak periods of the agricultural cycle, when labor requirements surpassed the capacity of the local population [1]. They were hired by labor contractors (<u>contratistas</u>), who came to the mission communities to recruit workers for the landlords. With the consent of the mission priests the <u>contratistas</u> brought entire families to work on the lowland estates. Many of these families were never allowed to return to their communities and were among the first settlers to establish new communities on the frontier after 1952.

The demand for laborers on the Santa Cruz estates increased after the agrarian reform, as commercial agriculture began to expand. Then too, land values rose as the frontier was rapidly incorporated into the national economy. Peasants from the highlands and valleys started to migrate in large numbers to Santa Cruz, because the fragmentation of their plots forced them to seek alternative subsistence activities. Wage labor on the burgeoning lowland estates provided an important source of additional income for many families, and the availability of unclaimed frontier land offered them the opportunity to own land and grow crops. Former tenants from the lowland estates settled on the frontier, after landlords, fearing that their claims would be contested, curtailed prereform tenancy agreements. Most received little or no assistance from the government, and although the state directed some economic assistance to peasants in certain parts of the country during the years immediately following the land reform, government policy increasingly sought to strengthen the large, lowland agricultural enterprises. Estate owners received a major portion of government assistance by the late fifties, and the small-scale peasant unit of production became subordinated to the newly constituted capitalist enterprise.

The agrarian reform and development strategy sponsored by the state strengthened capital-intensive agricultural enterprises and created a large group of impoverished peasants who were forced to adopt diverse strategies to meet their subsistence needs. The MNR allowed elites to retain large tracts of land in the lowlands, because popular protest was neither as strong nor as well organized as in parts of the highlands and valleys. The government--in conjunction with international development programs--then funneled economic investments to those regions and individuals less affected by the agrarian reform. The land reform constituted part of the MNR's initial response to rising militancy in such areas as the Cochabamba Valley. It was a political device intended to quell fears of rural violence, minimize tensions in the countryside, and galvanize support against the old oligarchy.

THE UNITED STATES AND THE OPENING OF THE ORIENTE

U. S. economic assistance to Bolivia began in 1942, when certain primary products obtained a strategic significance during World War II. The U.S. government sent an economic mission to Bolivia from December, 1941 to May, 1942 to study conditions and make recommendations for a long-range development program in the oriente. These recommendations were set forth in the Bohan Plan and included the following points: First, stimulate tropical agricultural products such as sugar, cotton, cattle, lumber and the export potential of rubber and quinine. Second, construct a highway network linking production centers with consumption centers. And finally, develop proven oil and natural gas reserves.

The principal agricultural areas in the 1940s lay within the southern boundaries of the provinces of Obispo Santiesteban and Sara, the southeastern part of Ichilo, the western half of Warnes province, and a fringe along the Rio Grande in the province of Nuflo de Chavez. The Rio Grande marked the eastern limit of the main agricultural area; Mineros, Santa Rosa, and Buena Vista marked the northern and northwestern limits; sandy soils and increasing dryness limited the area under cultivation south of Santa Cruz (Weeks: 1946).

The United States was quick to assist the economic expansion of Santa Cruz because it considered the MNR to be a reformist government and sought to maintain Bolivia within its sphere of influence. Beginning in the mid-1950s, it provided millions of dollars in aid to stimulate large-scale agro-industrial development in Santa Cruz and create an entrepreneurial-minded class of capitalist farmers. U.S.-sponsored development efforts gave first priority to the construction of a road between Santa Cruz and Cochabamba and to the petroleum industry. The highway, completed in 1954 and paved in 1956, linked important highland markets with the lowland department and greatly reduced the cost of transportation. The United States also provided funds for the construction of feeder roads between the sugar-mills and important sugarcane-producing properties. Further, it loaned considerable sums of money to local sugar mill owners to purchase new equipment and expand processing capacity. A state-owned mill--Guabira--also was built with American financial support in 1956.

The Point Four aid program, a precursor to the Agency for International Development (AID) in Bolivia, established a subsidized machinery pool for jungle clearance in 1954 and a credit program between 1956 and 1961. Large-scale sugarcane and rice producers enjoyed easy access to credit. They were the only ones who could post sufficient land and crop collateral to get substantial loans, and many became wealthy in a year's time with only a minimal investment in capital and labor (Heath: 1959b).

While millions of dollars were being spent to institute the recommendations of the Bohan Plan (see Table 1.1), the development of an industrial sector in the cities was ignored, and the highland and valley regions most densely populated by peasant families were left to stagnate. Consequently, large-scale migration to the department of Santa Cruz began with the opening of the Santa Cruz-Cochabamba highway. Settlements such as La Angostura and La Guardia sprang up on land made available by this road. The department grew at a rate of less than 1 percent from 1900 to 1950, but with the opening of new roads and the subsequent agricultural boom, the department experienced a 4.1 percent growth rate during the twenty-six years from 1950 to 1976. The five province region of northern Santa Cruz underwent the most significant growth because this was the center of agro-industrial expansion (INE: 1976).

Although migration was not new to Bolivia, the MNR strongly promoted the settlement of peasants in the lowlands through officially sponsored, directed colonization programs. Colonization, as the process of frontier settlement was called, was intended to redistribute the population more evenly throughout the country and relieve heavy population pressure in the highlands. Through its support for colonization, the MNR hoped to divert attention away from the possibilities of a more radical agrarian reform in the highlands and to place greater emphasis on the development of new areas. National unity was another goal of colonization. The expansionist tendencies of neighboring nations had gradually chipped away Bolivian territory. The mineral-rich Atacama territory was lost to Chile after the 1879 Pacific War; then Brazil took over the territory

TABLE 1.1
U.S. Expenditures on Agricultural Development: Santa Cruz 1953-1961

AREA	AMOUNT ($U.S.)	DESCRIPTION
A. Sugar		
1. La Belgica sugar-mill (1962)	2,500,000	Loan for equipment purchase.
2. La Esperanza sugarmill (1962)	486,414* 1,750,000	" " " "
3. San Aurelio sugar-mill (1962)	297,216 264,900*	" " " "
4. Guabira sugarmill (1954-55)	294,000	Grant for partial funding of the mill camps and construction.
5. National Sugar Commission (1959-60)	1,700,000 6,000	Machinery purchases. Grant to form commission and study problems of the sugar industry.
6. Sugarcane developmen= (1959-60)	240,000	Grant to subsidize sugar producers and promote large-scale production.
7. Sugar marketing	9,336,912	A.I.D. loan via the Grace Corporation to market sugar (1960-1962).
B. Rice		
1. Jack Steffan	36,229	Loan for equipment purchase.

(Continued)

Table 1.1 (Cont.)

AREA	AMOUNT ($U.S.)	DESCRIPTION
2. Hector Laguna	Unknown	Loan for working capital.
3. Lorgio Chavez	Unknown	"
4. Rice marketing	1,230,012	Loan for rice marketing via cooperatives (1961-62).
C. Agro-industrial credit (1955-61)	1,230,012	12,200 loans made to Santa Cruz landlords.
D. Machinery pool (1953-60)	7,000,000	Loan to provide subsidized land clearing machinery to commercial producers.
E. Muyurina Agricultural School	205,000	Construction of an agricultural school (1953-60).
F. Timber	Unknown	Loans to private entrepreneurs to buy trucks.
G. Saavedra Experimental Station	Unknown	Loan (1953-60).
H. Extension services	Unknown	Grant.
I. Colonization		
1. Resettlement of foreigners (1954)	47,000	Loans for resettlement of Mennonites, Italians, and Okinawans.
2. Resettlement of Bolivians and internal migration	72,000	Loan for resettlement of miners, peasants, etc. from the altiplano (1957).
3. Colonization studies (1961-62)	44,504*	Loan to study factors affecting success and failure of colonization.

4. Equipment acquisition	39,025*	Loan to purchase land clearing equipment for settlers (1956).
5. Okinawa Colony (1954)	28,000	Loan for community sanitation, equipment, and livestock purchases.

J. Transportation

1. Construction and maintenance of Santa Cruz-Cochabamba road	1,256,000	Construction loan.
2. Feeder roads	137,000	Loan
3. Sugar access roads	85,000	Grant to build roads from the mills to major sugar properties.
4. Northern road (1959-61)	42,000	Loan for construction of road to the north of Montero.
5. Pirai River bridge	451,000	Loan to build bridge.

Sources: a) *Progresso* - Aug. 6, 1962
b) United States Operations Mission to Bolivia Point Four in Bolivia, 1960.
c) White, Stanford "Contributions of the Alliance for Progress in Santa Cruz", 1968 (mimeo).
d) USAID, La Paz, Bolivia.

*Figure based upon the 1957 free-market exchange rate of 8,943 Bolivian pesos to the U.S. dollar.

of Acre in 1903; and finally, Paraguay appropriated a major portion of the Chaco in the 1932-1935 Chaco War. The losses were attributed to a failure to inhabit these nominally empty lands. Colonization was also promoted to boost agricultural output and satisfy national demand for various commodities--rice, cotton, sugar, and beef--through the creation of small family farms.

The seriousness of the MNR's much acclaimed goal of promoting family farms is called into question upon closer examination of development programs during the 1950s and 1960s. Funds for peasant colonization projects were minimal in comparison to the amounts received by the emerging agro-industries (see Table 1.1), and serious attempts to promote food crops other than rice never materialized. The sugar industry received the most funding during this period because of its export potential.

Colonization took place to the north and west of the main agricultural zone between Montero and Santa Cruz, where properties untouched by the agrarian reform were increasing sugarcane production. The initial strategy for populating the region in the 1950s and 1960s was through highly planned, directed colonization programs. In the mid-1950s, the MNR initiated several such programs in north-central Santa Cruz. Cotoca, founded in 1954, was the first government-sponsored colony, and it was followed by similar efforts in the late 1950s to aid peasants settling in the Aroma, Caranda, Huaytu, and Cuatro Ojitos colonies. These programs were extremely costly and did not achieve their stated objectives. Settlers abandoned their plots and returned to their home communities. The vast majority settled in a so-called spontaneous manner, with or without contact with government agencies and generally through the formation of their own organizations in frontier zones.

Foreign colonies of Mennonites, Italians, Japanese, and Okinawans also were sponsored during 1953 and 1954. These groups had greater success than the highland migrants for several reasons. Land granted to foreign settlers was generally more extensive, higher quality, and with better access to stable roads than those areas settled by Bolivian peasants. Also, the educational background and technical expertise of these immigrants were much more advanced. In the case of the Japanese colonists, additional aid was also provided by their home governments.

Foreign capital played an even greater role in support of large-scale commercial agriculture following the 1956 economic stabilization plan. The heavy U.S. financial support of the Bolivian government gave it considerable leverage in pushing for a harsh monetary stabilization program. Bolivia had been experiencing rampant inflation and serious balance-of-payment difficulties for several years, and these problems were not conducive to a favorable investment climate. The United States warned MNR leaders that continued aid would be difficult to obtain unless the nation's finances and currency were stabilized (Eder:1968), and under the threat of aid withdrawal, the Bolivian government adopted a series of fiscal austerity measures.

Commercial agriculture in the oriente benefited from the stabilization plan because the imposition of high tariff barriers restricted sugar and rice imports, and the nation was forced to rely heavily upon the eastern lowlands for these commodities. Wage freezes represented an attempt to control labor and keep salaries low, and greater expenditures by the U.S.-sponsored agricultural development program were a major stimulus, especially for the sugar industry. Foreign aid to Bolivia grew from U.S.$60 million from 1954 to 1956, to U.S. $140 million from 1956 to 1961 (Mitchell: 1977); sugar production increased from 4.4 thousand metric tons in 1956 to 41.1 thousand tons in 1961. The new reliance on foreign exchange led to the loss of Bolivia's economic sovereignty--a fact which was strikingly evident in agriculture, where less than 20 percent of state expenditures in 1964 were handled by the ministry of agriculture (Thorn: 1971).

While the national government and international development programs supported the increasingly powerful estate owners, despotic local caudillos vied for power in Santa Cruz. A local MNR party boss, Luis Sandoval Moron, organized the urban poor of the departmental capital around the issue of land reform and threatened many wealthy families that owned most of the land surrounding the city limits. His leadership antagonized many people, created conflicts with the national government, and gave rise to factions within the local party structure (Whitehead: 1973).

Some crucenos also resented the influx of highlanders who came to Santa Cruz following completion of the Santa Cruz-Cochabamba highway, which created additional tension in the department. The immigrants were often poor peasants who worked as seasonal agricultural laborers, but others, attracted by the new economic opportunities, invested in business and commerce and threatened to undermine local enterprises. Many of these aspiring merchants and small-scale entrepreneurs came from peasant backgrounds but benefited from the new opportunities in northern Santa Cruz to enhance their agricultural and commercial activities.

The upper class reacted to the new circumstances by rallying support to the rightist Pro-Santa Cruz Committee, founded in 1950 by members of the city's traditional, white elite. The Committee emphasized the Spanish, non-Indian heritage of its membership, and in 1957 the allocation of oil revenues provided it with a convenient issue to contest central government rule and the power of Sandoval Moron. The Committee demanded that a larger portion of the oil revenues generated in the department be earmarked for local expenditure, and in light of the historic neglect displayed by past national governments towards Santa Cruz, it's not surprising that the Pro-Santa Cruz Committee generated considerable support. Racist sentiments against the highland Indians also were whipped up, and strong emphasis was placed on the cultural superiority of the lowlanders. In this way the upper class, appealed to the urban poor and even many MNR members by encouraging them to support the interests of all crucenos (Whitehead: 1973).

The Pro-Santa Cruz Committee won its struggle for a larger share of the oil revenues and dedicated this income to a series of expensive regional development projects. The Corporacion Regional de Desarrollo de Santa Cruz (CORDECRUZ) initiated costly regional development programs financed by oil and natural gas income. These programs favored large-scale agriculturalists and urban-based industrial projects, and the agency also managed programs sponsored by the Inter-American Development Bank, the Agency for International Development, and West Germany.

By the 1960s the MNR had grown more divided at both the national and local levels. In the city of Santa Cruz, factions of the MNR and groups representing the upper class struggled for power and installed highly unstable, dictatorial, and short-lived local regimes. On the national level the stabilization plan of 1956-1957 had initiated a basic shift in the governing strategy of the MNR. The loose class alliances that comprised the MNR coalition had been seriously strained over the past four years because of high inflation and problems with the economy. It had been impossible for all groups to share wealth and power, and the pattern of decentralized power that had characterized the MNR to this point was unsuitable for the management of an unpopular economic program. Faced with the task of favoring some groups more than others, the MNR became more centralized and gradually alienated its constituency. Workers and peasants suffered the most under the stabilization plan and were gradually excluded from power. And such urban-based groups as small businessmen, sectors of the university, government functionaries, and journalists grew more and more disillusioned with the MNR's ability to govern (Mitchell: 1977).

By 1964 the MNR had become completely isolated from popular support, and General Rene Barrientos, backed by an army that had been rebuilt and re-equipped by the United States, overthrew the government and established military rule. Barrientos outlawed the MNR, and although the party continued to operate clandestinely, the army became the principal local ruler in Santa Cruz. The departmental army command also became fraught with factionalism, but the military clearly and unequivocally supported private enterprise in Santa Cruz. Barrientos followed many of the same paths taken by the national MNR leadership, such as weakening labor's political power, encouraging private business, and pursuing economic development. Like the MNR, the military did not begin any comprehensive agricultural development programs on the altiplano and continued to support commercial agriculture in Santa Cruz. Although Barrientos' economic development strategy differed little from the MNR, military leaders were willing to use more repressive force to control social unrest and such policies created favorable conditions for capitalist expansion. Agricultural investment continued to aid large private growers, and the threat of land expropriations in Santa Cruz diminished.

During the next decade the expansion of export-oriented agriculture enhanced the political and economic power of both the traditional cruceno elite and a number of new beneficiaries of state and international development programs. Peasants were excluded from participation in government organizations and forced to lead an increasingly precarious existence on undercapitalized, subsistence plots.

NOTES

1. The mission was founded by Franciscan fathers in the mid-nineteenth century, and the Guarayos remained under the tutelage of the Franciscans until 1948. The priests imposed a work routine that required three days of obligatory labor each week. This work was ostensibly designed to benefit all mission dwellers, but when the territory passed to the administrative organization of Nuflo de Chavez province in 1948, a decree stated that native labor had been exploited in previous years with little benefit to the community (Hermosa Virreira: 1972).

2
The Expansion of Capitalist Agriculture

The agrarian reform and the financial assistance directed to Santa Cruz during the 1950s and early 1960s set the stage for an economic boom. The completion of the Santa Cruz-Cochabamba highway opened highland markets to lowland growers, and new producers' associations formed to protect their interests. International banks opened branch offices in Santa Cruz in the 1960s, and foreign development organizations and the state continued to finance the expansion of cash crop cultivation. A new group of speculators, investors, professionals, and administrators--attracted to Santa Cruz by the economic opportunities and together with the prominent lowland families--successfully monopolized a large share of the economic support channeled to the region. Migrant laborers and land-hungry peasants also were drawn to Santa Cruz, hoping, on the one hand, to supplement their meager subsistence income through wage labor and, on the other, to establish their own independent farming activities on the frontier. The relationships between these groups was complex and characterized by intense competition for land, labor, and technical and financial assistance.

The agrarian structure that emerged during these years was characterized by inequalities in the access to and control over productive resources. To understand how this happened, we must examine state policies, the incorporation of the frontier into the national society, and the way prominent entrepreneurs struggled to control a labor force in a sparsely populated region that lacked large numbers of people willing to work as wage laborers. The province of Obispo Santiesteban, which became a center for sugarcane cultivation by the 1970s, was an important center where peasants, small-scale agriculturalists, and large-scale commercial growers struggled to gain a foothold.

THE GROWTH OF CAPITALIST AGRICULTURE IN THE 1960s

The reforms and upheavals of the revolution led to the rise of new leaders in Santa Cruz and a style of popular participation in politics that generated fear and uncertainty among many traditional lowland families. But unlike other areas of the country, the state encouraged large-scale cash-crop agriculture; plus, the provision of credit and technical assistance created new possibilities for economic expansion. Commercial banks, including Citibank, BankAmerica, the Bank of Boston, and the Bank of Brazil, started to operate in Santa Cruz and played an important role in financing cash-crop development and assisting both the large lowland landowners and a new group of beneficiaries to expand their investments in the region.

Sugarcane and, to a lesser extent, rice were the main cash crops from the late 1950s through the next decade. By the end of the 1960s, however, the influx of so many peasant settlers had effectively undercut the ability of capitalist farmers to grow rice profitably, and the state was unable to maintain the price subsidies that had been so attractive to large producers. Both the large landowners from Santa Cruz and a growing number of new arrivals, including ex-hacendados from the highlands, administrators, professionals, and speculators, made more lucrative investments in sugarcane and cotton cultivation. They concentrated these crops into areas of fifty hectares or more, and unlike the peasant producers, their operations were characterized by the exclusive use of salaried labor. They hired both temporary and permanent workers for distinct phases of the agricultural cycle, and harvests were destined for sale rather than domestic consumption.

The initial spread of sugarcane cultivation centered in an area of 1,500 square kilometers between Warnes and Santa Cruz. Its predominantly sandy soils were used by producers to serve the San Aurelio, La Esperanza, and La Belgica sugarmills during the 1950s. Few growers maintained soil fertility through programs of crop rotation and the use of fertilizers. Other crops did not offer similar rates of profit, and for considerably less than the cost of fertilizer investment, growers could acquire new, virgin land. Thus, sugarcane yields were either sustained or augmented by continually clearing forest, and production centers tended to move increasingly away from stable roads and consumption centers.

By the early 1970s, the province of Obispo Santiesteban was an important location for sugarcane cultivation. The completion of a paved highway to Montero and the opening of the Guabira sugarmill in 1956 created new possibilities for sugarcane investment between Warnes and Mineros. Two thousand five hundred square kilometers of land were cleared to replace exhausted soils in the south, and old lands were left under a regrowth of grass and bush, though some poor-quality sugarcane remained (FAO: 1972). Much of this area was subsequently converted into extensive cattle-ranching operations.

Producers organized to protect their interests. Sugarcane growers in 1961 founded the Federacion de Caneros de Santa Cruz. It represented the largest and most well-established cane growers in the region and was followed in subsequent years by beef, cotton, sorghum, corn, soy bean, rice and milk producers' associations. An umbrella agency--the Camara Agropecuaria del Oriente (CAO)--was established in 1966, and although it initially represented only sugarcane and rice growers, the CAO eventually included all such organizations. Its primary purpose was to formulate a coherent agricultural plan for the entire region and articulate demands of cruceno growers at the national level. The CAO and its affiliates negotiated policy concessions, especially concerning credit allocations and government price levels, and even though their constituency was relatively small and restricted to large growers, they successfully influenced government decisions and acquired considerable benefits for their membership.

In 1964, Santa Cruz agriculture made the nation self-sufficient in sugar, followed by rice and beef a few years later and cotton in 1969. Production became increasingly geared to the export market, and an emerging regional bourgeoisie gradually consolidated its control of the regional economy. As the economic importance of Santa Cruz grew, this group obtained new power at the national level. Their power reached its fullest expression with the 1971 coup d'etat that brought General Hugo Banzer to power.

The agro-industrial interests centered in Santa Cruz supported Banzer's August 1971 coup; Banzer and six of his ministers had their economic bases located in the region. The coup heralded the formation of closer ties between military personnel and lowland agro-industrialists, and a growing alliance between these two groups proved to be mutually beneficial. Military rule repressed social unrest and was supportive of the economic interests of cash-crop growers and agro-industrialists in Santa Cruz, which created favorable investment conditions. And the political support of the lowland bourgeoisie enabled Banzer to withstand political pressure from tin miners and to exclude both workers and peasants from significant participation in government. Military commanders thus could benefit from their control of the state apparatus by acquiring land in Santa Cruz and taking advantage of the export boom to accumulate personal profits.

Under the dictatorship of Hugo Banzer, lowland producers and large-scale commercial agriculture received unequivocal support. Production grew to include four principal crops: cotton, sugarcane, soybeans, and cattle. Rapid land clearing and the construction of a new sugarmill in Mineros facilitated the spread of sugarcane cultivation into the Obispo Santiesteban province. Cattle ranching--developed in those parts of the province exhausted by the cultivation of cotton or sugarcane--was stimulated in new areas by large grants from the state. Many formerly remote frontier settlements were engulfed by the spread of commercial agriculture, and their residents were confronted with a new set of conditions.

The rapid growth of capitalist production hinged on the ability of large-scale producers to lay claim to productive resources--particularly land, labor, and financial assistance. To this end, government policy favored capitalist entrepreneurs with concessionary credit and large grants of frontier land. Such policies tended to undermine the position of independent frontier settlers and transform them into tenant farmers and wage laborers. Moreover, during times of crisis the state acquiesced to pressure and openly assisted growers in mobilizing a labor force. These practices became most pronounced during the boom years of the early 1970s.

AGRICULTURAL CREDIT IN THE 1970s

The allocation of agricultural credit reflected the continuing desire of foreign lending institutions and the Bolivian government to finance the development of an export sector in Santa Cruz. This policy, which took shape after the 1952 revolution, became more pronounced during the late 1960s and early 1970s for a number of reasons. First, several years of military rule and economic aid had created seemingly attractive investment conditions. Second, during the early 1970s investors were lured by the possibilities of large profits, especially in cotton production. This was due to a rise in international commodity prices after the jump in oil prices announced by the Organization of Petroleum Exporting Countries (OPEC). Finally, agro-industrial interests in Santa Cruz were the mainstay of support for the Banzer regime and received generous loans in reward for their continued backing of the government.

To understand how the state and

international development organizations and banks shaped credit policies and influenced the direction of agricultural production, it first is necessary to outline briefly the structure of the Bolivian banking system. The Bolivian Central Bank controls and regulates commercial banks and the Bolivian Agricultural Bank (BAB). The commercial banks consist of a state bank, ten Bolivian-owned banks, and seven foreign-owned banks. The multinational banks became actively involved in financing commercial agriculture during the cotton boom, when Citibank, BankAmerica, and the Bank of Brazil loaned U.S. $11,266,460 to cotton growers in the 1971-1972 fiscal year (ADEPA: 1972).

BAB was founded in 1942 to provide exclusive service to the agricultural sector. Although it was restructured to provide financial assistance to small farmers following the 1952 revolution, mismanagement and pressure from both the government and foreign-aid agencies led to four more reorganizations after 1954 and a reemphasis on large capitalist producers. Its foreign capital base increased during the 1960s, as the United States pumped ever larger sums into commercial agriculture; most of the bank's operations ceased to be funded by internal revenues. Locally financed programs fell from 84 to 34 percent of total outlays from 1965 to 1969, and foreign-sponsored credit lines grew to five times the size of other credit programs. Peasants received virtually no money from international sources during this period, and they obtained little of BAB's own funds (Eckstein: 1983:125).

From 1966 to 1978, international development agencies made approximately U.S. $146 million available to both BAB and the commercial banks for agricultural credit. USAID controlled 46 percent of total foreign-financed credit, and the World Bank and the Inter-American Development Bank, which loaned directly to the government, provided the rest. By the mid-1970s, most of the agricultural credit passed through three special lines--D.S. 07911, FRA-1, and FRA-2--created by USAID. The Special Fund for Economic Development--D.S. 07911 --was established in 1967 to finance agriculture and other production-oriented industries. Prior to this time, credit had been available almost exclusively for sugarcane, but D.S. 07911 monies gave principal support to beef-cattle producers in Santa Cruz and Beni. It was followed in 1972 by the FRA-1 program, which made loans to medium and large growers of food crops and livestock producers; credit was overwhelmingly utilized to finance soybeans, however. A credit program for small farmers with less than fifty hectares of land was not founded until 1975 (see Table 2.1).

The favored position of capitalist agriculture in Santa Cruz is reflected in Tables 2.2 and 2.3. We can observe in Table 2.2 that from 1973 to 1978, 68 percent of all commercial bank credit went to Santa Cruz, and in 1973 alone, the department captured 96 percent of these funds. Similarly, BAB's preference for export crops grown primarily in Santa Cruz is shown in Table 2.3. From 1973 to 1975, for example, cotton received over 40 percent of the loans, while the more traditional crops--rice and corn--which are grown by peasants for internal consumption never obtained more than 6.5 percent of total funds.

The policy of loaning to large growers was economically unjustifiable and suggests that political factors were an important criteria for supporting capitalist farmers. First, the repayment record of large agriculturalists was worse than that of peasants, who had the lowest delinquency rate of any group of borrowers. Second, the banks continued to finance export crops even as yields dropped even though crops that actually demonstrated per-unit increases were being grown in the highlands and valleys by peasant households. By 1978, 68.8 percent of the delinquent BAB loans were in Santa Cruz, and cotton and soybean producers were the worst offenders. The Banzer regime did not pressure growers to repay their credit but instead issued a decree in 1977 that extended the repayment period for cotton and soybean loans from BAB and the state bank an additional eight to twelve years. Banzer then went a step further and purchased the credit portfolios of Citibank,

TABLE 2.1
FRA-1 and FRA-2 Credit Disbursements (1973-1978) (Thousands of pesos)

Purpose of Loan	No. Ha. Financed FRA-1	No. Ha. Financed FRA-2	Disbursements FRA-1	Disbursements FRA-2
Soy Beans	40,240	1,075	111,347,320	3,289,400
Corn	5,399	6,140	6,538,789	10,660,012
Rice	6,362	9,155	4,414,520	16,546,250
Dairy	-----	-----	10,118,394	303,442
Machinery	-----	-----	7,478,514	-----
Wheat	5,123	30	4,859,015	53,900
Pigs	-----	-----	674,000	652,780
Pineapple	5	-----	22,603	-----
Machinery repair	-----	-----	405,842	-----
Poultry	-----	-----	4,488,785	248,910
Peanuts	-----	4	-----	18,000
Marketing	-----	-----	900,000	1,350,000
Potatoes	-----	35	-----	339,150
Green Peppers	-----	2	-----	76,530
Tomatoes	-----	2	-----	84,500
Cacao	4	-----	166,800	-----
TOTAL	57,133	16,443	151,614,582	33,622,874
PERCENT	78	22	81	19

Source: Banco Central de Bolivia

TABLE 2.2
Distribution of Commercial Bank Agricultural Loans by Department (1973-1978)
(percent of total)

Department	1973	1974	1975	1976	1977	1978	Total
La Paz	.5	6.5	52.19	24.89	22.41	23.78	23.24
Santa Cruz	96.45	85.39	39.72	66.83	66.60	66.11	68.04
Cochabamba	---	2.18	3.34	5.46	4.16	2.73	2.97
Potosi	---	.30	---	.40	---	---	.08
Oruro	---	---	---	---	---	.28	.07
Chuquisaca	---	.10	.04	---	---	---	.02
Tarija	---	---	.08	---	---	.56	.17
Beni	2.97	5.81	4.65	2.45	6.85	6.59	5.44
Pando	---	---	---	---	---	---	---

Source: USAID, Bolivian Rural Financial Sector. La Paz: Ohio State University Report, 1979.

TABLE 2.3
Annual Distribution of Credit by Purpose of Loan BAB (1970-1978)
(percentage of total)

	1970	1971	1972	1973	1974	1975	1976	1977	1978
Cattle	12	27	17.2	21.1	19.5	19.4	17.6	23.3	14.1
Cotton	17.6	23.9	28.5	47.1	43	42.3	36.4	25.6	31.8
Sugar Cane	.3	24.2	37.2	4.3	8.3	19.7	20.4	11.2	4.4
Soy Beans	.4	---	---	6.4	5.9	1.1	4.3	9.2	7.6
Rice	---	---	---	.2	4.2	6.5	4.3	.1	---
Corn	---	.1	.1	.3	1.4	---	1.4	3.5	6.3

Source: USAID, Bolivian Rural Financial Sector. La Paz: Ohio State University Report, 1979.

where over 80 percent of the loans were overdue, and transferred them to BAB to prevent Citibank from pressuring delinquent borrowers. These policies had two effects: They facilitated an enormous income transfer to a privileged group of producers, since loan repayment constituted nothing of real value, because of the effects of inflation. And international banks escaped penalty by transferring their bad debts to the state. Domestic capitalists and the multinational banks thus benefited, while the Bolivian state became more decapitalized (Ladman and Tinnermeier: 1980; Eckstein: 1983).

LAYING PRIVATE CLAIM TO THE FRONTIER

As concessionary credit policies facilitated the growth of capitalist agriculture, land became a valuable commodity in northern Santa Cruz, and the struggle between settlers and large-scale producers to control it became the most important feature of commercial agricultural development. The Banzer regime encouraged frontier expansion with land grants on the fringes of the burgeoning agro-industrial zone, especially in those areas improved by a stable road network. And the creation of the Brigadas Agrarias Moviles in 1968 improved the process of land surveys and expedited bureaucratic titling procedures. Such grants were often located in areas previously settled by peasants, and not surprisingly, this lead to conflicting property claims. Although the outcomes of disputes varied from case to case, peasants generally lost out to the advancing agro-industries.
The rate of land distribution increased five-fold from 1971 to 1978. During this period some 5,973,648 hectares were affected by the reform, a figure that contrasts sharply with the 9,119,442 hectares repartitioned during the entire preceding period of agrarian reform (Grupo de Estudios Andres Ibanez: 1983). People usually received land in two ways: a <u>dotacion</u>, or grant, was the result of a written appeal to the state requesting either unclaimed lands or a parcel

that had been worked for several years on the property of a hacendado. Land consolidacion was the recognition of previous land rights by a particular individual. Consolidacion occurred when both the agrarian reform and the landowner recognized that the property belonged to the latter. Of the entire 8,742,760 hectares distributed in this manner, 82 percent of the land was received through dotaciones (Grupo de Estudios Andres Ibanez: 1983) [1].

In the province of Obispo Santiesteban the scramble for property resulted granting titles for 55 percent more land than the territorial area actually encompassed (CIDCRUZ: 1983). A closer examination reveals how the extreme inequalities developed. The beneficiaries of the agrarian reform are overwhelmingly small property owners with fifty hectares or less, but they control only 11 percent of the land (Table 2.4). In contrast, individuals in the sample who own properties of over five hundred hectares represent 10 percent of the total beneficiaries but control 83 percent of the land. Furthermore, if we next consider land distributed by the Instituto Nacional de Colonizacion (INC), the difference between large and small landholders becomes even more disturbing. By 1980, INC had distributed 1,270 parcels, averaging twenty-seven hectares each, to settlers in Obispo Santiesteban. Only 24 percent of the recipients possessed legal title to their land, and the total titled area encompassed a mere 7,625 hectares (CORDECRUZ), a figure that still falls far short of the percentage represented in Table 2.4 for a small sample of agricultural enterprises. This suggests that the number of settlers in Obispo Santiesteban province is even greater than the data in Table 2.4 indicate, and that unlike the large producers, a substantial majority do not hold title to their parcels.

The justification for granting such large extensions of land under the designation of cattle or agricultural enterprise was consistent with the government's import-substitution policy, which held that large holdings offered a greater productive potential than small parcels. Many recipients did use their grants to expand

TABLE 2.4
Distribution of Properties Affected by the Agrarian Reform in Obispo Santiesteban Province (1953-1975)*

Classification	No. Hectares Distributed	%	No. Parcels	%	No. Beneficiaries	%
Small Property (0-50 Ha.)	7,639	11	230	85	230	82
Medium Property (51-500 Ha.)	3,676	6	21	8	23	8
Medium/Large Cattle Property or Agricultural Enterprise (501 and more Ha.)	54,673	83	17	6	29	10
TOTAL	65,988	100	268	100	282	100

Source: Office of the Agrarian Reform, La Paz, Bolivia.

* This table is based on 15 percent sample of the available expedientes in the La Paz agrarian reform office which date from 1953 to 1975.

TABLE 2.5
The Sale of Land Grants over 2,000 Hectares in Obispo Santiesteban (1971-1979)

Name of Property	Size of Grant	Date Granted	Date & Quantity Sold	Stated Sales Price ($bs.)
El Porvenir(a)	10,058	10/13/72	4/18/73 2,224 Ha.	40,000
San Martin	5,000	4/28/73	8/31/73 2,500 Ha.	25,000
La Cola	3,912	3/20/74	3/28/74 3,912 Ha.	70,000
Banados del Rio Grande	7,023	7/29/74	11/21/74 900 Ha.	20,000
La Cachuela	3,000	6/11/76	12/8/76 1,000 Ha.	40,000
La Fortuna	19,987	8/29/78	9/4/78 19,987 Ha.	unknown
El Porvenir (b)	3,600	11/12/78	8/31/79 3,600 Ha.	100,000

Source: Derechos Reales

sugarcane, cotton, and cattle ranching operations, and some families placed several hundred hectares under cultivation. Others, however, engaged in speculative activity. By classifying land as pasture, individuals could receive larger land grants and then sell out for a profit to those eager to begin their own commercial farming ventures.

Several land grants of 2,000 hectares or more in Obispo Santiesteban were sold before contributing in a significant way to increasing agricultural output. These sales, which took place primarily in the seventies, are reflected in Table 2.5. (The properties indicated represent all such land grants recorded in derechos reales from 1971 to 1979, where land was sold in a period of two years or less.) Agrarian-reform legislation did not prohibit this practice, although in later years a detailed investment schedule was required to obtain an agricultural or cattle enterprise.

Such speculation was not unique to Obispo Santiesteban. In 1979 two companies began to operate in Santa Cruz that sold land previously granted by the agrarian reform along the Santa Cruz-Corumba train line in the province of Chiquitos. These companies--the Bolivian Land and Cattle Co. and the Bolivian Land and Forestry Co.--sold 2,500,000 acres at a price varying from U.S. $31.09 to U.S. $36.88 per acre.

In addition to government grants, growers also enlarged their holdings by buying or encroaching onto peasant lands that bordered their properties. Peasants, lacking capital and confronted with the many difficulties of frontier agriculture and crop marketing, often sold their parcels for a nominal price and then either moved further into the frontier, relocated to the towns, or remained in the region as low-paid agricultural laborers. While a number of wealthier settlers replaced them, the large-scale commercial growers increasingly dominated the emerging agrarian structure, and those settlers who retained their land were not immune to the expansionist tendencies of the most powerful producers. Growers often encroached onto fallowed land or areas still covered with forest and then

made use of legal confusion over property
boundaries and the frequent absence of titles
among the rural population to incorporate the
land into their own holdings. Dishonest officials
facilitated this form of land acquisition, and
the large-scale producers, who had access to the
legal bureaucracy, were able to prevail when
their claims were contested.

Moreover, agrarian-reform legislation,
although it was supportive of settlers' rights,
often acted as a double-edged sword. The reform
laws advanced the principle that those who farm
the land are its rightful owners and stated that
cultivated land should not be taken away from
peasants, even if they had not yet acquired legal
title. Nevertheless, using only family labor
settlers could not cultivate more than two or
three hectares of land; further, land had to be
left fallow in order to regain its productivity.
Large growers, who owned machinery and controlled
capital, could more easily place extensive areas
under cultivation, and after planting sugarcane
or some other crop, many moved onto neighboring
peasant lands and claimed it for their own.

The experience of settlers from a community
near Mineros exemplifies this process. In 1978
fifteen people from the community of Paichanetu
laid claim to ninety-six hectares of frontier
land in a newly opened settlement zone. They
sought additional land for cattle, which they
hoped to buy after several estate owners
purchased much of the land surrounding their
community. When the settlers initiated
proceedings to obtain a title, however, a
prominent individual from the town of Montero
claimed the property, although he could not
present legal title. The settlers were to become
the rightful owners, but while they awaited their
title and raised the money necessary to buy
cattle, this individual rented the land to a
group of Brazilian immigrants who were unaware of
the conflicting claims. The Brazilians owned
agricultural machinery and controlled
considerable capital reserves, and within a short
time they had placed sixty hectares under
cultivation. In 1982, the settlers protested the
matter before a local agrarian-reform judge, but

this time the individual appeared with a seemingly legal title to back up his claim, and the presence of cultivated land lent validity to his case. The judge ruled in his favor and thus negated the legality of the peasants' title, which was still being processed.

The concentration of landownership in northern Santa Cruz was a phenomenon that affected certain areas more than others. The penetration of commodity production was an uneven process, and settlers in some communities consolidated their own agricultural activities and resisted the advancement of large-scale producers more successfully than others. Some colonizers lived in the same location for many years and never experienced any threat to their property claims, but in other areas, particularly around Mineros, entire communities were engulfed by the expansion of the agricultural enterprises.

Table 2.6 illustrates the rapid accumulation of land by four growers in the Mineros region. The opening in 1976 of a new sugarmill in Mineros--the Union Agroindustrial de Caneros (UNAGRO)--stimulated sugarcane cultivation and moved many growers to acquire land in the vicinity. As indicated, three of these individuals purchased the bulk of their land in the 1970s, much of it representing small properties of fifty hectares or less purchased from colonizers. These growers own additional land in other areas of the northern zone and frequently control more land than that to which they are legally entitled. Lorenzo Soleto, for example, accumulated 195 hectares that represented the individual parcels of five peasant families, and as of 1981 it was not legally registered in Soleto's name. Several peasant families in the area said that debts to their former employers or the need for cash to pay for expensive medical treatment were the principal reason they sold their land.

That this process happened in one of the most dynamic parts of the lowlands is especially significant. The monopolization of land and financial resources by a small group of planters made it increasingly difficult for many settlers to establish themselves as independent small

TABLE 2.6
Land Accumulation in the Mineros Region
of Obispo Santiesteban Province *

	Size of Parcel (Ha.)			
Date	Hernan Arredondo	Martha Portugal	Lorenzo Soleto	Orlando Limpias
1954	--------	--------	------	83
1957	--------	--------	100	--------
1959	16	--------	--------	--------
1961	--------	--------	--------	42
1966	--------	--------	480	--------
1967	--------	--------	141	--------
1970	--------	--------	50	--------
1971	36.5	50; 50	50; 50	--------
1972	10;26;10;16	40	--------	55
1973	50	--------	--------	--------
1974	127	--------	50	50
1975	--------	--------	--------	50
1976	230.4;16.3; 16.3; 726.7	--------	--------	--------
1977	213; 273.4; 5 parcels of 16.3; 137	900	--------	55
1978	353.7	--------	--------	--------
1980	--------	--------	--------	25
TOTAL	2,356.1	1,040	921	360

Source: Derechos Reales

* Portions of this data appear in Grupo de
Estudios Andres Ibanez, <u>Tierra, estructura
productiva y poder en Santa Cruz</u>, 1983. Due
to the political conditions in Bolivia,
sources were not cited in this work.

farmers; consequently, an impoverished, wage-
earning peasantry began to emerge. This group,
described in detail in Chapter 3, could not exist
on the diminishing returns of subsistence
agriculture and was obliged to seek wage
employment in order to survive. Its development

was one solution to the labor shortages suffered by the lowland agricultural enterprises.

CASH-CROP PRODUCTION AND LABOR ACQUISITION

The rapid expansion of commercial agriculture led to further integration of the regional economy into the world market and generated additional demands for labor. Those entrepreneurs who hoped to profit by producing export crops first had to increase their labor supply, and their primary gauge for labor investment was the prevailing prices for sugar and cotton on the world market. In a sparsely populated frontier region such as Santa Cruz, however, the mobilization of an adequate labor force to meet the intensifying rhythm of export agricultural production posed a considerable problem. Although the transformation of settlers into wage laborers was one solution, growers also adopted other methods that combined economic incentives with coercion to meet their labor demands. Such tactics were a reponse to changes in regional and national economic conditions and political circumstances within Bolivia.

Prior to the 1952 revolution, lowland peasants and indigenous groups satisfied the limited labor demands of the lowland estates, but for a number of reasons, growers increasingly turned to the highlands and valleys for workers during the years that followed. Most lowlanders preferred to cultivate crops on their own land rather than endure the work routine on the sugarcane and cotton estates, which intensified as the agricultural boom gathered steam. The availability of frontier land offered them the opportunity to own their own parcel, and when they had to seek wage employment, most tended to do so only on a sporadic basis, working for a day, two days, or a week and then returning to their own agricultural activities. They also tended to move from estate to estate, seeking out the best working conditions, then moving on when the situation was not to their liking. For these reasons, the lowlanders gained a reputation for laziness and unreliability among the dominant class.

There is a more basic reason why lowlanders could not have constituted a major work force on the Santa Cruz estates. The region was too sparsely populated and settlement was too disperse to supply the ever greater numbers of laborers required by the agro-industries. Consequently, growers concentrated their recruitment efforts on rural people from the highlands and valleys, areas that were the most densely settled parts of Bolivia and contained the majority of the national population. Also, Chiriguano Indians of the southern province of Cordillera also became a focus of recruiting efforts.

People from Cordillera as well as the highlands and valleys had several reasons to migrate to northern Santa Cruz. The fragmentation of their plots due to population growth and inheritance made subsistence agriculture more precarious, and the lack of employment alternatives in their home communities forced people to look elsewhere for work. In Santa Cruz, the comparatively high wages offered by sugarcane and cotton growers constituted an incentive for many to migrate to the department and take up wage labor. The principal areas of out migration were the Cochabamba Valley and the department of Chuquisaca, but significant numbers also came from the departments of La Paz, Oruro, and certain provinces in Potosi. An influx of migrants from the lowland provinces of Chiquitos and Cordillera in Santa Cruz department also added to the total numbers (INE: 1980).

Many of the initial migrants to northern Santa Cruz were young men from sixteen to thirty-five years old who came as seasonal laborers for the harvest. The extreme seasonality of cotton and sugarcane production generated intensive labor demands only during the crucial harvest months. The cotton harvest began in March and extended into May, when the sugarcane harvest got under way and continued for approximately six months, from mid-May or early June through October. This schedule coincided with a lull in the agricultural cycle of the highlands and valleys and allowed migrants to engage in work for a portion of the year before returning home to plant their own crops in October and November.

Although some migrants came to Santa Cruz with other friends or family members to look for work, others were recruited from their home communities by labor contractors during the preharvest months. The labor contractors, or contratistas, worked for the sugarcane and cotton planters and represented the growing connection between the lowland agro-industrial sector and the largely subsistence economy of the highlands and valleys. Contractors controlled much of the migratory flow and channeled it to the large estates--thus constituting a key element in the planter's overall strategy of labor acquisition.

Most contratistas were residents in the regions where they contracted, as the job required an intimate knowledge of the local setting and fluency in both Spanish and an indigenous language, usually Quechua or Guarani. The majority were themselves former wage laborers who, initially at least, enjoyed a certain amount of influence and respect among their fellow workers. Growers would spot such individuals and offer them money if they would bring a specified number of men to work the following season. At first a contratista might bring only five to ten workers, recruited from his own network of friends and relatives, but many subsequently expanded their operations and provided laborers to more than one grower. New channels of upward mobility opened for a few individuals, as the highlands and valleys became more integrated into the expanding lowland commercial sector. In fact, the contratistas came to represent a new source of domination and exploitation in many rural communities.

The contratistas recruited workers primarily during the preharvest months, when they received money from the growers to advance loans to prospective laborers. On the eve of the harvest, trucks arrived at designated points throughout the regions of out-migration to collect workers and transport them to Santa Cruz. A certain amount of contracting also went on in the lowlands. Individuals who migrated independently to the department often were recruited in the towns and commercial centers as they set out to look for work; workers also were frequently re-contracted on the estates prior to their journey home. During periods of acute labor shortages, indebtedness was one way that growers, through their contratista, controlled workers and obliged them to return again the next year.

During the 1950s and 1960s, contratistas were the most important means of securing laborers for both cotton and sugarcane growers. The system, however, was flawed in a number of ways. Growers constantly complained about their inability to recruit a sufficient work force. First, migrant laborers often found it difficult to adjust to the climate and the demanding work routine. Many became disillusioned by the bad working conditions encountered on the lowland estates and the mistreatment suffered at the hands of the contratistas. The reality differed from the exaggerated accounts they had heard in their home communities about the quick wealth and limitless opportunities available in Santa Cruz.

Second, although indebtedness enabled growers to control their work force, it was a double-edged sword that cut both ways. Workers frequently accepted advances from several contratistas, and then when the harvest approached, they set off to work with one but did not repay the other loans. Furthermore, growers constantly had to deal with indebted laborers leaving their estates. Workers fled to escape debts and to seek higher wages elsewhere; finding them was not always an easy chore. Contratistas on neighboring properties would hire them, and although they were not always aware that the individuals owed money elsewhere, the contratistas were less willing to return them once they had advanced money. Thus, evasion softened the harsher aspects of indebtedness for the workers and increased labor costs for the growers [2].

Finally, the availability of frontier land lured many migrants away from the sugarcane and cotton estates. After working for one or two seasons in the lowlands, familiarizing themselves with the region and establishing contacts, many chose to initiate their own agricultural activities. They were eventually joined by other family members who assisted them in the difficult tasks of clearing the forest and establishing a home in the jungle. Like their lowland counterparts, they hoped to avoid the insecurity of wage employment and to exert more control over their own future.

Why, one might ask, did growers not restrict settlers' access to frontier land? State support for colonization projects declined under the military; still, it would have been extremely difficult, if not impossible, to limit access to the vast stretches of frontier land. Moreover, settlers facilitated the extension of cash-crop production by clearing the forest and cutting access roads. They also needed land to reproduce their domestic units, as the highly seasonal nature of the agro-industries could not support a fully proletarianized labor force. Land kept people in the region and prevented many from drifting away after the harvest, which contributed to the growth of a local, more settled, labor force. Nevertheless, by monopolizing both credit, the marketing system, and the land located near stable roads, capitalist growers insured that many settlers could do no more than eke out a subsistence existence, forcing them to work as wage laborers.

Throughout the 1950s and 1960s, then, growers struggled to meet their labor needs and contended with the problems inherent in the <u>contratista</u> system, but by the 1970s a massive increase in cotton cultivation moved them to pressure the government to help recruit more workers, and the state became directly involved in new methods of labor recruitment. A project known as PROMIGRA 73 grew out of an agreement between the cotton growers' association--the Asociación de Productores de Algodón (ADEPA)--and the Ministerio de Asuntos Campesinos. Its objective was to recruit enough workers to satisfy the labor demands of the 1973 harvest.

PROMIGRA agents organized a massive radio and newspaper campaign, promising workers generous salaries and fringe benefits. Their pledges were distorted, and in 1973, the newspaper <u>Presencia</u> published the following commentary:

> The first social problems in the cotton fields of this department began to arise when this activity had still not entered into an intensive phase. At least 500 harvesters, primarily from La Paz, abandoned various cotton centers in the last ten days arguing lack of contract compliance and bad treatment...PROMIGRA according to harvesters' declarations, exaggerated its promotional campaign, making offers that are far from being completed. (Presencia: March 29, 1973)

The PROMIGRA campaign failed: The number of workers required for the cotton harvest were not recruited. This led to more pressure on the government to conscript workers from various regions of the country, and in some cases the army was sent out to harvest crops. Not surprisingly, peasants suffered numerous abuses during this period [3]. The program was discontinued the following year, and growers were compelled to find other means of dealing with their labor problems.

By the mid-1970s, the new frontier society was evident. Social relationships and the pattern of landholding in northern Santa Cruz--and particularly the province of Obispo Santiesteban province--did not represent a radical departure from post-1952 productive arrangements. Rather than dismantling the large estates, state policies favored landowners who chose to convert their properties into modern commercial enterprises, and the economic support of U.S.-sponsored development programs and international banking institutions facilitated the expansion of capitalism in northern Santa Cruz.

The process of capitalist development integrated the department into national and international markets, and as the economic importance of the region grew, the presence of the state became stronger: First, through the activities of the MNR party and later, with the increased presence and intervention of the military. Military support for and participation in regional development established the beginnings of an alliance between the military and agro-industrial interests, which would become even more powerful in years to come.

The growth of the agricultural enterprises in northern Santa Cruz, however, would not have been possible without the participation of rural settlers as both wage laborers and subsistence cultivators. They facilitated the expansion of the agro-industries with their land and labor, and even as they were losing the fight with large, capitalist producers, their struggles defined the direction that capitalist development in Santa Cruz would ultimately take. It is to these people that we turn to next.

NOTES

1. A much smaller area (376,681) was granted to Indian communities and communal areas such as plazas and soccer fields.

2. See Michael Gonzeles (1985) for further discussion of these points.

3. In areas of the altiplano, individuals who did not have proper identification to show were taken against their will to harvest cotton (<u>Presencia</u>: 5/9/73).

3

Frontier Settlement and Proletarianization

As prominent lowlanders and investors from other parts of Bolivia amassed large properties and extended cash-crop production onto the frontier, migrants--primarily from the highlands and valleys--initiated subsistence agriculture on small holdings scattered across the periphery of the burgeoning commercial zone. The lure of free land and the hope of shaping a more prosperous future for themselves and their children attracted these men and women, who, often could not satisfy subsistence needs in their home communities. What they discovered in northern Santa Cruz, however, did not always correspond with their expectations.

The heat and humidity of the tropics was an unwelcome change from the cool, dry climate of their highland communities. The settlers were scorned by the crucenos, who ridiculed their personal habits and resented the influx of so many impoverished migrants looking for work. The newcomers also felt isolated from their kinfolk and friends. They experienced acute feelings of loneliness and depression, but as they initiated cultivation on remote frontier plots, they were quickly drawn into a new series of commercial relationships. These relationships were frequently unequal and exploitative, and many settlers found it difficult, if not impossible, to establish viable farming activities in northern Santa Cruz.

The migrants were not a homogeneous group. Some came from peasant origins; others were either small-scale merchants and agriculturalists or came from families in a position to help them. A significant number profited from the commercial opportunities that accompanied the growth of commercial agriculture, and new class divisions began to shape the relationships among settlers.

The creation and transformation of three communities in Obispo Santiesteban province--Nuevo Mundo, Rio Viejo, and Paichanetu--illustrate this process. Located near the present-day town of Mineros, they were among the first "spontaneous" communities to form in the aftermath of the revolution, and the spread of capitalist relations of production did not affect them in exactly the same way as other settlements in the province. Capitalism evolved more rapidly in Nuevo Mundo, Rio Viejo, and Paichanetu than in other areas where weaker market connections forestalled internal differentiation. Yet their histories demonstrate the essential meaning of capitalist development for rural people in northern Santa Cruz, and their stories are not unique.

THE SETTLEMENT PROCESS AND LAND ACQUISITION

Land itself is not a definitive element in the development of a capitalist economy, but the amount and forms of access to it as well as its condition vis-a-vis the presence or absence of virgin forest are important factors. Before the expansion of commercial agriculture, virgin land in northern Santa Cruz could be settled at no cost. As it was drawn into agricultural production it acquired value and was bought and sold. This value originated from labor invested in such tasks as land clearance, soil preparation, the construction of access roads, planting, etc., and was not the product of the natural qualities inherent in the terrain. A greater productive potential developed as land was cleared and incorporated into production because of the speculative possibilities of lumber extraction, infrastructural development, and cash-crop cultivation--but this productive potential could be realized only by those who controlled capital, and capital was a scarce resource among settlers.

According to Holmberg (1950) and many of the original settlers, Siriono Indians resided in the forest north of Mineros prior to the agrarian reform. During the early decades of the twentieth century much of the land in the province was ceded to latifundists connected with the import-export houses interested in extracting rubber and timber. When rubber was not found, the houses turned their attention to the large mahogany stands and constructed sawmills along several rivers that traversed the province. Small-scale commercial exploitation of the timber reserves generated conflicts with the Siriono; also, many Indians were being taken against their will to work in the northern rubber forests. Such harrassment compelled the Siriono to flee into the Beni lowlands, and by the time colonizers arrived in the mid-1950s, few remained. The agrarian-reform legislation did not recognize Indian land rights, and settlers gradually took possession of the land.

Lowland peasants were the first to enter the northern forests, and new communities initially grew up in the region surrounding Mineros, which at the time consisted of a few thatched huts and served as a frontier outpost for the Santa Cruz import-export houses. Many early colonizers were former tenants from the lowland estates who entered the forest along paths previously cut for lumber extraction. They left the estates in the aftermath of the land reform, when many landlords curtailed tenancy agreements out of fear that peasants would claim the land.

Groups of individuals, often kinfolk, founded several of the first settlements, including Nuevo Mundo, Rio Viejo, and Paichanetu. They had little difficulty obtaining land: the vast tracts of jungle seemed endless. And the agrarian reform, which sought to institute a regime of private landownership based on individual property titles, legitimized their claims. More important, landlords faced considerable difficulty enforcing their rights in this remote region. Most forfeited claims to retain property in the more favorable locations where cash-crop production was a viable possibility. Some, however, struggled to maintain a foothold. One latifundist denounced an agrarian judge and the local army commander when his 2,000-hectare claim was going to be reduced to eighty hectares. Through his personal connections, he had the judge replaced, and a more sympathetic one allowed him to retain 1,000 hectares. Other latifundists bribed agrarian-reform judges to prevent the virgin land that they claimed from being taken over by settlers.

The settlers formed syndicates to defend their rights to the land. The organizations governed life in the new frontier communities and maintained order in places where state power still was weak. They defended peasants' rights gained in the revolution and enforced claims even in the absence of legal title. Although their development goes back to the rebellions of the 1930s and 1940s in the Cochabamba Valley, the syndicates became a major political force in Bolivia after 1952 (Dandler: 1969). The first syndicates in northern Santa Cruz were never as militant as many of their highland and valley counterparts. Most formed in the aftermath of the revolution, prompted by the encouragement of MNR sympathizers who sought to rally popular support for the new government.

In Nuevo Mundo and Rio Viejo, the syndicates were organized in the towns among former peones from the haciendas surrounding Montero. Members (not more than 200) marched off to the frontier, where they claimed areas of forested land and divided it into parcels ranging from ten to fifty hectares. The names of many new communities such as Nuevo Mundo (New World) reflected the founding families' hopes and visions of a better life. Once established, the settlements extended for several kilometers in a long strip along the access route; families lived in a dispersed fashion, often at a considerable distance from each other. Nuevo Mundo, grew out of a syndicate called "La Cruz Seis de Agosto", which sought to expropriate a property of the same name that encompassed several thousand hectares (see Figure 3.1). Most of this property was covered with forest. The eighty-one lowland settlers and their families who formed the syndicate had little

Figure 3.1

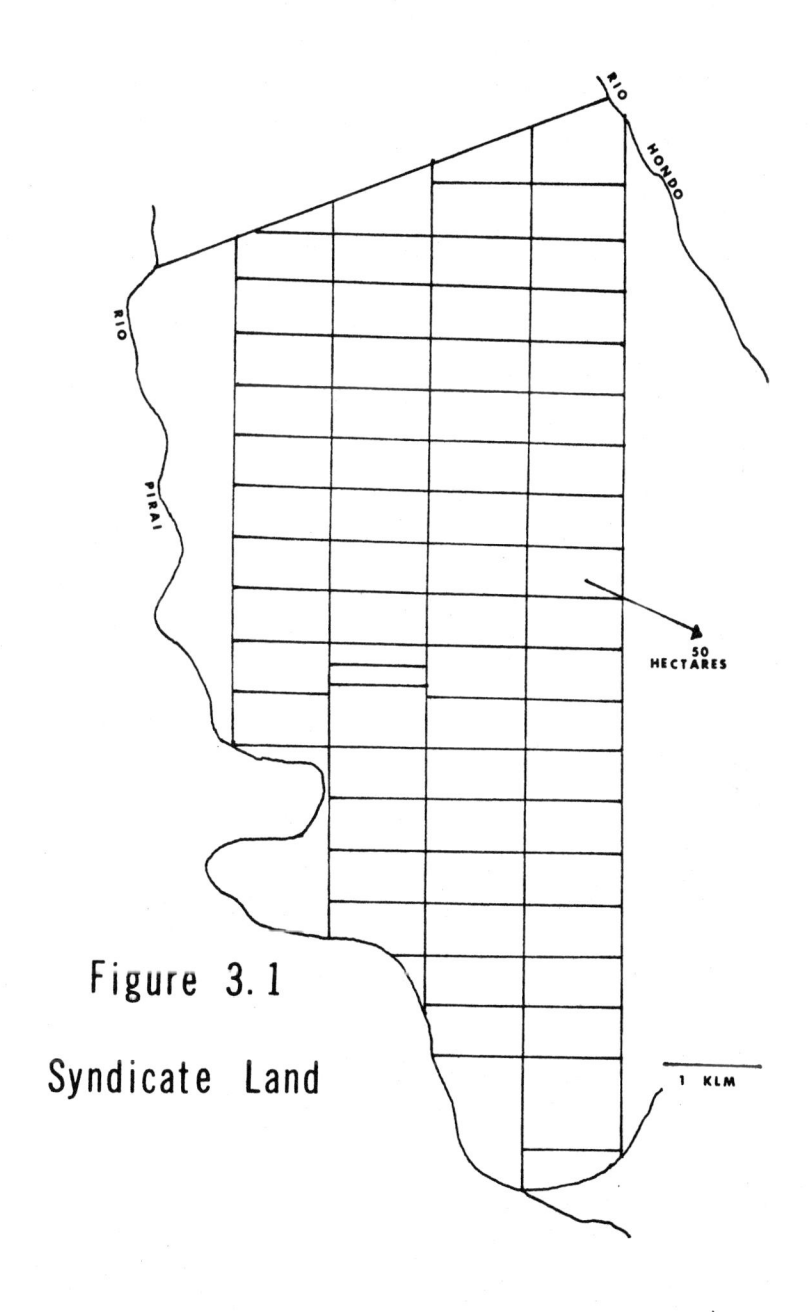

Syndicate Land

trouble occupying and initiating subsistence farming on the land--which the syndicate distributed in fifty-hectare plots to each adult male or head of household. In 1960 the agrarian reform recognized the settlers' land rights and also gave them 100 hectares for a future urban center and further settlement. The original landowners contested this decision, but they had to content themselves with plots averaging from twenty-five to one hundred hectares.

Syndicates also appeared after colonization had taken place. Around many of the old sawmills workers began subsistence farming on land slightly distant from the mills. Other workers, viewing the success and independence of the settlers, joined them, and as the settlements grew, the new members gradually organized syndicates to legitimize their land claims. Paichanetu developed in this way after sawmill workers on the Rio Hondo claimed several hundred hectares of land that had belonged to the mill owners. In the early 1950s, after the timber reserves were exhausted, the owners had no more use for the land and moved their operations further upstream. Several workers, mainly Guarayo Indians, remained behind and began to cultivate the land. After the revolution they were joined by a number of other Guarayo and Chiquitano families who left an estate near Montero. Together these people organized a syndicate to protect their land rights and confront the new problems brought on by increasing national integration.

The first pioneers were usually young men, joined by their wives and children after establishing both a tentative land claim and minimal living arrangements. Given the enormous labor demands associated with frontier agriculture and the creation of a new community, "woman's work," i.e., cooking, washing, mending, and helping with some of the agricultural chores, was extremely important to the survival of the domestic unit, and single men who could not count on the labor of female kin frequently attached themselves to households where women carried out these tasks. In the absence of state support, individual households depended heavily upon ties of kinship, compadrazgo, and interfamilial cooperation to survive in the inhospitable jungle environment. The syndicates were based on such ties and represented a village-level form of social organization that united households and directed social life to benefit the community as a whole.

The syndicates played an important role in the social organization of the frontier settlements and were initially synonymous with the communities themselves. Only through a local syndicate could a settler receive land, and land constituted the basic element for the organization and reproduction of the peasant family. The syndicates also directed and participated in a wide range of activities, including the distribution of land, the initiation of infrastructural development, and the resolution of such internal disputes as intermarital and property-boundary conflicts. A representative from each household--usually the male household head--was obliged to attend biweekly meetings, where people organized development projects, elected local leaders, and discussed community problems. Furthermore, the syndicates often called upon residents to participate in collective work groups. Such groups engaged in projects that included road clearing and the construction of wells and schools. The syndicates thus facilitated communication among settlers dispersed over a wide area by allowing them to share experiences, overcome feelings of isolation, and solve common problems.

After claiming a piece of land settlers were immediately confronted with the problem of placing enough of it under cultivation to produce food for the next six to eight months. They also had to earn a cash income sufficient to purchase a few basic necessities. Settlers practiced a system of tropical swidden agriculture that involved cutting down the primary forest, burning the dried debris, and planting crops for a period of two to three years. For this system to operate effectively, a large quantity of land was indispensable, since the cleared field (chaco) was subsequently abandoned and the natural forest allowed to regenerate. Lost soil nutrients were replenished, and weeds and diseases that lowered yields were eradicated. After five to seven years the regrowth (barbecho) could be cleared and burned for a second round of cultivation. Yields were high per cultivated hectare but low when distributed across the total territory required for the success of these practices. Rudimentary technology--the ax, machete, hoe and knife--was utilized; few settlers had the capital reserves necessary to hire wage laborers or use agricultural machinery. Consequently, the size of the domestic labor force and the availability of labor through reciprocal exchanges or simple collaboration between households determined the amount of land that could be cultivated.

Particularly at the outset, the labor demands associated with clearing the forest and planting the first crops were taxing. The cultivated area varied, but the available labor supply generally did not permit it to exceed a maximum of three hectares, thus maintaining the balance between planted land, barbecho, and virgin forest. Settlers mobilized labor through their ties with kin, neighbors, and friends because few had the money necessary to hire wage laborers. Such ties were particularly important to new households consisting of young couples with small children, who could not yet count on the labor power of several offspring.

Although reciprocal forms of labor exchange--ayni and minka--were not practiced as widely among lowland peasants as in the communities founded by highland and valley migrants (see Weil: 1980 and Blanes and Flores: 1982), interhousehold cooperation united the settlers in Nuevo Mundo, Rio Viejo, and Paichanetu. When labor demands were heavy, such as the rice harvest or clearing the forest, kinsfolk assisted each other, working first on the parcel of one household and them moving on to others. Relatives from different areas, often prospective settlers, would reside with family members for a period of time and participate in the daily work routine. This was particularly helpful to colonizers during peak periods of the agricultural cycle and also enabled potential migrants to acquire valuable information about the frontier settlements. Such links represented a broad system of cooperation and coordination of resources, which united families in the settlements and linked dispersed households to relationships extending beyond the boundaries of their communities.

The ability of traditional swidden agriculturalists in various parts of the world to use the tropical forest as a renewable resource and develop highly efficient patterns of food production is one of the salient characteristics of this system (Geertz: 1963; Nations and Nigh: 1980; Riester: 1977; and Rappaport: 1968). Unfortunately, the growing monetization of the regional economy did not permit most settlers to develop a stable agricultural base. Landlords no longer assumed any of the responsibility for the subsistence of peasant households, and settlers increasingly needed cash to meet a rising number of claims on their income, e.g., clothing, medicines, some manufactured goods, and basic food items not produced by the domestic unit. They were therefore obliged to plant crops that provided a quick cash income rather than cultivate food crops for domestic consumption.

Rice was the first crop sown and was one of the only crops that offered the possibility of a cash income to families located in remote settlement zones. Aside from its subsistence value, rice required little capital input and could be marketed in a relatively short time. The dry varieties common to the area were easily cultivated and stored, and they demanded little soil preparation. The intensive use of unpaid domestic labor allowed peasants to produce such rice in situations that were unattactive to the capitalist enterprises.

Yields were relatively high during the first year of cultivation on virgin land because problems with weeds were minimal. The second year brought a fall in output because of greater weed and pest infestations, and by the third year such problems were uncontrollable. Two weedings were the minimum by the second year, and to hire labor for additional weedings in subsequent years was prohibitively expensive. Settlers either left the

Settler Harvesting Rice

plot and cleared a new chaco or planted such
crops as corn, which were less sensitive to the
suffocating weeds. But preparing a field from
virgin forest required large labor expenditures;
the continual abandonment of old fields and the
creation of new ones placed heavy demands on
family labor. Most families could not afford to
hire additional laborers and plant a larger area
to compensate for falling yields, and their own
labor was poorly remunerated. This occurred for a
number of reasons.

    First, increased participation in the market
exposed settlers to new market-based insecurities
that jeopardized their income. Distance and poor
roads complicated the sale of goods, and unstable
prices affected the final value of the crop.
Second, the depletion of virgin forest, which
grew out of the commodification of agriculture,
reduced the resource base available to rural
families. Finally, a large number of middlemen
rose to dominate the marketing system in the
aftermath of the revolution. By acting as
moneylenders--buying cheap and selling dear--they
extracted a large surplus from peasant producers.
The number of middlemen grew in response to new
conditions created by the revolution. The estates
no longer acted as the principal recipients of
peasant crops. But the growth of urban centers
created new demands for agricultural products,
and peasant production played an important role
in sustaining the growing population of northern
Santa Cruz. Intermediaries, who possessed their
own trucks and some financial reserves, were able
to take advantage of the new opportunities for
profit. As a result, settlers did not accumulate
capital, and wealth was transfered to other
groups.

    As subsistence agriculture became
problematic and settlers could not establish
viable farming operations, families were forced
to find other sources of cash to meet the
subsistence needs. Wage labor represented one
alternative to agriculture. Some settlers left
the communities and either moved to the towns
where they found part-time employment as street
vendors, domestic servants, cargo carriers, and
construction workers, or tried to capitalize new

plots further into the frontier. Others remained in the countryside and worked as agricultural day laborers, dedicating a portion of their time to wage labor while continuing unprofitable farming in regrowth or attempting to reestablish subsistence agriculture.

Credit also was a solution to the cash shortage. Since banks did not deal with colonizers during the early phases of commercial expansion and the communities did not benefit from government assistance channeled to directed settlement programs, the colonizers' only hope was to approach merchants and sugarcane producers (often the same person) for loans. The creation of debt relationships eroded the more egalitarian forms of reciprocity and redistribution that initially characterized the settlements and replaced them with new, asymmetrical relationships based upon domination and dependence (see Chapter 5). Although the creation of creditor-debtor ties and wage labor represented different alternatives to the problems posed by subsistence agriculture, needy settlers could not limit themselves to only one option and most diversified their income-generating activities to include agriculture, wage labor, and indebtedness.

The stability of the communities grew ever more tenuous. While the charter community members abandoned the settlements or spent increasingly longer periods away from their homes to earn a cash income, new migrants from the highlands and valleys began to pour into Santa Cruz, many settling in the communities during the late 1960s. Some purchased land from the original settlers and started their own commercial farming ventures. Others joined the increasingly proletarianized rural labor force. This migratory process began after the completion of the Santa Cruz-Cochabamba highway in the mid-1950s but at first only affected Nuevo Mundo, Rio Viejo, and Paichanetu beginning in the early 1960s.

New families moved into the communites, and the settlements became tied to a broader network of commercial relationships. Northern Santa Cruz "progressed" as markets grew and money began to circulate throughout the region. Mineros changed

from a remote trading outpost to a thriving
commercial center. A civic committee formed and
inaugurated a town plaza; schools appeared, and
electric lighting illuminated the streets. State
presence in the communities became more apparent
with the appointment of corregidores. Meanwhile,
the state built new roads and upgraded old ones,
and buses and trucks began to operate between the
city of Santa Cruz and several new centers in the
northern zone. The constant arrival of new
settlers--both wealthy and poor--led to further
changes in the social and economic organization
of the frontier. New notions of ethnicity
developed, class conflicts sharpened, and many of
the syndicates became disorganized and ceased to
function.

IMMIGRATION AND SOCIOECONOMIC DIFFERENTIATION

Migrants came from a number of different
cultural, linguistic, and economic backgrounds.
Many were born in the department of Cochabamba,
where they grew up speaking Quechua. The women
wore long braids, dressed in many-layered skirts
called polleras, and carried their children in
brightly colored shawls on their backs.
Chiriguano migrants, from the southern province
of Cordillera, and Guarayos, from former mission
communities in the north, spoke different
dialects of Guarani. The Guarayos benefited from
an intimate knowledge of the flora and fauna and
utilized their fishing and hunting skills to
survive during the first, most difficult year in
the new frontier settlements.

Although their numbers did not fulfill the
government's hopes of redistributing the national
population, the newcomers exerted a profound
influence on Nuevo Mundo, Rio Viejo, and
Paichanetu as well as the entire department of
Santa Cruz. The vast majority were impoverished
peasants who migrated to northern Santa Cruz in
search of work. Like the pioneers from northern
Santa Cruz, they attempted to establish their own
claims to land, and to cultivate subsistence
crops after working as wage laborers for a season
or two. Although a few were successful, many

fared little better than their lowland counterparts and swelled the ranks of an emerging group of impoverished peasants who alternated between wage labor and subsistence agriculture.

By the late 1960s, acquiring land around Mineros had become difficult. Previous settlement had resulted in the complete privatization of land in this region, and rising land values in communities such as Nuevo Mundo, Rio Viejo, and Paichanetu precluded purchase for all but the wealthier migrants. The locus of frontier expansion now lay at a considerable distance from Mineros, and in order to gain access to free land, settlers had to migrate even further north. Migrants who could not afford to buy their own parcel entered into various forms of rental and usufruct arrangements with landholders in order to gain access to a small plot for subsistence cultivation. Such agreements typified the increasingly unequal control over productive resources exercised by local residents.

During the early 1970s, most of the land that once belonged to individual families in Paichanetu passed into the hands of a few sugarcane growers who were extending the scope of their activities. This process was aggravated both by serious flooding that spurred some migrants to sell their land and by illegal land sales arranged by a syndicate leader. The community shrunk to less than eighty hectares of land, which remained under the control of the syndicate and had never been privately owned. The syndicate originally intended to use the land for future settlement and for the construction of a plaza, but with the reduction of the land base available to settlers, the syndicate began to allot portions of this land to families in small plots of one to three hectares for subsistence cultivation.

Many of the original settlers had been replaced by new migrants who came to the region as wage laborers, and since this area was not large enough to provide for the needs of the approximately thirty families who lived in Paichanetu, people dedicated most of their time to wage labor, and the community began to operate as a labor reserve for the surrounding estates. Both the original settlers and the new arrivals grew to share a common poverty, as chances for economic advancement in the settlement became fewer and fewer.

Impoverished highland and valley migrants adopted subsistence strategies similar to their lowland counterparts. Some relocated on or near the large, cash-crop producing estates. In exchange for a plot of land and a small salary, they engaged in a number of tasks that varied with the agricultural cycle. To find temporary work, many also drifted in and out of the growing urban centers in the department. Although for some this was merely a stage in their life cycle, many others quickly saw their hopes of prosperity and visions of a better life in Santa Cruz vanish.

This pattern of productive activities adopted by peasant families was a flexible one. Sometimes they engaged in one activity more than another, but at other times both strategies were combined. Such tactics also were adopted by low-income urban inhabitants, whose work was affected by the seasonal nature of economic activity in northern Santa Cruz. Hired truck drivers, agricultural machinery operators, and their assistants, working during the dry months, often cultivated small plots of land during the November-April rainy season. Given the low pay and insecurity of wage labor and the precarious nature of subsistence cultivation, these strategies made a good deal of sense; they gave people access to a range of income-generating activities. Indeed, most families distributed personnel in a number of different occupations and maintained contacts in both urban and rural settlings.

Santiago Pasabare and his family are typical of other poor peasants. Santiago was born in 1950 in San Jose de Chiquitos, a provincial lowland town located midway between the city of Santa Cruz and the Brazilian border. In the late 1960s, he and two brothers left San Jose after a prolonged drought ruined the family's crops and his father became indebted to a local cattle rancher. They worked as seasonal laborers on an estate in northern Santa Cruz, and in 1971 they settled in Paichanetu, where the syndicate alloted them small plots of land for subsistence cultivation. They were joined by their families and elder parents, and over the next decade the family developed a diversified pattern of subsistence activities.

These activities usually, but not always, included the cultivation of one or two hectares of rice, corn, and cassava for domestic consumption. The men periodically engaged in agricultural day labor on the surrounding estates. They worked for a day or a week at a time, clearing forest, cutting fence post, planting, weeding, and harvesting the various crops. At times, Santiago also obtained seasonal employment in a Mineros rice mill and in the offices of a Mineros-based agricultural cooperative. His wife, in addition to her domestic chores, also contributed to the family's cash needs. She baked bread and empanadas, which she took to Mineros and sold to passersby in the town plaza, and from time to time she also worked as a domestic servant for town women.

There was a lot of sharing between Santiago's household and other members of the extended family. Children passed back and forth between related households, cash and subsistence goods were given to and received from relatives in time of need; Santiago, his brothers, his father, and an uncle collaborated with the agricultural tasks related to subsistence cultivation on their parcels. Thus, they created greater social security for individual family members during times of sickness or crisis and shielded themselves from the harsher aspects of the expanding capitalist economy.

The kind and duration of salaried labor varied in accordance with both the family's need for cash and the seasonal and long-term economic fluctuations. Although a semi-proletarianized labor force suited growers because it could support itself during the dead season and allowed planters to pay wages below the cost of subsistence, the apparent balance of this relationship was only superficial. During the 1960s and 1970s commercial agriculture threatened the very basis of subsistence agriculture, which was so crucial to its survival, by pushing settlers further into wage labor. This naturally created tension, and when the economic boom lost steam several years later and a severe economic crisis threatened the agro-industries, many poor peasants, as we shall see in Chapter 8, took to the offensive in an effort to reestablish subsistence agriculture and reassert their rights as small-scale agricultural producers.

Although the migratory flow that brought people to the department of Santa Cruz was primarily a migration of labor, it involved more than just the transfer of labor power to the region, and the expansion of the economy and the growth of commerce actually created the conditions for the emergence of an entrepreneurial group of small-scale agriculturalists. Some migrants with small, but significant, capital reserves hoped to benefit from the new economic opportunities and to increase agricultural production for the market. Many came from peasant origins; some were small merchants or members of various urban groups. Several resettled directly in the boomtowns of northern Santa Cruz; others bought land from earlier settlers in the first settlements established by ex-peones from the lowland estates.

Although many small-scale agriculturalists began their life cycle in Santa Cruz as wage laborers, they generally had some formal education or skill and came from families in a position to assist them. In their communities of origin, such families did not always have enough land to distribute equally among subsequent generations, but they still could afford to help migrating family members with subsistence goods and small sums of cash. These families often had better connections in both the settlement zones and the urban commercial sector. Consequently, migrants were able to initiate cash-crop cultivation or commercial activities with greater ease than either the original settlers or the more impoverished migrants from the highlands and valleys.

By the early 1970s, the international demand for sugarcane had begun to determine which crops were cultivated in Obispo Santiesteban province, particularly in Nuevo Mundo, Rio Viejo, and Paichanetu. Located from eight to fifteen kilometers from the major north-south highway, these settlements were well positioned for the development of sugarcane cultivation and attracted a number of better-off migrants as well as large-scale commercial growers. Unlike the charter community members, these individuals had the necessary capital to purchase labor power and expand the area under cultivation.

The development of greater social and economic differentiation strained the local syndicate organizations, which were already suffering under military control. New conflicts and problems arose in the settlements, and the syndicates were increasingly unable to manage these disputes. Many ceased to function or existed in name only, and the communities were profoundly transformed.

DECLINE OF THE SYNDICATES

In the early days of frontier settlement, the syndicates were able to mediate internal conflict and channel cooperation in ways that were beneficial to the communities, but their early success cannot be attributed to the harmony of frontier life. Rather, it was due to their ability to enforce the concerns and survival of the group over disputes at the individual or village level. They succeeded because of the existence of a collective settler interest and a shared enthusiasm that all settlers defined as their own. This meant that the syndicates were viable only so long as the settlers remained united and faced the rest of the world together. But the communities were integrated into the wider society, and land came to be regarded as a commodity that could be bought and sold. Gradually the communal solidarity and the influence of the syndicates dissipated.

The syndicates had initially supervised both the distribution and, to a certain extent, the use of frontier land, even though the agrarian reform established the basis for private property. If families failed to cultivate their parcels or abandoned the settlements, the syndicates reallocated the plots to other settlers, and by so doing exercised control over the composition of the communities. This changed with the increasing monetization of the regional economy: Instead of simply abandoning a parcel of land when they decided to leave a settlement, families were able to acquire cash for their parcels and began selling to the highest bidder. This was one way that they obtained funds, which they then used to capitalize a new parcel further into the frontier.

As new, entrepreneurial-minded settlers and large cash-crop producers bought the land, sugarcane production began to supplant subsistence agriculture. Most of the new arrivals came from the highlands and valleys and were carriers of different customs and cultural traditions, which gave rise to greater heterogeneity within the communities and aggravated emerging class distinctions. The highland and valley migrants initially identified themselves with a particular community or region of origin, but such distinctions gave way to new categories. These categories--<u>camba</u> for lowland inhabitants and <u>colla</u> for highland migrants-- did not represent fixed categories; in fact, such distinctions hid important differences. Membership in each group was negotiable; it was a way that settlers formed friendships, associations, and gained access to political and economic resources. Stereotypes associated with these more comprehensive categories developed as people gained access to different positions in the newly emerging frontier society, and they reflected growing class divisions [1].

Acceptance of newcomers by the lowland syndicate members was frequently charged with tension. Settlers not affiliated with the MNR were discouraged, for example. To maintain the solidarity of the group, so crucial to settlers during the early years of settlement, the syndicates were not willing to accept just anyone into their midst. This led to conflicts between the original settlers and the more recent highland and valley arrivals. The latter at first were told to go elsewhere, but they increasingly purchased land in the settlements, and cash-crop production began to supplant subsistence agriculture.

The cohesiveness of the syndicates weakened, and the very notion of community grew vague. Although the original settlers had always maintained ties outside the communities, the constant departure of families and the arrival of new personnel created an extremely fluid situation. Many newcomers did not participate in the syndicates and spent little time in the settlements. Several constructed houses in Mineros and Montero, where they lived for extended periods, and poorer families who resided in the settlements also spent long periods of time away from their families, searching for work on one estate after another and pursuing part-time employment in the towns. They formed stronger, more direct ties with intermediaries, landlords, and money lenders and established patron-client relationships with the small-scale agriculturalists. Thus, the formation of vertical alliances with other groups at the regional and even national levels acquired greater importance than the bonds that had united the charter syndicate members during the early years of frontier settlement.

Weakened by internal divisions, the sindicates also were undermined by government manipulation and intervention. Even though the MNR utilized peasant organizations for its own ends, its fall and the rise of the military in 1964 seriously restricted independent syndicate activity. The Pacto Militar-Campesino, instituted in 1968 under the dictatorship of General Rene Barrientos, sought to exert greater control over peasant groups and brought the syndicates directly under the tutelage of the armed forces. In exchange for the unquestioning support of the peasantry, the military promised to provide financial and technical assistance to rural people.

The Pacto Militar-Campesino decapitated the syndicate hierarchy at the canton and provincial levels, where leaders of the sub-centrales and centrales were replaced by military-appointed repesentatives. These changes restricted the ability of local community syndicates to channel their grievances to state organizations. At the community level the impact was varied and at times more subtle. In some cases the syndicates had already ceased to function, and no new attempts were made at reorganization. Then, too, settlers sometimes merely stopped attending meetings and the syndicate continued to exist in name only. In several other cases, however, existing syndicates were reorganized under new leadership and controlled by "coordinators" appointed by the military. The new leaders were not chosen by the people and did not necessarily represent local interests; they frequently used their positions as a means of personal advancement and enrichment. Factional conflicts broke out over partisan political concerns, and the settlers became suspicious of the syndicates and increasingly viewed the organizations as tools for government manipulation.

In Nuevo Mundo, for example, a new syndicate had formed out of the original founding organization, as the population increased and several separate communities grew out of the syndicate La Cruz 6 de Agosto. By the late 1960s, however, the community syndicate had grown moribund and was reorganized under the Pacto Militar-Campesino. Its new leader was a highland immigrant who had purchased land and initiated sugarcane cultivation in the settlement. Other settlers complained about the lack of interest this individual showed for community concerns. He did not pass long periods of time in Nuevo Mundo, preferring a home in Mineros to life in the countryside. Thus, he enjoyed little respect from local people. Under his leadership, the syndicate stopped functioning altogether.

By the mid-1970s, rural people in Nuevo Mundo, Rio Viejo, and Paichanetu were divided, and no organization effectively represented their interests. Large-scale commercial production for the export market was undergoing an unprecedented expansion and undermining subsistence production, as major capitalist producers, with the support of the state, incorporated ever more land into their holdings. The combination of numerous tendencies--the commodification of land, labor, and production; the arrival of new settlers; the continuing socioeconomic differentiation; and the increasing integration of the region into the national political economy--created profound divisions among community dwellers.

FRONTIER SETTLEMENT IN A BROADER CONTEXT

During the more than twenty years between the national revolution and the mid-1970s, the experiences of Nuevo Mundo, Rio Viejo, and Paichanetu were repeated in many areas of northern Santa Cruz. This process of class formation was, of course, not uniform throughout the entire region. In many settlements distance from roads and market centers precluded the introduction of sugarcane cultivation and thus forestalled the development of internal differentiation. The more homogeneous backgrounds and cultural traditions of settlers in some communities helped to maintain the strength and vitality of local syndicates to a greater degree. But even if the early development of Nuevo Mundo, Rio Viejo, and Paichanetu was unique, these communities are important examples of the implications of capitalist development for rural people.
Although originally there was much diversity in the groups, the majority of the 3,472 families who had settled in Obispo Santiesteban province since the 1950s had a lot in common by the mid-1970s. First, they suffered from a lack of capital and technical assistance. Second, 84 percent lived in dispersed settlements of fifty families or less that lacked potable water and adequate health facilities (Ortiz: 1977). Bad roads and dangerous river crossings hindered the sale of their produce, and volatile and seldom stable prices reduced their income. Third, middlemen siphoned off settler surpluses and reduced the possibility of capital accumulation. And finally, as land became an increasingly scarce and costly commodity, access to it was possible only through new tenancy arrangements with landholders.

The failure of government-directed colonization programs to relocate people from highland and valley communities to lowland colonies in the mid-1950s and 1960s did not justify the continued expense of such projects, and international aid was withdrawn for this type of funding. Efforts by USAID and church-related organizations in the 1970s focused on families already established in the area, and the Instituto Nacional de Colonizacion (INC), formed in the 1960s to direct the resettlement process, followed a plan called "semidirected" colonization. INC provided land at low prices to new arrivals and distributed minimal medical benefits, but in spite of this assistance some 72 percent of all settlers received no support from government or international organizations.
    Like Nuevo Mundo, Rio Viejo and Paichanetu, the Cuatro Ojitos colony, located fifteen kilometers north of Mineros, was another important center where the penetration of capitalist productive relations altered the nature of community social organization. The colony was founded in 1956 as one of the early, directed colonization projects sponsored by the state and consisted exclusively of migrants from the highlands and valleys. The population reached 1,200 families, but because of a lack of sustained government support and disillusionment on the part of the founding families, many settlers chose to return home, and the population declined to only 800 families by the end of the 1960s (Iglesia Evangelica Metodista: 1972).
    The colony was one of the few frontier settlements with a paved road that passed through the center. When sugarcane cultivation began to spread in the province, Cuatro Ojitos was well situated for the development of this crop. But, as in other communities, a new group of entrepreneurs--not the original settlers-- profited from these circumstances, and it subsequently evolved into an extremely vocal and powerful organization. The Asociacion de Caneros de Cuatro Ojitos represented the interests of many, and another organization--the Federacion Especial de las Cuatro Provincias--also had a number of adherents in this colony. The latter

was founded at the end of the MNR period and was subsequently consolidated under Barrientos. From the beginning it was characterized by dependence upon the government, particularly the military.

Landownership in the Cuatro Ojitos became more unequal, and as in other settlements, many settlers were obliged to work for wages to make ends meet. The frustrations of many poor settlers were briefly expressed from 1969 to 1971, during a period of left-leaning military rule when new, independent organizations formed in northern Santa Cruz. The Union de Campesinos Pobres (UCAPO) was one such group. Linked to the Chinese communist party, UCAPO grouped together settlers from both the directed and the spontaneous settlement zones and included many poor peasants who lacked sufficient land for their subsistence activities. Although much of its leadership came from outside the peasantry, UCAPO responded to a problem increasingly felt by many poor peasants in northern Santa Cruz: the growing concentration of landownership by a few individuals. It organized the invasion of several large estates in Obispo Santiesteban province, and although the peasants who participated did not succeed in redistributing the properties, they created considerable apprehension and discontent among estate owners in the region. In 1969, poor peasants throughout the northern zone also occupied the central plaza of Santa Cruz to demand solutions for their rice marketing problems (El Deber: February 7, 1969).

These experiences and other local attempts to address peasant concerns led to the formation of the Federacion Nacional de Colonizadores in 1971. The federation represented colonizers in northern Santa Cruz, and along with similar organizations in other settlement areas, it was incorporated into the Central Obrera Boliviana (COB), the largest workers' union in the country. The federation promoted the growth of independent peasant syndicates, and its principal concerns centered around securing land titles, overcoming marketing problems, and establishing settler control over various institutions in the colonization zones (Iriarte: 1980).

Paradoxically, settlers from the state-sponsored settlement project, Antofagasta, were the principal organizers and leaders of the federation in Santa Cruz. When their communities were established in the mid-1960s under Barrientos, the government forbade them to organize syndicates, and instead, encouraged them to form "cooperatives" or "community committees" that were more directly linked to technical concerns and dependent upon the government for support. This paternalistic relationship had never been satisfactory, and in 1971 settlers from Antofagasta took control of several tractors that belonged to INC. Following the coup d'etat that brought Banzer to power in the same year, peasant leaders in Antofagasta and other settlements were persecuted, the federation was disbanded, and the government-controlled INC withdrew its support from many areas.

These attempts to address the problems of rural people in northern Santa Cruz arose from the concerns of peasants to defend their interests as small cultivators. Such a desire did not imply autonomy or self-sufficiency, but rather, the need to control resources and meet subsistence needs that other activities, particularly the sale of labor power, did not allow. The invasions occurred during a time of economic expansion; new opportunities lured migrants to northern Santa Cruz while the expansion of the agro-industries undermined their hopes of becoming independent producers.

Like the poor peasants, many small-scale agriculturalists suffered from the domination exercised by the large, capitalist entrepreneurs. Particularly in the province of Obispo Santiesteban, they saw their own operations circumscribed and threatened by the advancement of large-scale, capitalist agriculture, and with the further suppression of syndicates under the Banzer regime these individuals emerged as local leaders and created new organizations to promote and defend their interests. Although they shared the concerns of other settlers for land titles, financial assistance, and marketing improvements, these individuals--unlike the poor peasants--were principally concerned with defending their interests as sugarcane producers and expanding production through the employment of wage laborers. They established asymmetrical relationships with other settlers to further their entrepreneurial interests.

Thus, the growth and expansion of commercial agriculture opened the eastern frontier to large-scale capitalist development, but small-scale settlement and the immigration of peasants and entrepreneurs from other parts of the country also occurred. The formation and transformation of frontier communities varied according to the strength and vitality of peasant syndicates, the composition of the communities, and the degree to which commercial penetration marginalized settler households. Unlike other still remote settlements, Nuevo Mundo, Rio Viejo, and Paichanetu felt the brunt of capitalist development, and they are good examples of the implications of this particular development strategy for people elsewhere.

NOTES

1. See Wolf (1982) and Bonacich (1972) for a discussion of the development of ethnicity and the split labor market. See also Painter (1985) for a discussion of class formation and ethnic conflict in Santa Cruz.

4

Proletarianization and the Peasant Household

With the development of capitalist relations of production in northern Santa Cruz, peasants found that they had to struggle more and more against the contraction of their subsistence base. Many could not accumulate because their resources and surpluses were siphoned off to be used by more powerful groups. Consequently, they had to intensify domestic labor and combine a variety of productive strategies, particularly the sale of labor power, in order to survive. The methods adopted by different household members proved to be extremely flexible and protected the peasant household from ultimate disappearance. In order to understand how this happened we must consider changes in the production process brought about by the agrarian reform and the strategies initiated by the state and international development agencies.

As we have seen, the agrarian reform and other state policies led to the growth of highly capitalized agricultural enterprises, but they also gave rise to undercapitalized peasant plots and the marginalization of many settlers. The commercial growers sought to maximize their profits by increasing agricultural output at competitive costs, but poor peasants could not expand production because of the constant shortage of capital, the domination of middlemen, and the adverse conditions confronted on the frontier. As a result, their small-scale production units were subordinated by the agricultural enterprises.

Peasants had to sell their crops in a market

where prices were established by the production costs of the large agricultural enterprises. Representatives from the major producers' organizations negotiated these prices with the government every year; peasants continually confronted a relative decrease in prices for their principal agricultural products--rice and corn--as compared to manufactured goods. A closer examination of labor costs for both peasants and large producers illustrates one aspect of the competition suffered by small-scale growers.

LABOR COSTS FOR PEASANTS AND CAPITALIST PRODUCERS

Labor costs are different for peasants and capitalist entrepreneurs. Although mechanization can greatly reduce the labor needs of the capitalist enterprise, large-scale planters also are in a more competitive position to secure workers than the peasant. Their ability to offer greater work opportunities gives them an advantage over other local growers, whose agricultural operations are more limited in scope, because they can pay lower wages. In contrast, peasants, struggling to expand production beyond subsistence levels through the employment of laborers, must pay higher salaries in order to attract workers and often provide a minimal food ration. These higher costs lower the profit margin of a small agricultural unit and can make expanding production for the market an unreasonable proposition (see Healy: 1982).

Both peasants and the major regional planters grow corn, so the costs of producing one ton of corn demonstrate the disadvantages suffered by small producers. Hypothetically, the labor bill for the peasant using hired workers in 1980-81 amounted to 78 percent of total costs and more than the value of the final product, calculated at average free-market prices for that year (see Table 4.1). Total costs equaled U.S. $189.29 (bs.4,732.44), but the market price per ton--U.S. $104.40 (bs.2,610)--received by the colonizer did not even cover these expenses, and the producer suffered a loss of U.S. $89.89 (bs.2,122.44). As Table 4.1 illustrates, the

TABLE 4.1
Corn Production Costs (1980/81) *

	Cost per Ton (bs.) **	
	Settler - 5 Ha. Manual	Large Grower 100 Ha. Mechanized
A. Machinery	0	2,091.87
B. Tools/ Equipment	151.13	11.27
C. Technical Assistance	0	43.48
D. Inputs	298.96	547.68
E. Transportation	589.39	463.00
F. Labor	3,692.96	384.31
Value of Corn =	2,610	3,913
Total Labor Costs =	3,692.96	384.31
Total Costs =	4,732.44	3,541.61
Profit/Hectare	-2,122.4 (-$US 84.89)	371.39 ($US 14.84)

Source: CORDECRUZ

* This table does not take into account capital investments in agricultural machinery.
** $US 1 = bs.25

larger producer of 100 hectares under mechanization enjoyed substantially reduced labor demands. Labor costs represented only 11 percent of total expenses and 10 percent of the settler's wage bill. These growers had access to higher official prices--at times greater than the free-market rate--and thus realized a profit margin significantly greater than the peasant. At an official price of U.S. $156.65 (bs.3,913) per ton their profits were to U.S. $14.85 (bs.371.39) per ton.

Faced with competition from capitalist growers and unable to raise labor productivity through investment in machinery, peasant households are forced to adopt new strategies to earn a cash income. More money is needed to buy clothing and basic food items, and to acquire it peasants must increase their participation in the market. As mentioned in the previous chapter, many peasant families combined subsistence production, wage labor, and indebtedness to survive. They also intensified domestic labor to reduce costs and compete with capitalist enterprises.

Domestic labor is neither valued as an investment nor as a cost even though it's the most important resource available to peasant families. By intensifying domestic labor, families continue producing long after production would be unprofitable for those capitalist operations based strictly on the employment of wage laborers. Thus, the participation of women and children in the domestic labor force is crucial. Women's work--giving birth to and raising children, going to market, tending animals, washing clothes, cooking and other domestic chores--centers around the care and reproduction of the work force and the creation of use values. It is vital to the maintenance of the peasant family. Children also are important assets in this labor intensive work. At very early ages children begin helping around the home: carrying water and firewood, looking after younger children, and assisting in certain phases of the agricultural cycle. When elderly family members can no longer work, children accept the responsibility of supporting and maintaining these individuals (deJanvry: 1977).

By reducing peasant expenses to a bare minimum, domestic labor insured the provision of a range of cheap commodities that included rice, corn, citrus fruits, cassava, bananas, and vegetables to urban centers. In this way, peasants on the frontier played an important role in sustaining the growing urban population of lowland Bolivia. Domestic labor also cheapened the cost of labor for capitalist farmers, as peasants were pushed further into wage labor during the 1960s and 1970s. This occurred because peasant families assumed the primary burden of

Woman Washing Clothes in Nuevo Mundo

sustaining the labor force in the absence of progressive state policies; thus, employers were able to pay wages below the cost of subsistence. For the laborer, however, the household offered important security against the threat of unemployment and market fluctuations in a dependent capitalist economy where the agro-industries were still too weak to support a completely landless, rural proletariat.

It is for these reasons that locating the proletariat in a region such as northern Santa Cruz is often difficult. Laborers still reside in households with access to land either through ownership, use rights, or some form of rental agreement, and these households provide important material support for their activities as wage laborers. The economy of the peasant household does not constitute part of a separate mode of production but is closely connected with the capitalist economy through both production and reproduction. To grasp the meaning of increasing capitalist penetration for rural people, however, we must further explore how impoverished peasants struggled to cope with the transformations affecting both the region and their families.

WAGE LABOR AND SUBSISTENCE ON THE FRONTIER

The founders of Nuevo Mundo, Rio Viejo, and Paichanetu were among the first settlers to experience the dramatic changes that began to transform the northern frontier. The experiences of a group of settlers who established the community of Nuevo Mundo provide us with an example of the upheavals that affected other settlers and the strategies they devised to survive.

Ebaristo Mejia and his brother Carmelo were part of the group of founding families who established the community of Nuevo Mundo. The two brothers had worked on an estate near Montero called Monte de la Vibora prior to the national revolution, but when the land reform left the property intact, they were forced to move elsewhere because the landowner began to expand cash-crop cultivation and to worry about ex-tenants claiming estate land under the new agrarian legislation. The Mejia brothers, however, were not the only peons to face this situation. Their sister Nolberta, and her husband, Antonio Tomicha, found themselves in a similar position, and Ebaristo's mother-in-law, Irene, and her husband, Nestor Ribeiro, could no longer remain, nor did they have any desire to continue working for a patron whom they all hated. Similarly, Julio and Manuel Antezana and their wives grew up on Monte de la Vibora, and Julio and Manuel had labored in the patron's fields together with Carmelo, Ebaristo, and Antonio.

In the aftermath of the revolution they eagerly joined the syndicate La Cruz 6 de Agosto because they wanted to own their own land and work for themselves. The men, with little more than the clothes on their backs, set out for the frontier on foot. Roads were still little more than dirt tracks, and there was no regular transportation to Mineros. They walked through the dense jungle for over thirty kilometers before reaching the site where the syndicate was redistributing land. Each male household head acquired a fifty hectare parcel from the syndicate and then faced the difficult task of establishing a homestead in this lonely and inhospitable environment. Some women accompanied their husbands to the settlement from the very beginning, while others arrived after an initial land claim had been staked out. They took over the domestic duties of preparing and cooking food, washing, etc. By assuming responsibility for household chores women enabled the men to dedicate more time to clearing forest and preparing the land for cultivation. This was extremely labor-intensive work, and few, with the exception of Nestor Ribeiro, could count on the labor of numerous offspring because they were still only in their early twenties. Consequently, settlers were very cooperative with each other and worked together clearing land on each individual plot.

They were frequently obliged to make the long trek back to Montero to buy provisions. Matches, rice, cooking oil, coffee, and sugar were among the items that they needed for subsistence until the first rice harvest was ready. In order to purchase these commodities they raised cash by selling the remaining mahogany trees on their properties to the sawmills that still operated in the region. They also hunted game in the forest; it was plentiful and provided settlers with valuable skins, which could be sold in the town markets and represented a source of food.

Nevertheless, establishing viable farming enterprises in Nuevo Mundo proved to be an extremely difficult task. Marketing their crops was problematic given the distance, poor roads, and lack of transportation. Occasionally an intermediary, usually connected with a rice mill in town, would come to the settlement looking for rice to buy. Such individuals brought their own weights and measures and often cheated settlers. They offered prices well below the going rate in

Montero, but families lacking their own transportation had little choice. As a result, their surpluses were accumulated by other groups, and they often became indebted to the intermediaries. In the process, the families could not create a stable economic base in the community.

The mahogany reserves were eventually exhausted and as more and more settlers and large commercial growers began to enter the region, game in the area became scarcer. By the late 1960s, the households still could not reproduce themselves independently, and their members found other means of generating a cash income beyond the meager returns provided by agriculture. They began to work as wage laborers for new settlers who bought land in Nuevo Mundo and large sugarcane growers expanding their presence in the region.

During the 1970s, Ebaristo and Carmelo Mejia, Carmelo's now teenage son Gregorio, Antonio Tomicha, and Manuel Antezana's sons, who also had come of age, began to work for a prominent cane grower expanding his cane fields in the vicinity of Nuevo Mundo. This individual, Lorenzo Soleto, was a descendent of the family that controlled the community land prior to the 1952 revolution. He inherited 100 hectares and began cultivating sugarcane in the 1970s, after yields began to fall on his estate near Montero. Throughout the 1970s, Soleto expanded his property by buying contiguous parcels owned by settlers and planting more and more land in sugarcane. He increased his labor needs and impoverished Nuevo Mundo settlers had no trouble finding work on his property.

A labor contractor advanced settlers money prior to the harvest. This money arrived at a crucial time when rice reserves from the previous year had run low, but the new crop still was not ready for harvest; The advance allowed them to satisfy their immediate short-term subsistence needs. Prior to the beginning of the harvest, the workers took a few belongings and moved onto Soleto's estate. The property was only a couple of kilometers from Nuevo Mundo, but the rhythm of the harvest did not allow them the luxury of living at home. They resided with other seasonal migrants from the highlands in long adobe barracks divided into small rooms. Individual families inhabited one room, and single men shared cramped living quarters in groups of three or four. The Nuevo Mundo men were usually not accompanied by their wives, but the women walked back and forth to the estate once or twice a day to bring meals to their husbands.

Workers labored in the cane fields twelve to sixteen hours a day. They worked in groups of four to six men who cut, stacked, and loaded the sugarcane onto trucks. The groups were usually comprised of friends and relatives from the same community or region of origin; thus, it was not unusual that the Nuevo Mundo group formed a small unit within the larger work force. Their work was supervised and closely scrutinized by an administrator, and every two weeks, Soleto himself traveled to the property from his home in Montero to oversee the estate affairs and pay workers.

Workers had difficulty saving their earnings and often ended the harvest in debt. If sickness or injury forced them to temporarily withdraw from the work force, they were not compensated for the lost time. Similarly, work days lost because of bad weather conditions were not recognized by the patron, and workers were frequently obliged to seek additional loans to see themselves through until the next payday. The crowded living quarters and lack of potable water and sanitary facilities caused numerous health problems, and a number of occupational hazards also jeopardized workers safety. Workers loaded the trucks with sugarcane by lifting heavy bundles onto their shoulders and carrying them up narrow wooden ladders propped against the sides of the vehicles. Slipping or loosing one's footing was a common occurence, frequently leading to injury. Machete cuts and snake bites, particularly when working at night, also plagued workers.

Second, to a large extent the condition of the sugarcane determined how much money a worker could earn. Workers were paid by the ton, and if the cane fields were old or filled with weeds,

Sugarcane Harvesters Loading Cane onto a Truck

this impeded their progress and reduced earnings. Sugarcane is a perennial crop, planted about once every five years in Bolivia. Old cane is substantially thinner and lighter than new plants, but it requires the same amount of work to cut, peel, and stack. And fields that have not been properly weeded prior to the harvest make the workers' task all the more difficult.

Finally, the estate's administrator controlled financial accounting and kept day-to-day records on each worker's production. The laborers had no control over these accounts, and many, such as Ebaristo Mejia and Antonio Tomicha, were illiterate. The administrator also ran a small store on the property which offered a range of basic goods for sale. These goods were priced well above prevailing rates in the towns, but workers were only free to go to town and purchase provisions once every two weeks. Consequently, many had to buy higher priced goods on the estate, which constituted one more factor that eroded their earnings.

It is not at all surprising that many workers were unable to pay back their preharvest advances and end the sugarcane harvest in November with a small savings. Although some years ended better than others, the group of laborers from Nuevo Mundo found that they often had little to show for their efforts and sometimes even left the estate in debt. The labor of these individuals and others like them and their subsistence-oriented household economies enabled Soleto and his family to regain their former preeminence in the region and embark upon large-scale sugarcane production.

Once the sugarcane harvest ended the Nuevo Mundo workers returned to their community and began preparing their fields to plant rice and corn. But because they still needed cash, they alternated work on their own plot with day labor for some of the small-scale agriculturalists from the highlands and valleys who were buying land in the community and developing their own operations. Although settlers resented the influx of these newcomers, they preferred to work for them, rather than large growers such as Soleto. Pay was generally the same or higher, and one had the option of working with meals included. The patron-worker relationship also was more direct without the intervention of a labor contractor or administrator, and the work routine was much less intensive. Individuals did not have to leave home to reside on the property of the owner, and the work day was punctuated with more frequent rest stops.

Throughout the 1970s, however, the position of many of these charter community members grew more unstable, and some were forced to sell their land. Ebaristo Mejia sold his property to Lorenzo Soleto to repay mounting debts. Luckily, however, his compadre Manuel Antezana extended him the use of a small plot on his property to cultivate rice and corn for the family's consumption. In this case, usufruct rights in this case were part of the general bonds of reciprocity that existed between the two households. Nevertheless, Manuel eventually sold off ten hectares of land to a highland immigrant, and when Carmelo Mejia's wife became ill, he also was forced to sell ten hectares to pay for her treatment. Unfortunately, she died.

These stories were repeated with numerous variations by other settlers. Sometimes families remained in the community cultivating land through rental of usufruct agreements. Usufruct arrangements were used between the poor and the rich and among the poor themselves. The small-scale agriculturalists extended usufruct rights to impoverished families as a means of attracting workers to their properties, but among the poor these arrangements were part of a broad network of cooperation and coordination of resources that linked dispersed households in a series of interlocking relationships. A land-controlling family would loan a small plot to other landless peasants, kinsfolk in the town, or relatives from their home communities. These people later were called upon for a wide range of services, including the care and education of children, assistance during periods of illness, loans during lean periods of the year, etc. Such arrangements permitted people without capital to continue producing minimal subsistence needs in an area constricted by the development of commercial agriculture and enveloped by capitalist productive relations.

At other times settlers left the settlement altogether. A former Rio Viejo syndicate leader, for example, returned to his home community, while another family resettled further onto the frontier. Similarly, two Nuevo Mundo families relocated to new settlements further north, and two others moved to a town and became employees of a sawmill. The pattern of landholding changed dramatically: We can see in Figure 4.1 that the area settled by the syndicate La Cruz 6 de Agosto to a large extent passed into the hands of new owners by the end of the 1970s.

A similar process was occurring in Rio Viejo. With the decline of the syndicate, settlers had no organization to protect their claims to the land, and many still did not possess legal title. When a large grower contested their rights to the land, the settlers, fearing the imminent loss of their parcels, sold their land to a bank official from Mineros to avoid complete loss through expropriation. The banker quickly produced a document attesting to his ownership, and the grower was eventually forced to desist. The settlers remained on the land through permission of the new owner, cultivating subsistence plots and working as wage laborers for the banker and more prosperous settlers.

Settlers who possessed legal title enjoyed more security than these families, but land rights again could become problematic when questions of marriage and inheritance arise. Like colonizers throughout northern Santa Cruz, many men and women in the communities established nuclear families without formalizing these unions through marriage [1]. Although most people were very religious Catholics and placed great value on church weddings, the cost of marriage ceremonies and the general lack of necessary identification (particularly among women) discouraged people from participating in formal weddings. The settlers, however, recognized male-female unions after a couple had children and lived together and expected these pairs to uphold the same behaviorial norms as their married

112

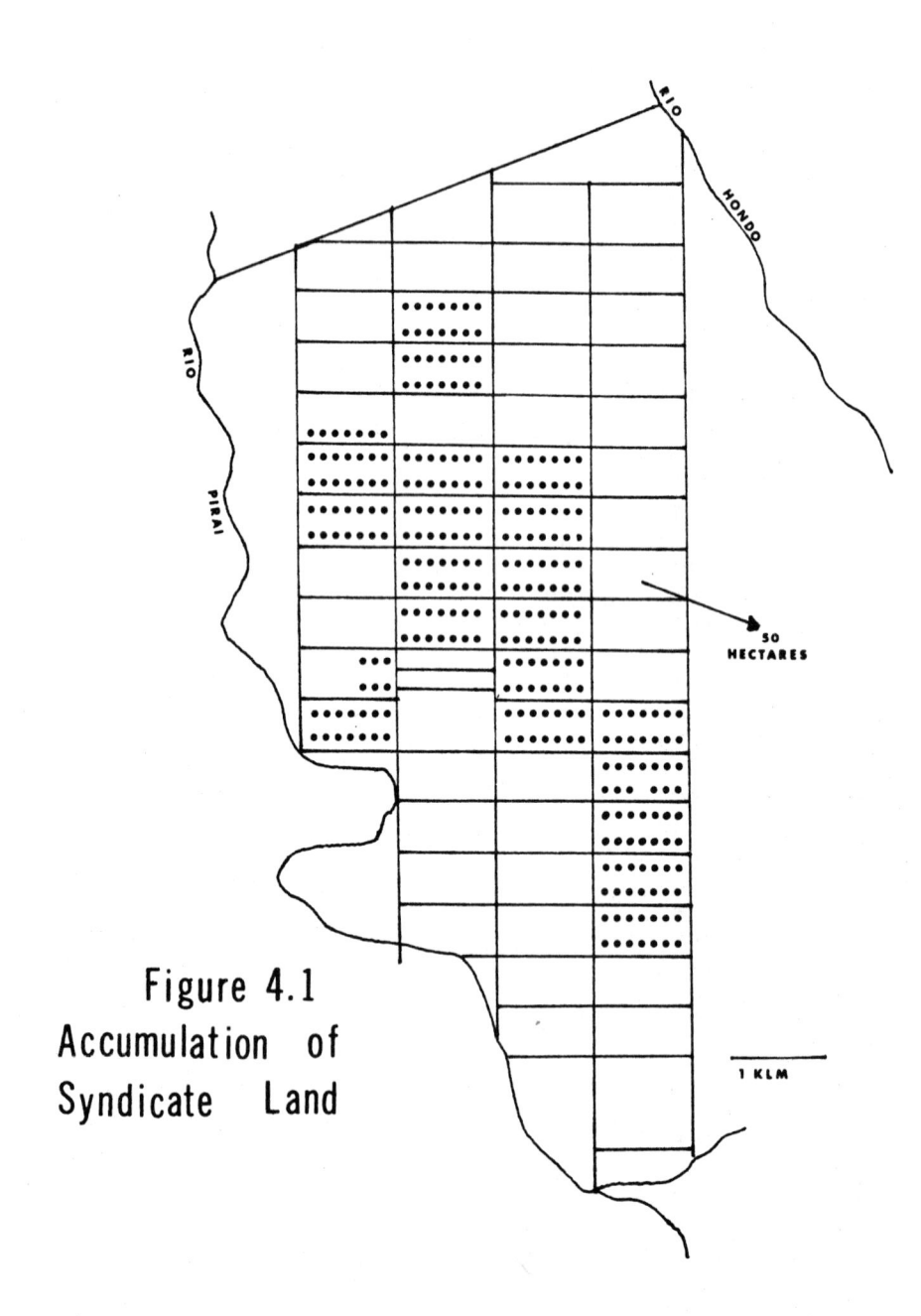

Figure 4.1
Accumulation of
Syndicate Land

counterparts. Nevertheless, in such cases the land title was held in the man's name, and the woman's rights and those of her children could become problematic in the eyes of the wider society if a conflict over inheritance claims arose.

Many large growers incorporated settler land into their own holdings without contesting settler claims. Also, the lack of financial and organizational support gradually forced peasants to sell their land to raise cash, and large-scale sugarcane producers were eager buyers. As settlers sold their land, turned to wage labor, and negotiated new tenure agreements, new families began to establish themselves in the communities. Although some of the newcomers were better-off families who could afford to hire wage laborers and initiate cash-crop cultivation, many were also poor peasant families who came from both the highlands and the lowlands and alternated between wage labor and subsistence agriculture. For these poor peasant families, settlement in either Nuevo Mundo, Rio Viejo, or Paichanetu was only the most recent of a series of different residences in the lowlands of Bolivia and did not necessarily represent their final destination. Some would eventually establish viable agricultural operations, but the majority formed part of a growing number of marginalized settlers that could not accumulate and moved back and forth between subsistence agriculture and wage labor.

Most of these people came to the communities through contacts with relatives or acquaintances. Fermin Cardoso, his two brothers, and their young families settled on the property of a small-scale agriculturalist in Nuevo Mundo, a fellow countryman from their home community. The brothers had worked for a couple of years as seasonal laborers, but hoped eventually to establish their own farming operations. To do this they assumed all the agricultural chores on this man's property in exchange for a small plot of land to plant subsistence crops. They also laid claim to land in a newly opened colonization zone further north, and traveled back and forth to this settlement when time permitted. Some poor peasants, such as Juan Terceros, came directly to the community from their homes with no prior experience in the lowlands. Juan settled on his uncle's property in Rio Viejo and hoped to work until he saved enough money to buy land in the community. Still others had no intention of remaining in the lowlands at all. Rigoberto Flores, who was twenty and single when he came to Paichanetu, wanted to earn money and return home to Potosi. Nevertheless, the presence of relatives and countrypeople in the communities offered such individuals important material support, information on the lowlands, and a wealth of accumulated experience.

The strategies of the poor families also expanded to include other activities besides subsistence agriculture and agricultural day labor. The cocaine industry developed in the 1970s and provided lucrative alternatives to agricultural labor (see Chapter 8). Also, when a family member migrated to an urban center, he or she became involved in a range of income-generating activities that broadened and diversified the family's access to resources. The strategies developed by the family of Carmelo Ortiz and his wife, Juana Melgar, were typical of other families in the communities.

Carmelo, fifty-five, and Juana, forty-eight, were born in the department of Santa Cruz and had nine children. They were originally from a small town near the city of Santa Cruz, but had more recently purchased a piece of land in an old frontier community called Ojosal. They worked the land for four years but never harvested a single crop because of a series of misfortunes. Convinced that the land was plagued with bad luck, they sold it and moved to Paichanetu, where the syndicate alloted them a small parcel to cultivate. But the family could not produce enough on one hectare to satisfy all its needs. Carmelo and an elder son worked as day laborers to earn additional income, and Juana and her three youngest daughters operated a small dry goods store into which she and her husband had invested all the money earned from the land sale in Ojosal.

Several of the couple's sons eventually left

the community and established residences in the Villa Primero de Mayo, a squatter settlement on the outskirts of the city of Santa Cruz; another settled land in a new colonization zone. The two oldest daughters married and moved out of the community: One became a seamstress in Santa Cruz--her husband drove a taxi--and the other married a truck owner and resided in Mineros.

The children in the town provided economic assistance in times of crisis, but they, too, benefited from their relatives in the countryside. When severe stomach problems obliged Carmelo to seek medical attention in Santa Cruz, the children offered important support and lodging. In addition, Don Carmelo's son-in-law, the truck driver, hauled his father-in-law's crops to market without charge when Carmelo decided to sell small portions. And in return, the children could count on gifts of food--e.g., cassava, corn, rice, and chickens--from their country relatives. Finally, young children were sent back and forth between these households to help with chores; they were cared for by an extensive network of relatives. Through these relationships and with only minimal economic remuneration for their own labor, the Ortiz family and others like it with little land and scant resources waged a successful battle against complete proletarianization.

As the struggle to control scarce resources intensifed, people's backs were pushed to the wall. Many long-time settlers saw their tenuous balance between subsistence and disaster grow more precarious with the arrival of new settlers to the community, and this led to growing ethnic conflict. Migrants brought a variety of distinct cultural traditions, and these differences were constantly reinforced through language, dress, dietary preferences, housing design, and segregated residence patterns. The strained ethnic relations are best understood as a manifestation of the emerging class struggle between an increasingly differentiated peasantry and a capitalist class striving to consolidate its power (Painter: 1985).

Threatened by the dissolution of their economic base, the original lowland settlers

faced new competition from an influx of migrants
from the highlands and valleys. Rivalry
intensified as the different groups strove to
control scarce resources and acquire employment.
And a number of wealthier settlers, primarily
from the highlands and valleys, established
small-scale commercial and agricultural
operations, employing poor peasants as their
laborers. Although these small-scale
agriculturalists employed poor peasants from a
variety of backgrounds, the social and cultural
affinity between them and the impoverished
migrants from the highlands and valleys could act
as a channel for upward mobility for this group
of poor peasants. Not surprisingly, this
aggravated tensions that were commonly
articulated as ethnic issues, with the alleged
behavioral characteristics attributed to
different groups.

For example, the highland and valley
migrants accused the lowlanders of laziness and
irresponsibility. They maintained that the
lowlanders did not appreciate the value of work,
spent money unnecessarily, and were content to
live a precarious, hand-to-mouth existence. The
lowlanders, however, felt that the newcomers were
greedy, dirty, and dishonest. Such tensions were
most acute during the early years of in-migration
and economic expansion. In the 1960s several shop
owners in northern Santa Cruz refused to serve
immigrants from the highlands, and many migrants
said that they feared walking about at night
alone. Graffiti that read "Be Patriotic, Kill a
Colla" summarized the hostilities of this period.
Although such tensions never completely
disappeared, they eased in subsequent years, as
more and more immigrants settled in northern
Santa Cruz and played crucial roles in sustaining
the local economy.

The dominant lowland bourgeoisie manipulated
and re-created the cultural differences among
settlers by stressing regional distinctiveness
and cultural contrasts. Through the Pro-Santa
Cruz Committee, for example, they appealed to the
regional sentiments of all <u>crucenos</u> to rally
support for a number of their own causes. This
enabled them to unify different factions of the

capitalist class, to pressure the government for a greater share of state resources, and to compete with the highland-based mining sector for national prominence. Their emphasis on the racial superiority and common Spanish origins of the lowland population divided the work force and prevented collective worker action on many of the large agricultural enterprises in northern Santa Cruz. Lowlanders, who felt both culturally and economically threatened by the increasing numbers of migrants settling in the region, at times aligned themselves with the bourgeoisie.

By 1981 the composition of Nuevo Mundo, Rio Viejo, and Paichanetu had undergone a marked transformation, reflecting the processes of change that had been under way for nearly three decades. Five hundred forty-nine people resided in the communities and were distributed more or less evenly among eighty-six households. Fifty-six percent of the population was in the economically active age category of fifteen to sixty years of age, and the birthplaces of the household heads attested to the different cultural backgrounds of these families. Most (sixty-six) were born in various parts of the Bolivian lowlands and came from the northern Guarayo communities, the southern province of Cordillera, and the Chiquitania to the east. But a significant minority migrated from the intermontane valleys of Santa Cruz and Chuquisaca departments, the highlands of Potosi, and the Cochabamba Valley. While the household heads spoke Spanish, 49 percent also spoke an indigenous language--Quechua, Guarani, or Chiquitano.

The residence period of the household heads highlighted the dynamic and constantly changing makeup of the settlements. The largest group (48) established residency from the mid-1960s to the mid-1970s and included many original settlers from Rio Viejo, founded later than either Paichanetu or Nuevo Mundo. Only 7 families, however, had lived in their current location for 20 years or more, and 19 households had been established since 1976. Only 28 (32.5 percent) of the 86 households were original community founders, and only 5 of these households still possessed the same amount of land received at the time of settlement. This condition and the fact that fully half of all households were landless attests to the instability of these communities.

The unstable nature of these settlements also was reflected across generations: Many children of the pioneer families who came of age on the frontier had not been able to improve their living conditions. Of the 28 charter families, 16 had a total of 23 children--14 men and 9 women--in the economically active age category of 15 to 60 who had formed separate households [2]. Seven of these children continued to reside in the communities; 7 migrated to urban areas, and 9 lived in other rural communities.

Subsistence agriculture supplemented with agricultural day labor was the most frequent combination of productive activities among this group. Twelve men and 4 women were a part of household units where such arrangements formed the basis of the domestic economy. This group included all 7 children who remained in the community of whom 4 were landless and practiced subsistence agriculture on rented land or land held in usufruct. Another nine people lived in newer frontier communities or close to the properties of large capitalist farmers, where they worked as day laborers. Finally, the urban-based group held low-paying, unstable jobs in the informal sector, although all maintained relations with relatives in the countryside. Five women worked as domestic servants, and two men labored on part-time construction jobs. None of the children substantially improved their standard of living; they continued to lead an impoverished existence.

Furthermore, the constraints imposed by market conditions and the lack of capital compelled a full 63 percent (54 people) of all community household heads to engage in wage-labor activities for 6 months or more of each year. These individuals had access to land through either rental, ownership, or usufruct, but could not survive on agriculture alone. They were joined by 70 additional community residents from the ages of 15 to 60 who contributed to the income of their families through wage labor.

During the 1960s and 1970s, the penetration of commercial relationships led to the internal differentiation of Nuevo Mundo, Rio Viejo, and Paichanetu and the marginalization of many peasant households. But while these decades witnessed a general trend towards proletarianization, the extremely flexible nature of the domestic economy protected the peasant family from ultimate transformation into an agricultural proletariat. Peasants combined migration, wage labor, subsistence agriculture, debt, and patron-client relationships, and an extensive network of reciprocity between related households in both urban and rural areas to offset the contraction of their economic base.

Mounting competition for ever more scarce resources led to increasing ethnic conflict between lowland settlers and immigrants from the highlands and valleys. New notions of ethnicity developed and became the idiom for an intensifying class struggle between a divided settler population and an emerging regional bourgeoisie seeking to consolidate its base of power. As many peasant families waged a battle against proletarianization, other settler families found that they could take advantage of the commercial opportunities in northern Santa Cruz to expand their agricultural and commercial operations through the employment of wage laborers. How they managed to do this is the subject of the next chapter.

NOTES

1. In 1981, 48 percent of the men and women heading each household were not legally married.

2. Nine families have no economically active offspring living outside the household, and insufficient data made it impossible to access four other households.

5
Settlers Become Entrepreneurs

The signs of the veritable explosion in cash-crop production during the 1960s and early 1970s were nowhere more apparent than in the Mineros region. The frontier was continually pushed back, and during the six-month, May-October harvest period, the region hummed with activity. Migrant workers arrived from the interior and swelled the local population. The roads, which were passable once again, became clogged with traffic, as trucks heavily laden with cane ground their way to the mills during all hours of the day and night. Businesses in Mineros thrived, both seasonal workers and settlers converged on the town during the weekends to purchase supplies, take in a movie, and visit with friends and relatives.

While many wealthy landowners and speculators from Santa Cruz and Montero were buying land and converting the forest into sugarcane and cotton fields, another group of small-scale cane producers and merchants also gained a foothold in the region. Most were immigrants from the highlands and valleys whose social origins were often in the peasantry. They established themselves as small-scale agriculturalists and entrepreneurs, making the transition, in many cases, from peasant agriculture to capitalist production, and emerging as a middle-level bourgeoisie with considerable influence in the rural communities of northern Santa Cruz.

SUGARCANE PRODUCTION AND COMMERCE

The generation of migrants who formed a sound economic base in northern Santa Cruz did so by investing in sugarcane production and commerce during the 1960s and early 1970s, and the roles of small farmer and merchant often coincided. Small farmers invested their sugarcane profits into businesses and truck transport. And merchants became sugarcane producers because the opportunities for profit associated with sugarcane cultivation were so attractive. Thus, they came to exercise new dominance over many impoverished peasant families in the settlements of northern Santa Cruz through their control of land and labor and their greater access to capital.

Sugarcane, and later cotton, were the only crops that were planted, cultivated, and harvested exclusively for sale, and compared with the staples of the region--rice and corn--they offered potentially higher profits. Because of its technical requirements, however, cotton production remained the domain of large capitalist producers, but sugarcane cultivation soon included many small- and medium-size producers. Despite its attractiveness sugarcane production demonstrated a number of special characteristics that excluded the poor peasants from its cultivation. First, sugarcane production tied producers more closely to unpredictable market changes in both national and international supply and demand. Second, cultivation was profitable only in those areas linked to factories located within fifteen kilometers of all-weather roads because of high transportation costs and the impossibility of storing cut cane (Royden and Wennergren: 1973). Sugarcane also required a capital investment more than three times that of rice and corn and had particularly strenuous and regimented labor demands during the harvest. Moreover, the gestation period forced the grower to wait a full year between planting and harvesting before the fruits of his labor were rewarded--which was extremely difficult, if not impossible, for the poor peasants constantly suffering from a cash shortage. Rice, in contrast, needed only five and corn only seven months before either could be harvested and sold. Clearly, sugarcane cultivation could only be undertaken by those who already controlled capital.

If not more important than its financial prerequisites, sugarcane marketing was strictly controlled by the large growers and sugarmill owners through a quota system that discriminated against the small producer. The state first instituted this system in 1965 to control the growth of the sugar industry for several reasons. National demand for sugar had been satisfied the previous year, but the area under cultivation superseded the amount necessary for national consumption, and temporarily low world prices did not favor exports. Confronted by these constraints, the state sought to control irrational expansion by imposing quotas on the mills. The mills, in turn, divided the quotas among their suppliers in accordance with the area cultivated by each individual, and--not surprisingly--the largest growers were favored with the most generous allotments.

Small-scale planters who could not acquire a quota were obliged to sell to large producers at a price considerably below that offered by the mills, but in the early 1970s, a boom in cotton cultivation lured the major producers away from sugarcane, and it became possible for many small growers to obtain direct access to the mills. With the rapid conversion of cane fields to cotton, the sugarmills began to suffer shortages, but growers resisted attempts to redistribute quota assignments among small producers. A struggle developed between large and small planters and a new organization--the Federacion de Campesinos Caneros y Productores Agricolas-- was created to represent the small planters. The mill owners supported this group; many formerly excluded producers gained direct access to the processing centers--a position from which they benefited in subsequent years with the renewed expansion of the sugar industry.

In addition to the boom in sugarcane cultivation, the expansion of the regional economy created profitable new opportunities in commerce. Since the revolution the lowland estates no longer fulfilled their traditional role as the primary recipient of peasant agricultural produce. Also, the rapid growth of the cities of Santa Cruz and Montero generated markets for agricultural products and a range of other commodities. Lowland products could now be shipped to other national and international market centers, as the completion of the railroads and the Santa Cruz-Cochabamba highway linked the department to a broader network of commercial centers.

A group of merchants and middlemen responded to these developments by stepping in to take advantage of the new circumstances. Like sugarcane production, however, involvement in various commercial ventures required the prior accumulation of capital. The control of financial resources to a large extent, determined the position occupied by a particular merchant or middleman in a hierarchy that extended from the most remote frontier settlements to the departmental capital Santa Cruz de la Sierra. Merchants did not constitute a homogeneous group, and they intervened at various stages and to different degrees in the commercialization of agricultural goods and the sale of commodities. The most influential commercial interests came from the agro-industrial bourgeoisie. They were the major sugarcane and cotton growers; they owned rice mills, controlled producers' organizations, and operated shops in the towns that handled consumer durables and other costly imported goods.

The majority of the highland and valley migrants never achieved such power and prominence, but they participated in petty commerce by buying and shipping peasants' goods to urban markets. They also operated small businesses (usually dry goods shops or restaurants). Such migrants were often exploited by the more powerful bourgeoisie, but through their involvement in commerce they avoided many of the risks associated with agriculture, e.g., unstable prices, labor problems, and bad weather and took advantage of price differentials between urban and rural areas and the lack of a standardized system of measure.

Through their control of capital, which had become the most important source of power in northern Santa Cruz, they were able to maximize profits by acting as money lenders and middlemen.

Merchants profited from peasants in northern Santa Cruz in a number of ways. Many settlers were unable to maintain a minimal subsistence income without entering into debtor relationships with more powerful, capital-controlling individuals. Small-scale rice producers, for example, faced a particularly difficult period during the preharvest months of January and February, when reserves from the previous harvest were exhausted, the new crop was not ready for harvest, and little cash remained to purchase a range of basic necessities. The rainy season, which engulfed the region from November through April, also reduced contact between urban commercial centers and rural communities because inundated roads and swollen rivers curtailed most forms of transportation and precluded the shipment of commodities to urban markets until well into June. As previously mentioned, many settlers turned to wage labor to make ends meet, but this often was not enough and they frequently formed ties with merchants to satisfy their subsistence needs. The relationship between merchants and peasants varied, but it always depended on the access to and control over capital.

Some merchants became directly involved in the production process by purchasing peasants' labor. During the rainy season, they extended loans to producers in return for the sole right to buy rice after the harvest, at a pre-determined price below market value. When the roads were passable, merchants then entered the communities in their trucks, picked up the rice, and transported it to the towns, where the product was sold at market value for a profit. The original sale of the rice, however, masked the actual sale of labor power. Even though in many cases peasants retained control over the land, their labor power was a commodity because they could not reproduce the conditions of their own existence through agriculture alone. The loans that the merchants provided were generally

Rice Stored in a Field

not used by rice growers to buy such production inputs as herbicides and machinery but rather to purchase medicines, basic food items, and clothing--thus satisfying the subsistence requirements of the domestic unit. Household labor was available for production, and the merchants acquired labor with the original loan and later received rice that had attained value as a result of the production process [1].

The central government has tried unsuccessfully since 1959 to develop a system of marketing rice that could benefit the interests of both producers and consumers, but its success has been limited, and intermediaries, rather than rice growers, often have benefited the most. In 1973 the government formed the Empresa Nacional de Arroz (ENA) after the failure of four previous institutions. Its objectives included the regulation of prices at the level of the producer and consumer, the purchase and sale of rice, the organization of rice transportation, and the sale of rice surpluses on the international market.

The ENA tried on several occasions to monopolize the rice market by establishing an official price and acting as the principal buyer. These attempts failed because of financial difficulties, and the ENA never purchased more than a quarter of the total marketable production. Nor did it ever represent a viable alternative to the intermediaries. Purchases often began after the harvest, which undermined the small growers, who had to prepare the next year's planting and could not wait long to be paid. Moreover, because of distance and poor road conditions, peasants often had no other choice but to sell their rice to intermediaries. The intermediaries then took advantage of prices in the towns where the ENA silos were located.

This relationship between rice growers and middlemen was possible only because the settlers did not completely control the means of production. Although they still retained a certain degree of control over decisions affecting a range of activities associated with rice production--land clearing, planting, weeding, and harvesting--they were forced to turn to middlemen for financial assistance. The middlemen, in turn, avoided the risks associated with agriculture. To increase output they expanded their ties with settlers--frequently through the creation of <u>compadrazgo</u> relationships, debt ties, and familial connections--rather than increase productivity through investments in machinery and other technical inputs. The intermediaries did not always develop these relationships for tradition's sake: they were the most effective way to generate a profit, and business associations based on real or fictive kinship blurred the unequal and exploitative nature of these relationships.

Rice growers were not alone in their exploitation; middlemen also developed similar relationships with banana and cassava producers. With these crops, however, they used somewhat different labor relations, combining the domestic labor of the direct producer with more purely free wage labor. Cassava and bananas could not be harvested in advance and stored as easily as rice. Thus, the middlemen contracted laborers to accompany them to a specified community, where together with the direct producer and his family members, they harvested the crop. It was then piled high on a truck and taken directly to market.

In the case of sugarcane, intermediaries with a quota--usually other growers--bought cane from planters below the market price when bad weather or flooded fields interfered with their own harvest and precluded the completion of their sugarcane quota in the mills. They also took advantage of periods when the mills temporarily suspended the quota system and allowed unrestricted shipments to acquire cane from other growers. They could then sell an unlimited amount of cane to the mills and increase their own quota assignment for the following year. During these times intermediaries generally purchased the cane in the field and then sent workers and truckers to harvest it and transport it to the processing centers.

The small cane growers often were forced to sell to intermediaries. In addition to lacking a quota in one of the mills, these planters confronted more acute labor and transportation problems than the major cultivators of the region. They experienced considerable difficulty organizing a sufficient and reliable labor force, and transportation inconveniences existed not only because of the greater distance of their parcels from the mills, but because few owned trucks.

To be permitted a shipment of one truckload a day, for example, a grower needed a total annual production of at least 1,500 tons. This signified an area of thirty hectares or more. Most colonizers cultivated five hectares or less and were assigned shipments spaced out over longer periods. A grower with five hectares of cane and a total production of 250 tons was assigned only one trip a week. This obliged the individual to have the necessary workers and transportation available at a specific time every week over a period of several months. If the

River Crossing in Northern Santa Cruz

grower could not employ the workers and crew with additional work during the interim, he had to maintain them with his own financial resources or see them take work elsewhere.

The same problems arose with transportation. Large growers owned their own trucks, but most small growers were obliged to hire truckers. The delays and long lines that formed at the mill gates often forced drivers to wait as long as twenty-four hours before delivering their cargo. Faced with such a situation, truck owners shunned small producers, preferring more lucrative possibilities for profit with the major regional producers. Consequently, those growers either unable to mobilize the necessary transportation and labor or without a quota chose to sell their cane at a lower price rather than see it rot in the field.

Not all merchants, however, became involved in the process of production itself, since they did not always have the capital available to advance to producers. Several limited their activities to the sphere of circulation by exploiting price differentials between urban and rural areas. Some traveled about the countryside in their trucks, purchased commodities when the possibility arose, and then resold them for a higher price in the towns. They also took advantage of an inefficient system of weights and measures. Rice, for example, is measured by the *fanega*, the equivalent of 408 pounds wet and 384 pounds dry. The degree of humidity thus becomes open to discussion, and the peasant, who frequently depends upon the middleman to purchase rice is not in a bargaining position. Finally, in the sugarcane marketing system, the so-called *rescatistas de cana*--who were not necessarily cultivators--bought truckloads of sugarcane at the mill gates from those who arrived without a quota. Some were former cane growers, but others had managed to obtain a quota by bribing or negotiating deals with mill personnel.

We see, then, how merchants benefited from their relationships with other settlers. Sometimes they became directly involved in the production process; other times they limited their activities to the sphere of circulation. The extent of their involvement in the production process depended upon both the amount of capital at their disposal and the kinds of labor organization best suited to particular crops. In all cases, their actions were based on the optimal way to achieve the highest profits.

Merchant involvement with settlers varied; not all were indebted to merchants for example. Some lacking their own means of transportation established contacts with merchants only during the sale of their crops. In such cases the settlers enjoyed more flexibility regarding when, where, and to whom they would sell their crop. And when it was in their interest, settlers also hired truck drivers to ship their goods to urban markets, where they realized the sale themselves. While this pattern of marketing was indicative of the degree of differentiation among settlers, it also reflected a pattern of inter-community differentiation which had developed as well.

By the early 1970s, Nuevo Mundo, Rio Viejo and Paichanetu, along with other settlements near Mineros, enjoyed better contact with urban centers than those located further north on the edge of the expanding frontier. Settlers were now in a much better position to market their produce--transport costs to the towns were cheaper, and there was a wider range of potential buyers. Then, too, more Mineros- and Montero-based truckers were willing to enter the communities. Paradoxically, such remote, recently established settlements as those located in the Chane-Piray colonization zone had become the center of rice cultivation, as sugarcane expansion and declining rice yields occurred in the older settlements. Settlers in these areas faced the greatest difficulties marketing their crops because distance, rivers, and impassable roads raised costs and inhibited transportation.

One might ask how some migrants acquired the initial capital to launch their profit-making ventures in commerce and sugarcane. To answer this question, we must examine the backgrounds of these migrants, the timing of their arrival in northern Santa Cruz, and the kinds of organizations and relationships they formed.

THE EMERGENCE OF SMALL-SCALE AGRICULTURALISTS

The basis for the emergence of a group of middle-level merchants, intermediaries, and small-scale agriculturalists was established by the first generation of highland and valley migrants. Although lowlanders also participated in petty commerce and cash-crop production, migrants dominated these activities by the 1970s. The explanation for their local-level prominence lies partially in their greater numbers. In 1976 nearly two-thirds of the residents of Obispo Santiesteban province were immigrants from other departments, mainly Cochabamba, Chuquisaca, and Potosi (INE: 1976). These individuals and their families often had savings from previous economic activities in other parts of Bolivia and foreign countries. Such activities included work in the mines, seasonal wage labor in Argentina, agriculture, and earlier commercial involvement with small stores. Lowlanders, in contrast, enjoyed fewer opportunities to accumulate small savings, as Santa Cruz, prior to the growth of the agro-industries, was a stagnent commercial backwater that suffered from poor communications with more economically dynamic areas.

The group of migrants who rose to local prominence in the Mineros region came from a variety of backgrounds. Many were from peasant origins, but others were urban dwellers, ex-miners and merchants. As mentioned in Chapter 4, several migrants began their life cycles in Santa Cruz as wage laborers, but because they possessed some formal education and came from families in a position to assist them, seasonal labor represented only a short phase of their migratory experience. Others avoided wage labor altogether and moved directly into commercial ventures either through the purchase of land or the initiation of mercantile activities.

While these individuals frequently benefited from prior savings and family assistance, the timing of their arrival in Santa Cruz also played an important role in their success. Most of those who established themselves in the Mineros region did so after the initial wave of settlement had already taken place. The impoverishment of the original pioneers provided new migrants with a source of labor, while the improvements already made on the land were of great benefit to them. The second wave of settlers often obtained the land with fruit trees and crops already planted. This represented a source of income for the first year and often proved to be a substantial help.

Juan Vega is a case in point. The circumstances that led to his arrival in northern Santa Cruz and the growth of his farming operations are similar to many other men like him. Juan is a native of Chuquisaca department, where he was born in the intermontane valleys of Azurduy province. His parents were independent peasants prior to the 1953 land reform and struggled to eke out a living for themselves and their ten children on the dry, rugged slopes of southeastern Bolivia. They owned several small parcels scattered across an ecologically diverse area and supported their large family through agriculture and cattle herding activities without seeking additional income through wage employment. But, although the land maintained the nuclear family, it was not enough to redistribute among subsequent generations of children and their families. Consequently, Juan and his brothers and sisters were obliged to look for alternatives to subsistence agriculture on the family land.

In 1957, Juan left home for the first time at the age of nineteen. He went to southern Bolivia, where he worked as an agricultural day laborer and as a mason's assistant. At the end of the year he returned home but soon left again for northern Argentina and the sugarcane harvest. Over the course of the next eight years, he traveled to Argentina on a seasonal basis to cut cane but always came home to help his father with the agricultural chores. Juan eventually saved enough money to purchase his own one-hectare plot and acquire a team of oxen; he subsequently married a young woman from the same province.

He and his wife became frustrated with the problems of supporting their own growing family on one hectare of rocky soil. Friends and acquaintances, returning from the eastern lowlands, recounted stories of the endless stretches of unclaimed land, the bountiful harvests, and the numerous opportunities for employment in northern Santa Cruz. These descriptions and the clear signs of economic improvement evidenced by many of the returning migrants moved Juan to think more and more about going to Santa Cruz. Finally, in 1970 he set out for the lowlands to assess the situation himself. He sought out his father's **compadre**, who had purchased land and settled in Nuevo Mundo, for information on life in the frontier settlement and the problems and prospects of agriculture in the tropics.

Juan was profoundly impressed by the man's rice and corn crops--the exuberant green vegetation amazed him after the dryness of Chuquisaca. After staying in Nuevo Mundo with the man's family for fifteen days, he went home, sold his land and animals, received a small cash gift from his parents, and returned to the settlement with money to buy land. Through the help of his friend, he arranged the down payment for a fifty-hectare parcel from one of the charter members of the settlement, a lowlander, who had already cleared four hectares of forest. The lowlander, according to Juan, was "lazy and didn't know how to work", and he was forced to sell his land in order to obtain money.

Juan purchased this land on June 1, 1970, with a down payment of half the stipulated sales price; he remained in Nuevo Mundo for the next four months to insure the transfer of the property and to begin planting. He then returned briefly to Azurduy to bring his wife and two children back to Santa Cruz. The first year in Nuevo Mundo proved to be difficult for the entire family, but the rice harvest provided them with sufficient income to purchase a one-half hectare plot of sugarcane on a neighbor's land during their second year in Nuevo Mundo. They cultivated the cane with hired help and sold it at the end of the season to a large grower who had a quota in one of the sugarmills. Although the sale was not wildly profitable, it allowed them to plant a little cane on their own land and pay off their debt to the former owner.

After this initial success, disaster struck. The following year a fire, brought on by a drought and strong winds, burned everything and the Vega family harvested none of its sugarcane. But by 1974 their luck changed again. A good harvest and high sugar prices allowed Juan to not only recuperate his previous losses but also to expand cultivation to eight hectares. At this time the mills were desperate for raw material and accepted cane from anyone, whether or not they had a quota assignment. Juan hired a trucker to ship all his cane to the La Belgica mill, and on the basis of these shipments the mill granted him a quota for subsequent years and recognized him as a small cane grower. In later years he and a group of small cane growers from Nuevo Mundo and a neighboring community collectively organized transportation. During one season, Juan and four other Nuevo Mundo growers (all migrants from the same region in Chuquisaca department) also contracted a group of ten Chiriguanos from the southern province of Cordillera to harvest their crops. Thus, they avoided many of the difficulties that plagued individual small producers.

We see, then, that a number of factors were responsible for Juan Vega's initial success. Unlike other settlers, Juan had the capital to purchase land in a region that was rapidly being incorporated into capitalist production. Moreover, he invested in cane production at a time when it was becoming an increasingly lucrative and viable undertaking. He distinguished himself from other settlers in the community, who either lacked the necessary capital or came to the region when it was still a frontier and cash-crop production was not yet a feasible endeavor. And Juan benefited from the previous experience of his father's compadre as well as the initial forest clearing by the former owner.

Julio Aguilar also successfully established a small capitalist enterprise on the other side of the river from Juan Vega. Julio came to Santa Cruz in 1967 from the town of Comarapa, located in the western valleys of the Santa Cruz department. Unlike Juan Vega, Julio's family was not peasants but successful merchants in the town of Comarapa. Julio had studied in Cochabamba and La Paz, where he completed secondary school and one year of university education. He and his wife traveled to Santa Cruz in their truck to expand the family's commercial operations, but sensing the possibilities for profit in the region, the couple decided to stay. They purchased a house in Mineros, and with a small dry-goods store, they eventually accumulated enough money to buy fifty hectares of land; three years later they planted fifteen hectares of sugarcane.

Segundino Villa represented another path to accumulation, one which combined agriculture with some intelligent commercial ventures in Mineros. Although his early experience was similar to that of Juan Vega, he soon branched out from agriculture and initiated urban-based businesses that ranged from a carpentry workshop, a general store, and later, an extremely lucrative trucking business.

Don Segundino was born in 1941, the same year as Juan Vega. He grew up in the intermontane valleys of Santa Cruz department and migrated to the lowlands in 1961, at the age of twenty, when frontier settlement was still in an early phase. Like Vega, he left his home community in the hope of finding sufficient land and work to support his young family and provide his children with a more promising future.

Through the help of an acquaintance, he located a twenty-five hectare plot of land eight kilometers from Mineros, near the community of Paichanetu. At first the local syndicate that represented lowland peasants was hesitant about accepting a "colla" into their midst, but through the intervention of an agrarian judge, Don Segundino eventually established a claim to a piece of land. His wife soon joined him, and during the first year he worked alternately on his own land and as a hired day laborer. The growth and urbanization of Mineros was just beginning, and through the urban land reform Segundino and his wife acquired a small lot in the expanding town to build their home. By the end of 1963 they had constructed a small wattle and daub house in Mineros and had made the decision to bring their belongings from Vallegrande and reside permanently in the oriente.

Agriculture--primarily rice cultivation--and temporary wage labor provided them with a subsistence income for the first three years. After each harvest they briefly returned to Vallegrande to visit their families and reestablish old acquaintances. They took rice and cassava to their relatives and always returned with potatoes, cheese, and mote, a special kind of corn not produced in the tropical lowlands. These items, which were staples in their home community, were absent in their lowland diet and sorely missed by both Segundino and his wife.

In 1964, Segundino, with the help of a relative, opened a carpentry shop in Mineros and no longer worked exclusively in the countryside. For the next six years, Segundino and his wife made a modest living, constructing furniture and cultivating rice and corn on their land. They eventually sold their lot in Mineros, bought a new one on the town plaza, and constructed a larger, more durable house of brick and concrete. Their initial step into capitalist agriculture and more extensive commercial activities did not come until 1970, however.

Segundino decided to plant tomatoes and green peppers with the money he had saved from the carpentry business. Although these crops had a high commercial value, they required a relatively large capital investment and entailed considerable risk because of their perishability and erratic prices. Aware of these pitfalls, Segundino decided to take the chance. Transportation from his property to Mineros had greatly improved; a proper dry-weather road now existed where once there was only a narrow path. The construction of this road represented the collaboration of several local syndicates and the combined labor of many settlers. And the growth of urban centers over the past decade provided a ready market for his produce. Mineros had not only become a dynamic market center, but paved roads connected the town to larger cities such as Montero and Santa Cruz de la Sierra. During the 1970 season weather conditions favored his crops and prices remained high. By the end of the harvest, Segundino's venture paid off when the tomatoes and peppers brought him an income of some 42,000 pesos.

With these earnings he decided to open a general store in Mineros instead of reinvesting in more hazardous vegetable cultivation. Then, through help and a loan from one of his wife's relatives, Segundino began traveling back and forth to the highlands, bringing merchandise to stock the store. The relative was also a skilled merchant who had considerable experience transporting contraband goods from the Peruvian border and Brazil and reselling them in Santa Cruz. He allowed Segundino to accompany him on several trips to the highlands and shared his knowledge as well as the use of his truck to transport the commodities.

This business proved to be extremely

remunerative, as Segundino earned 100 percent profits on the merchandise shipped from La Paz. Pleased with his good fortune, he decided to leave the carpentry shop under the supervision of his younger brother and dedicate more time to commerce. By the time Banzer devalued the Bolivian peso in September 1972 from twelve to twenty to the U.S. dollar, Segundino had already accumulated some 70,000 pesos, and through a combination of good business sense and a fortuitous occurrence he maintained the value of his capital after the devaluation. The day before the announcement of the new exchange rate, Segundino arrived from La Paz with a shipment of goods that represented one of the largest investments he had made to date. When the devaluation was decreed, he stored the merchandise and shut down the store until prices stabilized at a new level. He then reopened the shop and sold his wares at much higher prices, maintaining the value of his investment.

Unlike Juan Vega, Segundino Villa obtained his prosperity through commerce while maintaining a base in agriculture. Agriculture provided the family with an initial subsistence income, but the carpentry business allowed Don Segundino to accumulate the necessary capital to launch his investment in commercial tomatoe and pepper production when the right conditions existed. Subsequently, agricultural earnings and strategic familial assistance helped establish him as a prosperous Mineros-based merchant; thus, he diversified his income generating activities to include both agriculture and commerce.

While familial support and previous accumulations proved to be of great importance to migrants, they also gained access to another resource that had not been available to past generations of small producers in Santa Cruz. That resource was bank credit. Prior to the mid-1970s, regional banks had been unwilling to deal with small farmers, but the growing indebtedness of large producers and a series of problems which began to plague the sugar and cotton industries moved many banks to reconsider their policy. North American development organizations also became interested in financing small-scale cultivators in the aftermath of the Vietnam War. Government officials and development planners believed that the most efficient means of channeling financial resources to the local level was through the formation of agricultural cooperatives.

Although the formation of agricultural cooperatives actually began in Bolivia after the national revolution in 1952, the promotion of these organizations among settlers in the colonization zones did not really get under way until the late 1960s and particularly the 1970s. Government planners and foreign lending institutions became concerned with the rapidly growing colonization areas for a number of reasons. Che Guevara's aborted guerrilla movement in 1967 gave rise to fears over the long-term stability of the region, and the inequalities caused by nearly two decades of growth were creating growing unrest among settlers.

On the international scene, the failure of the Alliance for Progress and the inability of the United States to defeat the Vietnam rebels moved Congress to exert greater control over foreign policy; the "New Directions" guidelines for aid allocations were passed in 1973. They required the Agency for International Development (AID) to direct a larger percentage of development assistance to rural areas, and as an outgrowth of these measures, AID financed a variety of agricultural projects in Santa Cruz from 1976 to 1979 with some 132.1 million dollars (USAID, La Paz, Bolivia). Unlike the earlier directed colonization programs, these projects were primarily aimed at those families already established in northern Santa Cruz. Much of this money was channeled through agricultural cooperatives for such things as technical assistance and credit. In addition to AID, a number of smaller organizations --church groups, private volunteer agencies, and government foundations--became actively involved in similar rural development projects.

The shift in international emphasis also affected the credit allocations of Bolivian banking institutions since foreign capital constituted a large portion of their portfolios.

The Bolivian Agricultural Bank (BAB) and other banks started to make loans to peasant cooperatives in the mid-1970s. Small producers had proven themselves to be better credit risks than the large growers, and a fall in commodity prices made continued finance of sugarcane and cotton less attractive. In order to make these loans profitable, the banks used cooperative structures to extend credit to collective groups that assumed all responsibilities for making subloans and collecting debts from their members, and "pre-cooperatives" were created to expedite the paperwork. A pre-cooperative was essentially the same as a cooperative but could be organized more quickly with only a resolution from the Ministry of Agriculture; thus, it sidestepped the lengthy bureaucratic procedures for establishing a legal cooperative.

By 1977 cooperatives proliferated throughout Obispo Santiesteban province, and a survey of 3,472 families conducted by the Centro de Investigacion Agricola Tropical found that 40 percent belonged to agricultural or livestock cooperatives (Ortiz:1979). The most important goal of these organizations was to increase productivity through the provision of financial and technical assistance to small-scale agriculturalists so it should come as no surprise that they were in the best position to take advantage of such programs. Unlike many of the poor peasants, small-scale agriculturalists were able to sustain the necessary risk that greater production for the market entailed.

A number of small- and medium-size producers' associations also formed in Obispo Santiesteban province during the late 1960s and 1970s. These organizations sought to promote and defend the particular interests associated with specific crops, and the sector most thoroughly represented was sugarcane, which accounted for twelve of the twenty-four producers' associations active in the province. Those settlers who cultivated sugarcane were thus in a better position to defend their political and economic interests than any other group of settlers, but such organizations often divided settlers by addressing the production and marketing problems connected with particular crops instead of the common difficulties shared by most settlers. Consequently, many small producers' associations tended to identify with the demands of larger growers of the same crop, despite the considerable class differences that existed between them.

The Federacion Nacional de Cooperativas Arroceras (FENCA), which was created in 1965, attempted to represent the interests of rice growers in the Camara Agropecuaria del Oriente (CAO) and provide technical assistance to small producers, but the organization never functioned as a true support. Rice growers did not exercise the same power within the CAO or with government ministers as the sugarcane, cotton, and beef producers--and not surprisingly, they did not benefit from the financial support granted to other producers. Government intervention also prevented smooth functioning. Twice during the Banzer regime elected FENCA leaders were persecuted and replaced by leaders more sympathetic to military policy.

Understanding the need for credit and other assistance for their agricultural operations, Segundino Villa and Juan Vega joined cane producers' organizations and founded cooperatives in Paichanetu and Nuevo Mundo through the help of a Maryknoll priest. Created in 1974, these cooperatives gradually provided a growing number of services to the membership, which included crop transportation, heavy machinery, credit, rice milling, and a dry-goods store. A central office soon was established in Mineros that coordinated services to the local affiliates and solicited funding and support from both national and international agencies (see Chapter 6). Segundino and Juan rose to prominence in the cooperative, holding important positions at both the community and Central levels, and through this affiliation they greatly expanded their own entrepreneurial activities.

Juan Vega considerably extended his cane fields through cooperative assistance. A ready supply of credit enabled him to hire laborers on a consistant basis for the increased work load, and with cooperative transportation he was no longer forced to depend on hired truckers to ship his cane to the mills. Equally, if not more important, the opening of a state-owned mill in Mineros during 1977 greatly reduced his transportation costs. The cooperative quickly purchased shares in the mill, which gave members the right to sell their cane directly to it. Juan and other cooperative members gained direct access to the processing center in Mineros, and their transportation costs diminished as they no longer had to ship their cane to La Belgica.

By 1980, Juan cultivated twenty hectares of sugarcane in addition to rice, corn, potatoes, cassava, and tomatoes, and he had adopted a number of techniques to mobilize labor for his expanded operations. By granting use rights for small plots of land, he attracted a small, but relatively permanent and reliable work force, which every year numbered from two to three male adults, in addition to their spouses and children. These individuals most commonly represented relatives or fellow countrypeople from Chuquisaca who were recent migrants seeking to establish themselves in the region. They usually resided on Juan's property for a year or more before moving on and constituted the core of his labor force.

At peak periods of the agricultural cycle, however, Juan sought additional assistance from other Nuevo Mundo community members who were in need of employment. During the sugarcane and rice harvests and at times of heavy weeding, for example, his work force swelled to include fifteen to seventeen day laborers. Several of these men--both highlanders and lowlanders--were Juan's <u>compadres</u>. Others asked for and received cash advances from Juan to satisfy a range of necessities for their own households, and most were endebted to him. Through a series of interlocking rights and obligations with other community members, Juan was able to attract laborers from among the most impoverished residents of the community.

Finally, he and others like him profited from the collective labor supplied by the community cooperative. On one occasion, the cooperative initiated a cattle project with help from a foreign development agency. Cooperative members first cleared several hectares of land and also benefited from the cattle subsequently acquired by the cooperative (see Chapter 6).

It is perhaps tempting to construe the variety of labor relations used by Juan Vega as a precapitalist form of producing, but such an interpretation is erroneous. By the mid-1970s, Juan Vega was in the process of establishing an essentially capitalist, small-scale agricultural operation in Nuevo Mundo. Production was geared well beyond a level of basic subsistence, and its primary impetus was profit, in order to reinvest and expand. When Juan used such seemingly traditional techniques as loaning portions of his land to attract workers, he did so because it was the cheapest and most efficient way of planting, cultivating, and harvesting his sugarcane.

Juan no longer resided in Nuevo Mundo. He purchased a more substantial brick-and-cement dwelling for his family in Mineros and spent large portions of his time in town, attending to various business at cooperative headquarters, but when not otherwise engaged, he traveled to Nuevo Mundo on a motorcycle to supervise the agricultural tasks. Several of his children attended school in Mineros, and Juan and his wife hoped the children would eventually acquire sufficient education to become professionals.

Segundino Villa benefited from the cooperative and the economic boom of the late sixties and early seventies in much the same way as Juan Vega. Through cooperative assistance, he expanded his farming operations to include sugarcane. He also bought a truck, an investment that not only aided his agricultural and commercial dealings but also enabled him to extend his entrepreneurial activities into new areas.

Segundino became a rural transporter and no longer relied upon others to haul his crops. During the dry season months, he worked long hours shipping goods from rural settlements throughout the province to markets in Mineros, Montero, and Santa Cruz, and he found a ready supply of settlers eager to hire his services or sell their crops. He reactivated many former relationships in his home region of Vallegrande province and initiated commercial dealings with many old acquaintances from the area. Potatoes were a primary crop grown in the temperate valleys of this province, and producers had come to rely heavily on fertilizers to generate the required yields. Segundino shipped fertilizers from Santa Cruz to Vallegrande, which he sold at a considerable profit, and returned with potatoes to sell in Santa Cruz.

With the growth of his various commercial activities, Segundino expanded his network of social relationships. While his wife attended to business in their Mineros store, he developed a series of arrangements with more poor peasants to carry out the agricultural tasks on his land, in much the same way as Juan Vega. He utilized old relationships from his home community to extend his commercial activities and created new ties with settlers in Santa Cruz through debt and patronage.

During the years following the national revolution the stories of Segundino Villa and Juan Vega were repeated with several variations in other communities surrounding Mineros and throughout northern Santa Cruz. A group of entrepreneurs, many with peasant backgrounds, began to invest in new agricultural and commercial enterprises, as the opening of the eastern lowlands presented fresh opportunities for profit. Although they constituted a diverse group, these individuals also shared many similarities. The vast majority were migrants from the highlands or the intermontane valleys who benefited from important connections or prior accumulations made in other places. Many were from a second wave of settlers, who built on improvements carried out by the original pioneers. Finally, they gained access to financial and technical assistance through banks and cooperative organizations that had not been available to previous generations of lowland peasants.

These new entrepreneurs began to exert a stronger influence over more impoverished rural settlers and often came to exercise prominent leadership roles in their respective communities.

The influence of these individuals varied from community to community, depending upon the degree of social and economic differentiation, the amount of state involvement in local affairs, and the history of commercial penetration.

NOTES

1. See Roseberry (1983) for further discussion of this point.

6

Agricultural Cooperatives and Rural Development

The preeminence of the emerging group of small-scale agriculturalists in Nuevo Mundo, Rio Viejo, and Paichanetu was most apparent in the agricultural cooperatives that organized in these communities during the mid-1970s. The cooperatives added a new dimension to life in the settlements by enabling a small number of migrants to successfully establish commercial operations and to consolidate power at the local level. They were promoted by international development organizations to diffuse potential conflict between poor peasants and large-scale capitalist producers. The organizations, however, only further aggravated the process of social and economic differentiation which was already underway in the communities.

This chapter examines how the emergent group of small-scale agriculturalists profited from cooperative services and gained control of these new community institutions. Through the cooperative, they strengthened their agricultural and commercial activities and, in several cases, made the transition from subsistence agriculture to small-scale, capitalist farming. The community cooperatives replaced the syndicates as the most important local-level organizations, supplanting the broad political concerns of the syndicates with narrowly defined, technological preoccupations of the cooperatives. Premised on the false assumption that peasant agriculture was backward and low-yielding, the cooperative--the Central de Cooperativas Agropecuarias Mineros (CCAM)--directed previously unavailable services to the countryside and promoted greater productivity and market integration. While it helped to create new opportunities for wealth and power within the existing status quo, CCAM did not aim at rearranging the social relationships that generated patterns of surplus extraction and impeded capital formation among peasants.

The new "cooperative" ideology became a weapon used by both the small-scale agriculturalists and the poor peasants as the differences between them grew more pronounced. It served as a vehicle for both class struggle and class transformation: Those who benefited from the cooperative's services used the organization as a means of obtaining political power and justifying their pursuit of profit, but poor peasants called upon notions of cooperation and redistribution to defend their right to subsistence. To understand how this occurred, we must first consider the development and organization of the cooperative in these communities.

THE FORMATION OF COMMUNITY-BASED AGRICULTURAL COOPERATIVES

The organization of agricultural cooperatives in Nuevo Mundo, Rio Viejo, and Paichanetu began in 1973. A Maryknoll priest, who regularly visited the communities, and three prominent residents of Nuevo Mundo--Ignacio Betanzos, Juan Vega, and Julio Rodriguez--began to discuss the possibility of forming a cooperative in Nuevo Mundo. These men were recent migrants from Chuquisaca department, where they had known each other since childhood. Upon arrival in Nuevo Mundo, they had purchased land and initiated small-scale sugarcane cultivation. They wanted to invest and continue to expand their agricultural operations, and the possibility of forming a cooperative to acquire credit and technical assistance greatly excited them.

Like other members of their community, they had serious reservations about the syndicate's ability to address community problems. The syndicate had suffered badly from the shifting winds of Bolivian politics, and community residents were divided and suspicious of one another. Illegal land deals by a few unscrupulous syndicate leaders, financial mismanagement, and partisan political conflict, arising from the reorganizations suffered under the Pacto Militar-Campesino, had diminished the organization's prestige in the eyes of many settlers. For these reasons, rising new community leaders such as Juan Vega and Ignacio Betanzo saw the formation of a new organization--an agricultural cooperative--as a possible solution to their problems.

A cooperative, they were told, maintained political neutrality, although individual members were free to participate in the political party of their choice. In this way, a cooperative avoided the partisan political rangling and government repression so characteristic of many syndicates. Furthermore, a cooperative had a well-defined administrative structure with built-in checks and balances to discourage corruption, and this, they believed, was an attribute lacking in the syndicate. Finally, and perhaps most importantly, Bolivian banks and international development organizations began to finance small farmer cooperatives in the mid-1970s, and fortuitously, the local priest, a North American, had connections with foreign development organizations. These organizations did not display the same generosity to the syndicates. On the basis of these facts, then, community leaders decided to form a cooperative in Nuevo Mundo and encouraged other residents to participate.

A similar pattern of local initiative developed in Rio Viejo. The Mamani brothers--Pedro and Eusebio--were the prime movers behind the cooperative. As the sons of a mine worker, they had grown up in the highlands of Potosi department but migrated in 1966 to Santa Cruz department, where they worked as laborers on the sugarcane estates and bricklayers in Montero. The brothers traveled back and forth between Potosi and northern Santa Cruz for several years. Pedro eventually married and purchased twenty-five hectares of land in Rio Viejo with financial assistance from his wife's family. He was the first highlander to buy property in the community, which consisted entirely of Chiquitano and Guarayo families. Pedro and his brother planted a little sugarcane, and they eagerly embraced the notion of a community-based agricultural cooperative, hoping to develop agriculture still further.

In Paichanetu such men as Segundino Villa first seized upon the idea of a cooperative. They did not live in the community but rather, resided in Mineros and owned parcels scattered around the surrounding countryside. The settlement served primarily as a location for the monthly cooperative meetings, which had to be held in the countryside according to cooperative rules. Although some community residents eventually joined, the cooperative represented the interests of the leadership more than the concerns of Paichanetu dwellers.

In all the communities, the cooperative leaders were landowners, and the majority were already producing sugarcane when the cooperatives formed. They came almost entirely from the relatively privileged stratum of small-scale agriculturalists, who could benefit from the cooperative services that aimed to increase production. Unlike the original syndicate members, they were not elected by the communities at large but by a more limited number of cooperative partners.

In this way, CCAM emerged in Nuevo Mundo, Rio Viejo, and Paichanetu during 1973 and 1974. Eleven other community-based affiliates organized during the course of the decade. By 1980 they included recently settled zones such as San Julian and the northern parts of Ichilo province as well as the older settlements closer to Mineros. A central office (the Central) opened in Mineros to coordinate the distribution of services to 300 partners, and it became the site of monthly meetings for delegates from the base cooperatives to discuss policy.

The CCAM's organizational structure reflected a model developed among textile workers in Rochdale, England during the late nineteenth century. The cooperative was organized and administered on a dual level: the Central directorate and locally, by branch affiliates. Each level elected an administrative and oversight council. The administrative board consisted of a president, vice-president, treasurer, secretary and two alternates who served when others were absent. The oversight committee, which had a similar structure, oversaw the affairs of the former and reported problems to the partners (see Figure 6.1). The Central directorate met twice each month, once to review cooperative business and, later, to present their reports to delegates from the affiliated cooperatives. Two elected representatives from each branch cooperative attended the delegate meeting. They had full voting rights and the responsibility to report all the issues and decisions of the Central in the monthly affiliate meeting held in their respective communities. In addition to these meetings, a yearly assembly, which every branch member was required to attend, was held at the Central. The Central directorate was elected at this meeting and such important questions as the entry of new base cooperatives were discussed.

    The membership handled much of the day-to-day management of the cooperative. Men like Ignacio Betanzos, who formed the first cooperative board of directors, initially spent the week working at cooperative headquarters in Mineros and returned to their communities for the weekend. However, the Maryknoll priest also played an important role in cooperative affairs. He subsequently left the priesthood to marry a Bolivian and devoted himself to a full-time position as the cooperative's advisor. Over the next several years, he obtained a variety of loans and grants from both national and international agencies to finance projects (see Table 6.1). He negotiated credit with local banks and exercised an important role in cooperative policy. He also provided numerous benefits to the cooperative through his influence (muneca) with local authorities and contacts in the United States. Such benefits ranged from securing the release of members unjustly imprisoned to acquiring used clothing and agricultural

FIGURE 6.1
Organizational Structure of the Cooperative

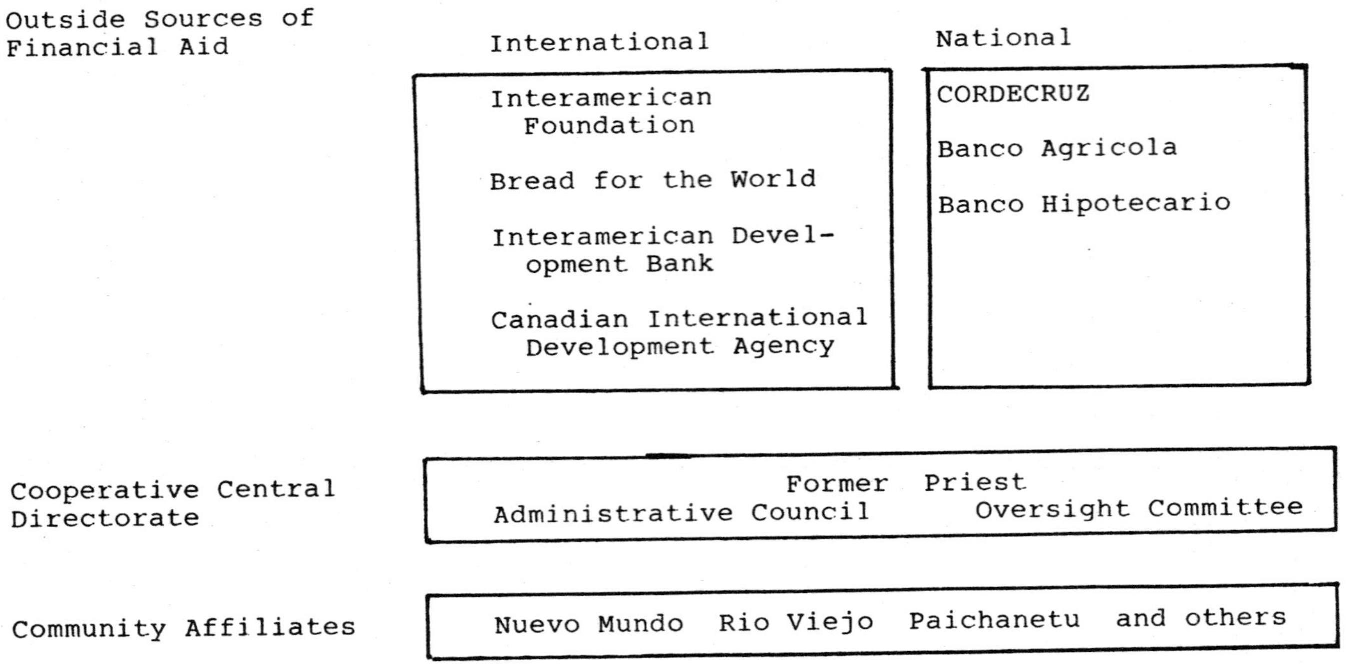

Outside Sources of Financial Aid	International	National
	Interamerican Foundation	CORDECRUZ
	Bread for the World	Banco Agricola
	Interamerican Development Bank	Banco Hipotecario
	Canadian International Development Agency	

Cooperative Central Directorate: Administrative Council — Former Priest — Oversight Committee

Community Affiliates: Nuevo Mundo   Rio Viejo   Paichanetu   and others

152

TABLE 6.1
Sources of CCAM Financial Assistance

A. International Sources	Amount ($US)
1. Bread for the World	
a) Revolving credit fund	500,000
b) Shares in UNAGRO mill	3,500
c) Rice Marketing	40,000
d) Mechanic Workshop	18,457
e) Education	23,750
f) Cattle project	40,500
Sub-total	626,207
2. Inter-American Foundation	
a) Capital investment funds	45,000
b) Consumer store	39,550
c) Emergency fund	12,560
d) Silos and grain dryer	64,936
Sub-total	162,046
3. Inter-American Development Bank	
a) New Cooperative Formation and Credit	500,000
4. Canadian International Development Agency	
a) Lathe for Workshop	?
B. National Sources	
1. CORDECRUZ	1,200
2. Banco Hipotecario	128,000
3. Banco Agricola Boliviano	16,882
Sub-total	146,082
TOTAL	$1,434,335

machinery from U.S. individuals and organizations.

He also acquired a D-7 bulldozer, two road graders, a backhoe, and two tractors, largely through the assistance of a policeman in the U.S. midwest; moreover, he obtained exemption from heavy import taxes through his connections with the Church. Shipping charges were the only major expenses, and the total "purchase" cost was therefore considerably less than local Bolivian prices. Such practices created an artificial situation, but they nevertheless shielded small producers from competition with more powerful capitalist growers and enabled the small-scale agriculturalists to expand their activities.

Because of the advisor's connections and the assistance granted by several foreign development agencies, the Central was able to provide numerous services to the affiliated cooperatives: crop transportation, a rotating credit fund, a rice mill, heavy machinery rental, a dry goods store, a mechanic shop, and a quota for sugarcane shipments to a local mill. The services did not appear all at once but rather developed over a period of years in response to the specific needs expressed by the membership. Based on these requests, the advisor and the Central directorate wrote project proposals articulating the desires of the membership, and the advisor then passed them along to his contacts in several international agencies. Over one million dollars was acquired between 1974 and 1982 (see Table 6.1).

Although cooperative membership represented a cross-section of community residents, some settlers found themselves in a better position to take advantage of cooperative services than others. Credit and transportation, for example, were the first services offered by the cooperative, and they were crucial to those settlers ready to switch from subsistence cultivation to the commercial production of sugarcane. Reliable transportation was necessary to swiftly ship cut cane to the mills and to avoid the intervention of middlemen, and credit was crucial for hiring wage laborers for the numerous demands of the agricultural cycle.

Several small-scale agriculturalists produced sugarcane before the cooperative formed, but they all suffered from transportation problems and difficulties mobilizing an adequate labor force. The cooperative services reduced these handicaps and helped them expand their operations.

Several families began to prosper. They extended the area under sugarcane cultivation, and some constructed second homes in Mineros, where they increasingly spent their time. Ignacio Betanzos purchased a small house near cooperative headquarters, moved his family in from the countryside, and left the day-to-day administration of his agricultural activities under the direction of a hired hand. Although living in Mineros was costlier than in Nuevo Mundo, town life offered a number of distractions and amenities. The numbers of mosquitos and other insects that plagued people in the countryside were less numerous in Mineros. Particularly, the vinchuca beetle, an insect which lived in the mud walls of rural dwellings and spread the dreaded Chagas disease, was less of a threat in the family's new wooden home. Don Ignacio's five children also could receive a better education in Mineros than in Nuevo Mundo, where the small schoolhouse had only two grades, and the teachers were frequently absent. In Mineros, the children could complete high school and then, hopefully, obtain professional occupations in the city instead of repeating the hardships endured by their parents in the countryside. Finally, the hustle and bustle of Mineros was often a welcome change from the tedium and monotony of farming an isolated field in the countryside.

The ability of some cooperative members to utilize cooperative services more than other community dwellers is best illustrated by the cooperative's mechanization program. It demonstrates the problems inherent in a policy aimed at boosting agricultural production solely through the diffusion of technology.

MECHANIZATION

Mechanization, as opposed to the traditional

slash-and-burn method, was most aggressively sought by the small-scale agriculturalists. When these families capitalized their holdings, they were obliged to expand the scale of their operations and to increase labor productivity. The introduction of heavy machinery made this goal possible, but it presupposed a change from swidden agriculture to more intensive land use. When combined with existing agricultural practices that sought only to maximize financial gain, mechanization led to extreme environmental degradation. In northern Santa Cruz, soil erosion was confined almost exclusively to those areas where mechanized soil preparation was practiced by large sugarcane, cotton, and soy bean growers.

The use of bulldozers to clear jungle and regrowth frequently leads to the removal of top soil as well as tree trunks and other debris. During the 1980-81 agricultural year, for example, I observed several corn fields that had been cleared by bulldozer. Tall, healthy plants grew on mounds formed by the bulldozer, but the corn planted on the cleared field itself achieved neither the same height nor fullness. Moreover, once the protective cover of forest was removed, repeated plowing to eradicate weeds was a primary factor contributing to soil erosion. Plowing was done during the dry season, when the wind attained velocities of up to fifty knots. In the absence of winter crop cover, wind breaks, and other precautionary measures, the winds rapidly carried away the fine particles of topsoil. Naturally, yields fell under these conditions, although they usually increased during the first year of mechanization. A study conducted by the British Tropical Agricultural Mission demonstrated that, in fact, yields declined during the second year of cultivation (personal communication).

Traditional slash-and-burn agriculture avoided many of these difficulties. By rotating the land under cultivation with regrowth, organic material was conserved, and weeds and pest infestations were controlled. Planted areas were small, and much of the vegetable matter remained on top to protect the soil from erosion. This form of cultivation also prevented excessive run-off that aggravated flooding, created large silt deposits, and harmed aquatic wildlife. Long-term residents in the communities stated that flooding caused by the Rio Hondo was worse than twenty years ago, when the area was still a frontier [1].

While mechanization helped some families embark on small-scale capitalist agriculture, many families, as we have seen, subsisted mainly from wage labor activities and the cultivation of small plots; they walked a thin line between subsistence and economic ruin. For these people, assuming the greater risk involved with mechanized cultivation could lead to disaster in the event of crop failure, impassable roads, or low market prices. This is exactly what happened to some Nuevo Mundo partners who used the cooperative's bulldozer in 1980-81. Rental costs were 950 pesos (U.S. $36) per hour, and approximately two to three hours (1900-2850 pesos) were necessary to clear one hectare of regrowth. The same work done manually cost 1,260 pesos (U.S. $50.40) per hectare if only hired labor was used but less if household labor was also utilized. Thus, the minimal difference between the two methods ranged from 640 pesos (U.S. $25.60) to 1,540 (U.S. $61.60) per hectare.

Twelve partners rented the bulldozer from five to eleven hours to clear their fields in October and November of 1981. The Central allowed them to rent on credit and did not demand payment for its services until after the harvest. No criterion was established to screen applicants, and some community residents, eager to increase their production but lacking a sound economic base, opted for mechanization. Unfortunately, the 1980-81 agricultural year was a bad one. Heavy rains and problematic road conditions damaged the corn and rice crops and inhibited marketing, and prices remained consistently low. In July 1981 only five sugarcane-producing households were in a position to repay their loans after the harvest, and by 1982 fully half of the partners had still not paid their debts, which ranged from 4,750 pesos (U.S. $190) to 10,450 pesos (U.S. $418).

The Central did not threaten debtors but exhorted them to pay back their loans. When these loans continued to be unpaid, however, the Central adopted stricter policies; people were obliged to pay half the cost upon requesting the services and the remainder immediately after completion of the work. The possibility of using harvest profits for payment was thus eliminated, and all but the most prosperous families were excluded from this service. Mechanization therefore benefited only those families capable of sustaining the greater risks that accompanied increased production for the market.

COMMUNITY DIFFERENTIATION AND CANE GROWER DOMINANCE

The cooperative, then, was instrumental in permitting some settlers to make the transition from subsistence agriculture to small-scale capitalist production, and it aggravated the process of social and economic differentiation that had begun two decades earlier. By 1980 a small group of seventeen families had planted sugarcane, but only six were original settlers. Some had initiated capitalist production through the cultivation of sugarcane, and others were in the process of doing so. A few successfully re-established small-scale capitalist agricultural activities after immigrating from another region of Bolivia and passing through an initial period of economic insecurity in the lowlands. These families employed between two and ten workers depending upon the season and the availability of household labor. Some, who were considered rich by local standards, had for most of the preceding nine years ended the agricultural year with a surplus beyond their subsistence requirements. The remaining sixty-nine households, however, could not insure the maintenance of the family unit through agriculture alone and frequently worked for the small-scale agriculturalists to earn cash to satisfy their basic domestic needs. Although they occasionally hired one or two wage laborers at peak times of the agricultural cycle, they did not realize a yearly surplus sufficient for expanding acreage though the use of additional laborers or agricultural machinery.

At this time, the community cooperatives consisted of 61 partners who represented 42 (49 percent) of the 86 households of the three communities. Forty-two of these partners were household heads, and 19 were sons or other relatives from their households. All but one of the sugarcane producers were affiliated with the cooperative, but only half of the other families were represented. The cooperatives regularly met once a month to discuss policy and make decisions on a range of affairs. They had become the most influential local institutions in the settlements.

Fiestas commemorating the founding of the community cooperatives were most indicative of this fact. Although residents of many frontier settlements in northern Santa Cruz planned celebrations for the days that their communities were founded, settlers in Nuevo Mundo and Paichanetu no longer made special preparations for these occasions. Rather, cooperative partners organized fiestas on the anniversary of their cooperative. Leaders from both the community and the Central came to the settlements, gave speeches extolling the virtues of working together, and exhorted individuals to continue united in the future. A large meal, prepared by the partner's wives, and quantities of beer, brought especially from Mineros for the occasion, followed the speeches. There was always lots of dancing as well, which was particularly lively if the cooperative advisor came with a generator to produce the electricity necessary to operate a tape or record player.

Only the families of Rio Viejo maintained the tradition of annual fiestas to mark the anniversary of their community. The incursion of outsiders had not disrupted social life to the same extent as in the other settlements. Although the Mamani brothers had become leading figures in the cooperative, more charter community members continued to reside in Rio Viejo than in either Paichanetu or Nuevo Mundo. Many of the original settlers had sold their land to outsiders, but the new owners were often wealthy people from the cities. They did not live in the communities, and as of 1980, they had not planted any crops. The original occupants were thus able to squat on their former parcels and continued producing subsistence crops, even though their own economic position had grown more tenuous. They recognized both the founding of their settlement and the formation of the cooperative with lively fiestas each year.

Those cooperative partners who controlled the distribution of cooperative services exercised considerably more power than either the government-appointed corregidor or the local-level syndicate leader who still remained in Paichanetu. The role of corregidor was largely confined to securing community school teachers and attending to various legal matters. The corregidor also was empowered to levy fines for minor infractions, but the real power of the position resided not in the office itself but in the person who held the title. In Nuevo Mundo, for example, a poor peasant was the corregidor during the research period and exercised only minimal influence over the affairs of the community. He had little backing to implement any major decisions, and residents recognized cooperative leaders as the primary figures in local affairs.

The situation in Paichanetu similarly reflected cooperative power. There, however, the corregidor was a sugarcane grower who belonged to the cooperative, and a nominal syndicate organization also existed in the community. The corregidor had been appointed several years earlier but no longer lived in Paichanetu. His participation in community affairs was restricted to the monthly cooperative meetings and visits to his own parcel, located on the opposite bank of the river. His prominence as a cane grower and his positions on the directive boards of both the Central and Paichanetu's cooperative were the basis of local influence and lent weight to any decisions he made as corregidor.

The syndicate leader was the caretaker (casero) on the Paichanetu corregidor's property and worked as a wage laborer. Although the syndicate had diminished in importance during the

Cooperative Leaders

Banzer years, it was revived by community members in 1979 (after the fall of Banzer), when conflict broke out in Paichanetu. Residents elected Felix Landivar as the leader and principal mediator in the dispute, but after the 1980 military coup, the syndicate again stopped meeting openly.

Since the cooperative's inception, the small-scale agriculturalists dominated the important leadership positions of the Central directorate and in Nuevo Mundo, Rio Viejo, and Paichanetu. These cane growers played a role in the cooperative disproportionate to their numerical significance, as only 45 (15 percent) of the 300 partners in all the base communities were sugarcane producers. A cane grower occupied the presidency of the Central for the first 8 years, and during 1981 cane growers held 6 of the 11 positions on the Central directorate boards and managed the cooperative transportation section. In the communities, sugarcane producers were not only the charter members and principal organizers of the cooperative but had also controlled the presidency of the base affiliates since the cooperative's formation. Their increasing prosperity distanced these leaders from the settlements.

Although many of the new cooperative leaders were well on the way to becoming small-scale capitalist producers, they experienced a certain ambiguity about their new role as profit maximizer. On the one hand, the origins and social relationships of these men were often firmly rooted in the peasantry, where reciprocity and the redistribution of goods and services were crucial to the survival of the domestic unit. On the other hand, the demands of numerous kin, fictive kin, and the poor peasants constituted a strain on their economic resources and hindered the process of accumulation. Managing these contradictions was a delicate task.

Kinfolk or poor community residents, faced with the deterioration of their own situation, called upon a "subsistence" ideology and reciprocity to remind the small-scale agriculturalists of their responsibility and to others to defend their right to subsistence [2]. They often asked wealthier individuals for loans in time of sickness or to sponsor a wide range of events that included weddings, soccer matches, and ceremonies marking the first hair cut of a young child. The sponsors were required to spend money on food, drink, jerseys for the soccer team, or locks of hair cut from the child's head. These activities represented important duties that the poor expected them to fulfill, but they also created a series of interlocking relationships based on mutual obligations and reciprocity that gave the small-scale agriculturalists access to the labor of other community residents. By extending loans and favors to poor peasants, prosperous families established a moral basis for their claims to the labor power of others.

These obligations, however, could be extremely onerous to a family struggling to launch commerical farming ventures because they drained resources, but the families, who had not yet consolidated their operations, found them difficult to refuse. They needed access to poor peasants' labor, and those men and women who failed to fulfill their civic duty quickly obtained reputations as "bad" patrons. They were chided by poor peasants for their greed and selfishness; this could affect their ability to mobilize workers.

With the advent of the cooperative, new ideas about "progress" and "development" through "cooperation" provided these men and women with an ideological justification for their upward mobility. Rather than encouraging competition and espousing the unbridled pursuit of individual profit, cooperative ideology held that helping one's neighbor and working together was the best way to insure the financial prosperity of everyone. In this way, it was consistent with peasant concepts of reciprocity and redistribution, but given the structure of the cooperative and the nature of its services, the new ideology also legitimized the dominance of the emerging group of small-scale agriculturalists. The cane growers of Nuevo Mundo, Rio Viejo, and Paichanetu were also well aware that they would have great difficulty acquiring individual loans from regional banks or development organizations, because their agricultural activities operated on a very small scale. They were thus eager to work as a group and were the foremost promoters of the new ideology. During meetings they referred to each other as brothers, and slogans such as "force comes through unity" were commonly heard. The poor peasants' inability to improve their situation was then more easily explained as the result of laziness, a lack of hard work, and the behavioral characteristics associated with certain groups, particularly the "cambas".

The subjects debated and discussed in the cooperative meetings reflected the concerns of the small-scale agriculturalists. From 1980 to 1982 the author recorded the major points discussed in ten monthly Central meetings as well as those debated in the Nuevo Mundo affiliate. The three topics most frequently discussed were credit and cooperative finances, international support for cooperative projects, and internal organization of the cooperative. A primary concern with credit and international support is not surprising. The small-scale agriculturalists relied heavily on cooperative credit to hire wage laborers, and credit and other forms of assistance had been available predominantly through the aid of international development organizations.

By examining the internal workings of the cooperative, we see how the small-scale agriculturalists in both the Central and the community affiliates manipulated events and beliefs to their own ends. The conflicts and accommodations that molded social relationships and shaped cooperative policy are highlighted. Two cases are presented below to demonstrate these processes.

Case 1: Cattle and the Nuevo Mundo Cooperative Affiliate

In Nuevo Mundo the influence of the small-scale agriculturalists is immediately apparent during the local cooperative meetings. These small-scale agriculturalists, and primarily three prominent sugarcane growers, monopolize the meetings, which do not occur without their presence. The poor peasants, who work for them as day laborers, rarely express strong public opposition to their motions, even though they voice considerable discontent in private. A conflict that developed around the purchase of cattle for cooperative partners in Nuevo Mundo illustrates this point.

Bread for the World donated money to the cooperative for cattle. Each partner was to receive one cow, but by the time the money arrived, its buying power was drastically reduced by a devaluation, and the cooperative's membership had increased. Only ten cows could be purchased, which were not enough for each partner to own one. The ensuing debate, which transpired during the course of two meetings, concerned whether the cattle should be sold to individual partners or managed collectively. The small-scale agriculturalists, led by Juan Vega and his brother, argued for individual purchases, but many of the poor peasants, who did not have the necessary funds, supported collective care and use of the animals. The small-scale agriculturalists stressed their position most forcefully. They maintained that their long-time affiliation with CCAM gave them more right to the cattle than others. Although the poor peasants outnumbered them, a vote was not taken, and the membership resolved the issue only after pressure from the Central administration moved them to accept collective ownership.

Central pressure came from Ignacio Betanzos, then Central president and also a Nuevo Mundo cane grower. At this time, Don Ignacio was struggling to buy a truck and did not want to invest in cattle. But, he did not wish to see the other small-scale agriculturalists be the sole beneficiaries of the cattle, and he also maintained a bitter personal rivalry with the Vega brothers. For these reasons, he backed collective ownership. Don Ignacio's influence as Central president and his charges that others behaved inappropriately strengthened the position of the poor peasants, who opposed the cane growers, and he (with support from the U.S. cooperative head) eventually obliged the small-scale agriculturalists to reverse their stand. The cooperative assigned each partner a number of days to care for the animals, but the small-scale agriculturalists did little of the actual work, more commonly sending a hired worker or a son to do their chores.

This case illustrated the conflicts that divide cooperative partners and how the small-scale agriculturalists used the organization to further their own interests. The small-scale agriculturalists sought individual gain from a project intended to benefit the entire cooperative. By supporting collective maintenance, Don Ignacio was able to further his own economic interests and appear as a defender of the poor. He not only maintained partial control over the care and use of the cattle at a time when he was unprepared to buy his own, but also strengthened his position as a leader in the eyes of the poor peasant partners.

Case 2: International Aid

When cooperative practices are scrutinized by representatives of international funding agencies, the sugarcane growers unite and emphasize the solidarity of all cooperative partners. By presenting a united front to representatives of international development organizations, they hope to acquire more credit and technical assistance from these organizations. This is particularly apparent when representatives periodically visit Mineros to check on current projects or discuss new ones and the possibility of new financial aid arises.

Late in 1982 three prople from a U.S. development agency came to Mineros to check on CCAM projects. They spent two days in Mineros and resided with the cooperative advisor. On the first day the advisor took them to cooperative headquarters where a "welcome committee" composed primarily of Central directorate members was on hand to greet them. This group had been encouraged to assemble by the cooperative head to give the representatives an opportunity to "talk to the people," and it was dominated by the sugarcane growers, the most articulate and outspoken cooperative partners. Leaders such as Ignacio Betanzos and his rivals put aside their differences, and along with cane growers from other communities, they presented the problems of settlers in northern Santa Cruz in terms of their own needs. The difficulties experienced by the poor peasants, insofar as they did not coincide with the leaders' own, were left unspoken and unheard. The few poor peasants who were on hand for this meeting deferred to the small-scale agriculturalists.

In this context, the cooperative leaders described the membership as one group of poor settlers who worked together, and they explained the greater poverty of certain families as the result of insufficient credit and support from outside sources or of simple laziness. These views were reiterated by the cooperative head. I, too, was told by the cane growers to say nothing that might damage the cooperative's image and was encouraged to express my support for the organization to these representatives.

THE COOPERATIVE AND THE POOR PEASANTS

It is instructive to take a closer look at the poor peasants and their involvement CCAM. In the early days of the cooperative, many of these families actively participated in the community organizations, because they hoped to benefit from the cooperative's services and did not want to be excluded from the "progress" that they hoped would improve living conditions in their communities. Nevertheless, the growing dominance of the sugarcane growers and repeated frustrations, increasingly disillusioned poor peasant families, and their participation in the cooperative gradually declined.

They made only limited use of the cooperative's services, because much of their income was derived from wage labor, and they were unable to bear the risks of greater production for the market. The remaining partners attended monthly meetings because of occasional opportunities when they could utilize the cooperative for hauling small amounts of rice or corn to the towns. The rice mill also benefited these partners when its prices were higher than those of other local mills, and some poor peasants obtained jobs in the rice mill. In addition, the Paichanetu cooperative, vis-a-vis the Central, oversaw the lengthy and costly bureaucratic procedures for legalizing community land claims. The cooperatives also played an important role in the communities. The monthly meetings and occasional cooperative-sponsored fiestas or soccer matches brought settlers together from dispersed households and constituted the primary social events in the settlements.

Nevertheless, the cooperative was unable to integrate all community members because it did not address many of the specific needs of agricultural wage laborers. Seasonal workers complained about working conditions on the sugar estates and the lack of rights for working people. Many believed that the estate owners should raise salaries and pay a half-day's wage when sickness or weather forced them to stop work. They expressed the need for an organization to protect workers from the abuses of employers and frequently cited pay received for weeding as an example of such mistreatment. Payment for a given area was determined by the quantity and thickness of the weeds. This naturally involved negotiation before a rate was set, and laborers, lacking strong organizational support and often indebted to the growers, were frequently obliged to accept the landowner's rates. The growth of the cocaine industry during the mid-1970s and the subsequent problems experienced by large growers in recruiting a labor force, however, weakened their bargaining position somewhat.

Any attempt to reorganize the unequal relationships among cooperative partners and within the communities would threaten the small-scale agriculturalists. Such changes are unlikely, given the current cooperative policy that aims to increase agricultural production through the dissemination of services and technological innovations. In addition, changes in cooperative administrative practices at the end of 1982 extended the term of elected officials. This change not only helped entrench the leadership but also distanced the cooperative even further from local control.

Yet, even as poor peasants were losing their fight against marginalization, they refused to give up, and their struggles continued to shape the contours of the emerging frontier society. As the cooperative increasingly reflected the concerns of the sugarcane growers, many poor peasants joined new organizations that formed in early 1980 during the brief democratic opening under the government of Lidia Gueiler. These organizations--the Comite Ad-Hoc de Trabajadores de Cana and the Federacion Sindical de Cosechadores de Algodon attempted to address the concerns of sugarcane harvesters and cotton pickers respectively, and they attracted both seasonal migrants and poor peasants. Several poor peasants from Paichanetu joined, and the comments of one man, who participated in the cane harvesters' association, reflected the frustrations and feelings of many others toward the community cooperative. He said that "the cooperative doesn't worry about these things [the problems of wage laborers] because the people have land and they are the rich ones." Although the agricultural laborers' associations were repressed by the military after a coup d'etat in July 1980, they resurfaced two years later when a new democratic government came to power (see Chapter 7).

The poor peasants also continued to use notions of reciprocity and redistribution as weapons in the intensifying class struggle. By constantly reminding the rich of their obligations to the poor, they defended their right to subsistence and limited, to a certain extent, the process of accumulation. Moreover, with the development of the cocaine traffic, they increasingly found more lucrative employment processing coca leaves into cocaine paste and earned wages up to ten times more than the going rate for agricultural day labor. The impact of this trade on the local economy receives more detailed discussion in Chapters 7 and 8.

CCAM AND SOCIAL CHANGE

Clearly, there was no development strategy that would benefit all the families of Nuevo Mundo, Rio Viejo and Paichanetu, nor all the cooperative partners. In response to political, social and economic changes in the wider society, the cooperative strengthened a limited number of small-scale agriculturalists whose demands and aspirations found important expression in the organization. It acted not only as a financial support to their growing commercial activities but also played an important role in legitimizing their desire for upward mobility. It did so by avoiding the broad social and economic concerns of the syndicates, concentrating instead on more narrowly defined technological problems.

The well-being of most community households depends upon employment opportunities and wages rather than agricultural productivity. Improvements in their living standard will come only after important changes are made in their status as poor peasants, but the cooperative does not address many of their concerns. This neglect is evident not only in the kinds of services offered by the cooperative, but also in the individualistic orientation of its services, despite the rhetoric of cooperation and the possibility for more collectively organized projects. Although communally organized projects have been attempted, they have enjoyed only limited success; services continue to be directed primarily to individual households. The potentials of the cooperative education program to promote a genuinely collective ideology have not been actively pursued. This program, which is financed by Bread for the World and directed locally by the U.S. cooperative advisor, emphasizes two major areas, the technological skills of farming and the administrative aspects of cooperative management, without reference to the social inequalities among cooperative partners.

By avoiding an activist stance and not espousing radical social changes, the cooperative survived several military dictatorships and withstood the shifting winds of Bolivian politics. Survival is also due to the cooperative head's extensive relationships with local politicians. In addition, CCAM fills a vacuum in the countryside left by the Bolivian state which, particularly under military rule, has been unwilling to seriously address the needs of poor peasants. It has chosen instead to manipulate and undermine peasant organizations to its own advantage. Financially weak and politically unstable, the state has responded to the economic demands of lowland agriculturalists and surrendered rural development to international agencies. CCAM emerged at a time when community syndicates were waning or had ceased to exist. Its policy sought to prop up subsistence agriculture and recreate the social relationships necessary for continued capitalist accumulation. In this way, it could create political stability by strengthening the position of the small-scale agriculturalists, who became linked economically to the agro-industrialists through the cultivation of sugarcane. The small-scale agriculturalists could then act as a stabilizing force between the two groups. Their presence was particularly important in a frontier region like northern Santa Cruz, where state control has traditionally been weak.

This development strategy, however, generated important contradictions; the same inequalities which made CCAM necessary were recreated and strengthened among the settlers (deJanvry: 1981; Feder: 1976). Those settlers making the transition from subsistence agriculture to capitalist production used cooperative services to strengthen their position and called upon the principles of cooperativism to further justify their pursuit of profit. The problems and difficulties experienced by the increasingly large numbers of poor, wage-earning peasants should be addressed more directly by rural development projects. By supporting the concerns of this group and strengthening local organizations committed to social concerns, such projects could establish the basis for comprehensive social change and a genuine improvement in the living standards of the majority of rural people.

NOTES

1. In an attempt to avoid the pitfalls inherent in mechanization, several rural development organizations have proposed animal traction as an intermediate technology more suitable to the conditions of small-scale agriculture in northern Santa Cruz (Graber: 1977). Although this method is used successfully among Mennonite settlers, the cooperative partners emphasize that it is inadequate for clearing stumps and roots. They point out that the Mennonites use animal traction in combination with more capital intensive equipment.

2. The *corregidor* of Nuevo Mundo, for example, even raised a local problem before the monthly cooperative meeting for the membership to

resolve. The issue involved a family temporarily residing in a house designated for the school teacher. The family was not maintaining the area properly, according to the corregidor, and he sought cooperative support to substantiate his demands, despite the fact that such affairs are technically outside the scope of cooperative activities.

3. See Scott (1979), Brocheux (1983), Polachik (1983) and Thompson (1971) for more discussion on the concept of moral economy.

7

The Agro-Industrial Bourgeoisie, Economic Crisis, and the Cocaine Trade

While growing class divisions transformed frontier settlements, a new bourgeoisie began to take shape at the regional level. State and international policies allowed both the traditional landowning families and a new group of beneficiaries to emerge as a powerful entrepreneurial class, concentrating wealth and power until they achieved considerable influence in departmental and national politics. The M.N.R. and U.S. development programs laid the basis for the appearance of this class, and the rise of the military strengthened and confirmed its hegemony; first, by supporting cash crop production, and later, through the traffic in cocaine.

The privatization of large tracts of the frontier and the marginalization of rural settlers constituted an important element in the emergence of a capitalist class, but the strength of the new entrepreneurs also rested upon their control of important regional organizations, urban-based commercial investments, and contraband, particularly cocaine. The development of the cocaine industry in Santa Cruz enriched several members of the bourgeoisie and strengthened a faction of the military tied to the illegal traffic. This, in turn, led to the rise of a repressive military dictatorship that was linked to the drug traffic and closely involved with local affairs. To understand the growth and consolidation of this class, we must first examine how families profited from the agricultural boom and how they responded to an economic crisis that began to develop in the late

1970s.

GROWTH AND CRISIS IN THE SANTA CRUZ AGRO-INDUSTRIES

The expansion of the regional economy not only allowed long-established <u>cruceno</u> landowners to consolidate their position and reap large profits but also attracted a new group of investors and speculators to the eastern lowlands. The newcomers consisted of ex-hacendados and mine owners from the highlands and valleys, military officers, administrators, professionals, and a substantial number of foreigners. Together with their lowland counterparts, they invested in both agriculture and a number of urban-based business ventures that grew out of the commercial boom. Such investments not only increased their possibilities for capital accumulation but also molded a number of common economic interests among these men and women. Their participation in important clubs and organizations, connections with the military and more established families--either by alliance or association--allowed them to further these interests.

Examples of these new investors are abundant. Juan Godoy, a former mine owner from Oruro, came to Santa Cruz at the height of the cotton boom and constructed a cotton mill with cheap credit that he received from a regional bank. Jose Sanchez, a Spaniard, arrived in 1959, after losing an inheritance battle with his brother over custody of the family estate. For the next twenty years, he bought land in northern Santa Cruz, acquired large land grants, invested in rice, cotton, sugarcane, beef cattle, soy beans, corn and sorghum production, and became involved in a number of urban-based businesses and import operations. He controlled the Mercedes-Benz concession in Santa Cruz, owned an agricultural machinery import firm, and through yet another agency, he sold refrigerators, freezers, and air conditioners. Further, the business carrying the family name--Sanchez, Ltda.--sold bathroom and kitchen fixtures manufactured in Argentina. Rigoberto Candia is another example. When his family's estate in the Cochabamba Valley was expropriated, Candia moved to Santa Cruz, bought land, and became a successful agricultural entrepreneur.

Contraband of various sorts also played an important role in the process of accumulation. The railroads to Argentina and Brazil facilitated a thriving contraband trade. Automobiles, cigarettes and clothing were among the many items illegaly shipped into Bolivia. A range of such consumer durables as stereos, tape recorders, kitchen appliances, and photographic equipment were also smuggled into Santa Cruz from Miami and Panama. One man, Gene Hansen, an American from a middle-class, Oklahoma family, made large profits exporting tropical birds to North America. Although certain species could legally be sold abroad, the sale of many rare, endangered birds was officially prohibited, and Hansen's operations were shut down from time to time when such species were discovered. Nevertheless, Hansen, who had married into the traditional cruceno elite, benefited from important connections in government ministries and was always able to renew his operations.

Foreigners, dispossessed landlords, mineowners, and other investors from the highlands and valleys were not the only individuals to prosper in Santa Cruz. Prominent lowlanders consolidated and enhanced their position after 1952 in several ways. With the increase in land values brought on by the economic boom, many dragged out old property titles or forged new ones to substantiate their claims to land, and as we have seen, agrarian reform legislation and U.S. economic assistance enabled them to convert their properties into agricultural enterprises during the 1950s and 1960s. The urbanization of Santa Cruz and Montero allowed several families to reap windfall profits by dividing their properties into lots and selling them to newcomers at vastly inflated prices.

The most prominent latifundists prior to 1952 were represented in the Junta Rural del Norte, an early forerunner of the CAO. This organization was dissolved after the revolution, but many of its approximately sixty members or their descendents continued to play prominent social, political, and economic roles in northern Santa Cruz. Descendents of the Soleto family bought land in Nuevo Mundo that had once been claimed by a family member, and they initiated sugarcane and cattle production during the 1970s (see Chapter 2). Manuel Jesus Mendoza became a prominent cash crop producer in the 1970s and made a handsome profit from the sale of his land to the state for the construction of a new sugar mill in Mineros. The Nunez brothers also initiated large-scale sugarcane and cotton production; one brother developed an import business and became a major shareholder in the Banco de Santa Cruz de la Sierra. Many others followed similar paths.

Perhaps more than any other, the Schweitzer family best represents the power and prominence attained by the lowland bourgeoisie in Santa Cruz. The family has played an important role in northern Santa Cruz because of its ownership of a large sugar mill and its important social and political connections. A German immigrant, who settled in Cochabamba around the turn of the century, established the family in Bolivia. He married twice to local women, had three sons by each marriage, and operated a business in Cochabamba that supplied the big tin mines with food prior to the national revolution. With the outbreak of World War II, the Bolivian government, under pressure from the American embassy, blacklisted the Schweitzers because of their German background, and the business gradually disintegrated.

A younger son, Erwin, left for the eastern lowlands, eventually married a woman from the local elite, and began smuggling contraband rubber from San Ignacio de Velasco in Santa Cruz to a border town in Argentina. All Bolivian rubber was being shipped to the United States at this time to support the war effort, and prices were only a fraction of those offered in Argentina. Over a four-year period, Erwin Schweitzer made large profits as a <u>contrabandista</u>, but at the end of the war, he turned his attention to agriculture and the construction of a sugar mill. In conjunction with three brothers, he purchased an 800-hectare property. The brothers acquired a rudimentary cane press and planted twenty hectares of sugarcane during the first year. In 1946 they bought an alcohol distillery, and in 1952 they installed the first machinery for a sugarmill and produced 265,000 pounds of sugar. The political upheavals of the revolution caused them initial concern, but neither the mill nor their holdings were disturbed. Through the Point Four program, the U.S. government, in a reversal of its former policy towards the Schweitzers, granted them a U.S. $2.5 million loan to purchase new equipment for the sugarmill and expand its processing capacity. Previous financial restrictions had prevented the Schweitzers from modernizing their mill and increasing its capacity, and Erwin Schweitzer attributed much of the enterprise's later success to this initial infusion of capital.

Annual output increased, and by 1964 it reached nearly 8.5 million pounds. Production continued to expand into the 1970s, and one brother returned to Cochabamba to establish a distribution center for the large highland and valley markets. The family expanded its own cane fields near the mill to include 400 hectares and worked closely with large-scale growers to insure a continual supply of cane to their mill. They also diversified into cattle ranching with the acquisition of a large estate in the Beni department.

The Schweitzers and other increasingly prosperous entrepreneurs became influential at both the regional and national levels as the economic importance of Santa Cruz grew, and their power reached new heights with the 1971 coup d'etat of General Hugo Banzer. As we saw in Chapter 2, Banzer rewarded them for their support with generous financial assistance and land grants. This support further strengthened the bourgeoisie and reinforced ties between the military and lowland entrepreneurs.

The Ocampo family exemplifies the growing connections between the military and commercial agriculturalists in Santa Cruz. Three brothers and their families live in the city of Santa Cruz where they operate a fiberglass factory and a carpentry business. During the early years of the Banzer government, Aldo Ocampo, the oldest brother and a carreer military officer, was one of the president's personal bodyguards. Such a position demanded a considerable degree of trust and confidence, and it is generally believed that through his military connections he received a 2,432 hectare grant in 1972 and other large grants for both brothers. He obtained a cattle estate in the western portion of the northern zone near Yapacani.

Hernan Arredondo represents still another pattern of accumulation. He benefited from the favorable policies of the Banzer administration and the booming regional economy. Born in Obispo Santiesteban province to a socially prominent family of modest economic means, Arredondo began to accumulate land in the 1970s. He steadily purchased peasant land, ranging from ten to fifty hectares in the Mineros region, and also received large land grants from the state. In this way, he amassed holdings of over 2,300 hectares in the course of a decade. Because of his close ties with regional banks and a prominent sugarmill owner, he began to plant sugarcane and cotton on a large-scale and eventually diversified into cattle, soy beans and corn. His operations expanded rapidly in the early 1970s, and when he was occasionally unable to mobilize enough workers to harvest his cotton and sugarcane crops, Arredondo's connections in the military provided him with enough recruits from the local garrison to complete the harvests. His success in agriculture allowed him to open an agricultural machinery import firm in Santa Cruz, to acquire an impressive array of machinery for his own operations and to sell equipment to other growers. He also invested in urban real estate and purchased several houses that he rented for a profit.

We see, then, that both lowland families and new investors established impressive agricultural and commercial operations in Santa Cruz. The sectoral distinctions that divided the various agricultural and urban commercial activities were largely artificial because most families had investments in both. If we examine the province of Obispo Santiesteban, this fact becomes more apparent. During the 1970s, approximately 130 private sugarcane growers constituted the backbone of the sugar industry in this province. Seven of these people occupied either the presidency or the vice-presidency of a major producers' organization during the decade. One man, Abelardo Suarez, moved between three different organizations and held key positions for five years. In addition, three sugarcane growers enjoyed ties with other powerful regional institutions. Juan Carlos Valverde was the president and vice-president of the Pro-Santa Cruz Committee. Another man, Abraham Telchi, was a vice-president of the Departmental Federation of Private Entrepreneurs and president of the Chamber of Commerce and Industry, and Hugo Pessoa was involved with the rightist Falange Socialista Boliviana (FSB). Many growers also occupied positions on the board of directors of cooperatives, sugar mills and other institutions as well as these more prominent posts.

The power of this new class of landowners and businessmen who benefited from government policies and several years of favorable economic conditions became ever more apparent. Although conflicts occasionally divided them, the economic strength of the region and a benevolent military regime enabled them to manage their disagreements. A number of common beliefs reinforced their unity. First, they wanted continued state and international support for private enterprise and no end to military rule, as only the military had the power to support the interests of such a minority. Second, they opposed the reorganization of mass political parties and peasant and worker unions, because they correctly understood the impact that such organizations could have on the status quo. The upheavals of the 1952 revolution in the highlands and valleys were well within the living memory of these individuals. Finally, they were prepared to quickly repress any opposition to their hegemony, as they were fully cognizant of how redistributive programs would affect their own welfare (see Whitehead: 1973).

The rapid expansion of commercial agriculture and its orientation towards the export market posed a series of new problems for these entrepreneurs. As we saw in Chapter 2, growers confronted mounting difficulties with the organization and control of an adequate labor force. After the failure of the PROMIGRA campaign in 1973, they were obliged to return to the use of labor contractors and the old system of contrata. This system was unsatisfactory not only because it was unable to mobilize the required number of workers but also because it merely intensified existing forms of labor exploitation. It did not proletarianize the rural population nor did it adjust well to the increasingly sophisticated demands of the export-oriented agro-industries.

Growers were obliged to carry out a series of technological improvements and invest more heavily in mechanization and agro-chemicals such as herbicides and insecticides. They hoped these measures would not only minimize their needs for laborers but also increase yields and reduce their overall costs. Moreover, higher levels of capitalization and greater labor productivity were necessary in order to compete with rival producing nations. The use of airplanes for heavy fumigation tasks quickly developed, and several commercial airline companies opened to service the needs of the cotton growers. The first two cotton harvesters appeared in 1974, and by 1975 the number of these machines had increased to fifty. The construction of mills also advanced, and in 1976 there were sixteen mills operating in northern Santa Cruz.

Although agricultural machinery and greater investments increased the productivity of labor, it required a large area under cultivation in order to be profitable. Only those growers who enjoyed access to credit could make the required investments, as machinery and other manufactured items had to be imported at great expense. These expenditures rose substantially with the world oil crisis of the mid-1970s and made high production costs increase still further. This eroded the competitive position of Bolivian crops on the world market, even though prices were not always unfavorable.

As a result of such mounting difficulties, the cotton boom collapsed in 1974. Acreage declined from a peak of 60,333 hectares in 1973-74 to 28,545 hectares the following year, and the industry entered into a serious depression from which it has still not recovered. Several factors gave rise to this crisis. In addition to labor problems and high production costs, a lack of planning existed at the regional level. A strict selection of credit recipients was not planned nor were loans properly supervised. Many individuals who received credit had no previous experience with agriculture, and loans were provided for production in areas where the soil structure was inappropriate for this crop. Disbursements were delayed, and this naturally disrupted important phases of the agricultural cycle.

Marketing problems continually plagued the industry as well. Cotton could not be stored after the harvest but had to be immediately taken to the mill for processing. Properties without direct access to all-weather roads suffered from transportation difficulties, as the harvest began when roads were still impassable because of the rains and flooding. Moreover, ADEPA monopolized the marketing of all cotton grown in northern Santa Cruz and frequently delayed payments to producers for six months or more. This exacerbated problems with loan repayments and postponed planting and soil preparation activities the following year. Finally, multinational enterprises such as the Cotton Import and Export Corporation, Misin and Company, Ralli Brothers and Company and the Mitsubishi Corporation controlled the sale of Bolivian cotton on the world market and extracted a substantial portion of the profits generated by Bolivian producers. When production and marketing problems delayed contract completion with these organizations, heavy fines were levied against Santa Cruz growers in the mid-1970s, and the industry lost its international credit rating.

The sugar industry, which had experienced a brief recession due to a drought and a cane blight, recuperated in the midst of the cotton disaster. Prices rose sharply on the world market in the mid-1970s, and the opening of new lands produced higher yields. World prices had averaged between five and six dollars per quintal since the 1950s, but in 1974 and 1975 the price shot up to twenty-nine dollars [1]. The belief that prices would continue to rise led growers to increase the area planted in sugarcane, which jumped from 39,200 hectares in 1974 to over 56,000 hectares the following year. Sugarcane growers, too, experienced a lack of workers as acreage surpassed its previous limit; subsequently several began to mechanize harvest operations.

The sudden price rise after years of relative stability led to excessive world sugar production and the accumulation of large reserves. This caused prices to fall drastically in 1976 and 1977, and the ensuing crisis moved the majority of sugar producing nations to sign the "Geneva Agreement" in 1977 that sought to regulate the relation between supply and demand through the assignment of an export quota to each country. Bolivia was alloted 73,350 tons and an additional 25,000 tons in 1979. This quota was subject to renegotiation each year, and its maintenance in years of low world prices required the government to subsidize exports at an average price of five dollars per quintal, which occasioned a strong erosion of foreign exchange.

Confronted by the deepening problems of sugarcane and cotton production, growers began to reorganize the structure of commercial agriculture in Santa Cruz. Many switched to new crops such as soy beans, which could potentially yield higher profits but also led to greater indebtedness. Cattle ranching also became a more attractive activity. It represented a stable, if less profitable, investment and was practiced extensively with little investment in land or labor. It could also be carried out on lands exhausted by the previous cultivation of cotton and sugarcane. The new crops relied less on the availability of seasonal migrants. They required a small number of full-time employees experienced in the use of agricultural machinery or able to

fill administrative positions.
　　While the crisis in commercial agriculture moved many local entrepreneurs to turn their attention to ranching, soy beans and other crops, some became involved with a new, "non-traditional" export. That product was cocaine. The growth of the cocaine trade in the mid-1970s responded to rising demand in North America and Europe and opened lucrative opportunities for the lowland bourgeoisie. As prices for all other Bolivian exports remained low, the value of cocaine soared, and this relatively new commodity became the basis for both a new export boom and closer ties between military commanders and Santa Cruz capitalists.

THE DEVELOPMENT OF THE COCAINE TRADE
IN SANTA CRUZ

　　The illegal production of cocaine has existed in Bolivia on a small-scale for some time, but with the onset of an economic crisis in the 1970s, it grew to immense proportions [2]. Coca leaves (Erythroxylum coca), from which cocaine is derived, have been an important part of Indian culture in the Andes for centuries, but during the 1970s, the country started growing more coca than it legally consumed. The rest was transported from the intermontane valleys, where it was grown, to clandestine factories in the lowlands, where it was transformed into cocaine.
　　Santa Cruz became a center for cocaine manufacture at this time for a number of reasons: First, the department was connected to the main coca leaf producing zone--the Chapare--via a highway that passed through the city of Cochabamba. Second, the region had access to a number of waterways that tied the department to the Beni lowlands further north as well as Brazil. More significantly, the vast tracts of remote, frontier land were ideally suited for the creation of clandestine landing strips. Transportation constituted a key element in the cocaine business, and in a nation such as Bolivia, airplanes were the most efficient means of shipping cocaine out of the country. Finally, and

perhaps most important, the lowland bourgeoisie was one of the few groups with the capital and the connections necessary to mount an international drug smuggling operation. Their properties enjoyed access to a stable network of roads that linked them to the departmental capital, and they could also accomodate airstrips for small planes.

While there is no direct evidence linking the Banzer regime with the drug traffic, the government did little to discourage its growth and expansion and seems to have maintained a generally benevolent attitude toward major drug traffickers. It is extremely improbable that the military was ignorant of the cocaine traffic given the problems of obtaining credit and chemicals, organizing transportation, paying for protection, and establishing marketing contacts in other countries that the drug traffickers faced. The number of military personnel and cruceno agro-industrialists subsequently implicated in the cocaine traffic suggest that a considerable amount of planning and coordination of activities took place well before the story burst onto the pages of the international press in 1980 (Marka:1981; Bascope: 1982; Dunkerley: 1984).

The emergence of one prominent cocaine dealer--Widen Razuk--illustrates how prominent lowlanders became involved in the drug trade and how political and economic power were interrelated in the Bolivian cocaine traffic [3]. Razuk was born in Bolivia, but his family migrated from the Middle East. His father--a prosperous merchant-- had been a member of the Junta Rural del Norte and had owned a large estate called La Empresa.

By the late 1970s, Widen Razuk was widely considered to be a major cocaine producer in Santa Cruz, where he produced some thirty kilos of cocaine a day on one of his rural estates near Montero (Narcotrafico y Politica: 1982). Razuk married the daughter of a prominent latifundist, and he acquired partial ownership of an estate called Perseverancia in Obispo Santiesteban province. His in-laws had managed to retain over 9,000 hectares and skillfully sold off portions of the estate to highland migrants who formed the

Colonia Aroma. With his portion of the property, Razuk embarked on large-scale agricultural production, and with Banzer's rise to power, Razuk, a militant of the FSB party, was named prefect of Santa Cruz department.

During the next several years, he gradually bought up land controlled by other in-laws and acquired additional holdings through purchases and government grants. In 1971 he obtained one hundred hectares of land that bordered his estate and in 1972, bought the 972-hectare hacienda, Santa Barbara, from ex-president Walter Guevara Arce. By the end of the decade, he owned over 5,000 hectares in Obispo Santiesteban province, in addition to a cattle estate located in a neighboring province that he received through a government grant.

Razuk used his influence and connections during the cotton boom to borrow U.S. $240,700 from the state agricultural bank to clear 600 hectares of land and plant cotton. At the end of the year, no cotton had been harvested and the loan remained unpaid. Bank assessors concluded that a large portion of the product or the funds were used for other purposes. Nevertheless, bank officials permitted Razuk to borrow an additional U.S. $43,640 the following year to plant 330 hectares of cotton, but once again nothing was produced, and the loan was not repaid.

At about the same time, Razuk and a group of associates formed an agricultural society ostensibly dedicated to livestock raising and cotton cultivation. This organization--the Sociedad Agricola Ganadera Perseverancia--was administered by Razuk and obtained over U.S. $1 million for cotton production, but in a similar fashion, these loans were never returned. It was generally believed that Razuk and other members of this association used cotton loans to invest in the production and marketing of cocaine. They all benefited from important political positions and connections and were eventually implicated in the cocaine traffic.

Mario Quintela Vaca Diez, for example, was named mayor of Santa Cruz in 1980 by General Garcia Meza, whose corrupt regime was implicated in the drug traffic. He was also a prominent cattle rancher and had acquired a 5,000 hectare land grant in Obispo Santiesteban province during Banzer's rule. Julio Malky Salomon, a textile manufacturer, and Lina Badini Merlin maintained close relationships with members of the Colombian drug mafia and Colonel Luis Arce Gomez, who was the minister of interior under Garcia Meza and closely tied to the cocaine traffic (<u>Narcotrafico y Politica</u>: 1982). Like Razuk, these men and women carried large individual cotton debts that they never repaid. Finally, his brother, Miguel, was arrested in Miami in June 1980, after trying to cash checks valued at U.S. $3 million, that were allegedly payments for cocaine shipments to North American dealers.

These new cocaine millionaires jealously guarded their wealth and resisted any attempt to threaten the status quo. Razuk's 1972 prefectoral address to Santa Cruz aptly summarized the views held by many others towards groups and individuals who tried to rectify the gross social inequalities that plagued the region. He ridiculed those priests committed to changing conditions among the rural population and referred to poor peasants of the short-lived UCAPO movement who invaded large properties in Obispo Santiesteban province as "assailants that plant disorder, destroying the tenacious work of the pioneers of the countryside " (<u>Presencia</u>: June 2, 1972).

During the late 1970s, the cocaine traffic burgeoned to astronomical dimensions in Santa Cruz. The lowland producers processed coca leaves into an intermediate sulfate base. To do this, they dug pits, lined them with plastic, and filled them with dry coca leaves. Then, they mixed the coca leaves with diluted sulfuric acid and hired laborers to stomp the mixture until a mash formed. This mash was subsequently bathed in kerosene to extract an alcoloide that rose to the surface and was scraped off and dried in the sun. The result was a basic paste that could be mixed with tobacco and smoked as a cigarette. Most, however, was exported--primarily to Colombia--and sold for approximately U.S. $5,000 per kilo. Colombian dealers then transformed the base into pure cocaine hydrochloride and smuggled it into the United States and Europe where a single, unadulterated kilo acquired a value between U.S. $40,000 and U.S. $60,000 (Narcotrafico y Politica: 1982). Pure cocaine, however, rarely reached the streets, but was usually diluted with amphetamines, sugar or talcum, which further increased the retail value of the original kilo of hydrochloride.

By the end of the decade, returns from cocaine sales were estimated to be nearly double the annual value of all Bolivian exports, which did not exceed U.S. $850 million. The impact of such a voluminous and disproportionately large trade in comparison to the economic reality of Bolivia was felt at various levels in northern Santa Cruz. Cocaine profits centered in the hands of sulfate and chlorohydrate producers and to a much lesser extent, coca leaf growers, transporters, middlemen and workers. Part of the money entered the country through the money exchange houses, which multiplied rapidly in the city of Santa Cruz. The rest arrived in the form of such consumer durables as radios, stereos, automobiles, agricultural machinery, and televisions, which traffickers purchased in Panama and Miami and shipped to Bolivia in the form of contraband. During the research period, for example, expensive European automobiles could be seen negotiating the mud-filled streets of many small northern Santa Cruz towns. A major part of the cocaine profits, however, never entered the country but rather, passed directly into bank accounts in Switzerland, Panama, Nassau, Taiwan, and Miami, the only branch of the federal reserve that consistently has a dollar surplus.

Traffickers were obliged to launder their coca dollars to erase the tracks of smuggling. The purchase of merchandise abroad was one way that they disguised their profits. Many cocaine producers formed businesses, or connected themselves with established enterprises, to facilitate the entry of merchandise into Bolivia. This created an intertwining of interests, which were often very difficult to separate, between legal and illegal business, and it is not surprising that the principal cocaine producers of Santa Cruz were linked to important businessmen through the Chamber of Commerce and Industry.

The growth of the cocaine trade in the countryside aggravated the deepening crisis in agriculture. High wages drew workers away from traditional types of salaried labor to clandestine factories. Workers were paid 10-times the going rate for agricultural day labor, and this generated labor shortages in other sectors of the economy. Wages in general were also forced up as competition for workers grew.

Meanwhile, the Banzer regime had grown increasingly unable to manage the mounting economic crisis in the country. Popular outcries for a return to democracy mounted, and the Carter administration insisted that the regime improve its human rights image. Succumbing to these pressures, Banzer called elections for July 9, 1978 and allowed a limited democratic opening, but after massive fraud led to the annulment of the election results, the government's candidate--Juan Pereda Asbun--overthrew Banzer and seized power for himself. During the two years that followed, Bolivia experienced a period of extreme political instability in which five presidents held office, coup rumors and threats were constantly reported in the press, and two additional elections were held.

This period of instability, and particularly the short-lived government of Lidia Gueiler (1979-1980), gave rural people all over Bolivia the opportunity to reorganize local syndicates and grassroots organizations outside the hierarchical stuctures imposed by the Pacto Militar-Campesino. Settlers managed to restructure the Federacion de Colonizadores despite the fact that representatives of the Pacto Militar-Campesino remained in their positions, often with the support of local army garrisons. The federation stressed even more firmly the importance of independent peasant unions and strongly advocated a non-partisan political stance, encouraging settlers to vote according to their own consciences (Alcoreza and Albo: 1979). Associations that represented the interests of agricultural laborers also appeared for the first time and were encouraged by Catholic priests and nuns who worked in the countryside.

On June 18, 1980, right-wing mobs lead by the FSB looted several buildings in Santa Cruz city, including the U.S. consulate, and killed two people in protest over elections scheduled later in the month and U.S. efforts to insure them. The vigilantes had the implicit support of local military commanders, and throughout the morning of June 18th, they broadcast diatribes over a local radio station, demanding that U.S. ambassador Marvin Weissman, who had warned the military against a coup, be expelled from the country (NYT: June 19, 1980). Earlier the same month, three union halls in the city were bombed (NYT: June 5, 1980).

The country finally elected a president by popular vote on June 29, 1980. The Unidad Democratica Popular (UDP), a coalition of left-leaning political parties led by Hernan Siles Suazo won a plurality of votes in the elections. The Bolivian Communist Party (PCB), the Movement of the Revolutionary Left (MIR) and the National Revolutionary Movement of the Left (MNRI) comprised the UDP. The MNRI, which was Siles Suazo's own party and an offshoot of the MNR, dominated the coalition. Although scheduled to assume power on Bolivian independence day, August 6, 1980, a military coup led by General Luis Garcia Meza on July 17th curtailed the democratic opening and plunged the country back into oppressive military rule. Peasant and worker organizations were immediately repressed, and opposition leaders were systematically tortured, exiled, and imprisoned. The organization of the coup and the repression that followed displayed a level of brutality previously unknown in Bolivia. Much of this repression was carried out by paramilitary squads that were organized under the direction of the new Interior Minister, Colonel Luis Arce Gomez. They received advice from Argentine military personnel and recruits from Nazi war criminal Klaus Barbie, who resided in Bolivia (see Excelsior April 8, 1981; NYT: Aug. 7, 1981 and Aug. 11, 1981; LAT: Aug. 31, 1980).

Stories began to circulate in the

international press, suggesting that cocaine interests in Santa Cruz had bought the loyalty of key military officers prior to the coup (<u>Excelsior</u> April 7, 1981; <u>NYT</u>: Aug. 31, 1981; <u>FT</u>: Aug. 31, 1980). One knowledgeable U.S. diplomat stated that, "This may be the first government in history primarily financed by illegal narcotics and whose primary purpose is to protect and promote the drug trade" (<u>LAT</u> Sept. 11, 1980). The cocaine clique feared a UDP government for two basic reasons: First, they expected the UDP to collaborate more closely with the U.S. Drug Enforcement Agency and clamp down on the drug traffic. Second, many strongly disliked Siles because of his liberal attitudes and association with the MNR of 1952. They dreaded a return to popular politics and mass organizations signified by a UDP government.

Several prominent businessmen and agro-industrial entrepreneurs from Santa Cruz have been linked to the 1980 coup. Former presidents of the Santa Cruz Chamber of Commerce and Industry, Erwin Schweitzer and Pedro Bleyer, reportedly passed a large sum to Garcia Meza in order to insure the loyalty of important garrison commanders (<u>LAT</u>: Sept. 11, 1980). By 1980 the Schweitzer family's influence extended well beyond the sugar industry. They owned several large rural estates, operated various businesses in the city, and belonged to the most exclusive clubs and organizations in Santa Cruz. Schweitzer's son, Roberto, was arrested earlier the same year in Miami on charges of conspiring to smuggle 850 pounds of cocaine into the country. But after paying a U.S. $1 million bail, he returned to Bolivia. Pedro Bleyer is also a prominent agro-industrialist whose interests include a large poultry farm, a veterinary and agro-chemical business, and two animal feed factories. In addition to the funds delivered to the military, the weekly newspaper <u>Aqui</u> reported in an edition published in clandestinity that a prominent Montero landowner, Jose Paz, paid U.S. $800,000 to the military to support the coup (<u>Aqui</u>: #4, 1980).

Cocaine elaboration received state protection for two years after the coup. The president and minister of interior, Colonel Luis Arce Gomez, were among the high officials involved in the traffic, and foreign and national paramilitary groups provided the repression necessary to insure large profits for the drug traffickers [4]. The ties between certain military personnel and members of the lowland drug mafia facilitated the cocaine traffic that flourished almost without restriction during this period. The collaboration of the military and drug dealers seems to have been closest in the realm of transportation (Dunkerley: 1984). Military commanders, customs officials, and inspectors permitted the shipment of coca leaves to lowland factories and the export of cocaine, in exchange for large sums of cash (NYT: Aug. 30, 1980; Narcotrafico y Politica: 1982:61). They established an elaborate system of taxation through which several individuals amassed impressive fortunes.

According to Bascope (1980), three different groups controlled the large-scale production of cocaine sulfate in Bolivia by 1980. The timing of each group's emergence varied, but their membership reflected a combination of prominent cruceno businessmen and agriculturalists as well as military officials. The first group that Bascope identifies developed in the aftermath of the mid-1970 cotton failure and consisted of military commanders and several civilian cotton producers who belonged to the cotton growers' association, ADEPA. These men controlled a production axis that extended from the town of San Javier in the east, through Montero, and westward to Portachuelo, because several owned large estates connected by the road network that integrated the region. The group's uncontested leader was Roberto Suarez Gomez, a member of a prominent lowland family and the cousin of Garcia Meza's interior minister, Luis Arce Gomez.

The early success enjoyed by these drug traffickers led almost immediately to the formation of another group comprised more exclusively of military men. Their operations, according to Bascope, centered around the population centers of San Ignacio de Moxos, San Ramon, and Santa Ana de Yacuma in the Beni lowlands. They faced greater difficulty supplying their factories with coca leaves because of the region's isolation from commercial centers, but at the same time, outside intrusion was less likely than among the San Javier-Montero-Portachuelo producers. The almost complete absence of air traffic control facilitated the easy shipment of cocaine to Colombia, Brazil and Venezuela.

Finally, Bascope cites a third grouping, fundamentally civilian in character and closely connected by kinship, which began to develop in the late 1970s. Its activities were based in the valley region of Santa Cruz department, around the towns of Comarapa, Vallegrande, and Moromoro along the Cochabamba-Santa Cruz highway, and its principal leaders consisted of several traditional landowning and merchant families from this region.

Although the timing of their emergence and the composition of these groups varied somewhat, we should not conclude that each one constituted a discrete entity. Group boundaries appear to have been fluid and a fair amount of cooperation as well as competition seems to have taken place among them [5]. Moreover, as the cocaine boom exploded in Bolivia, a growing number of smaller producers who did not enjoy official military protection, or support and who increasingly competed with large-scale producers, began to appear on the scene. The military carried out highly publicized campaigns to squash the activities of these upstarts. On the one hand, they hoped to stifle competition, and on the other hand, they wanted to show the international community, particularly the United States, that they were making serious attempts to control the drug traffic. Their only problem was that they convinced nobody (Dunkerley: 1984).

We have seen how members of both prominent cruceno families and a group of new beneficiaries concentrated land and capital and emerged as a powerful bourgeoisie under military rule. By investing initially in cash crop production and urban-based commercial activities, these individuals forged a series of common bonds among themselves and with military officials, permitting them to further their interests and maintain political hegemony. The booming economy and military backing of the 1960s and early 1970s allowed them to manage conflicts and exclude peasants from the rewards that economic prosperity brought to northern Santa Cruz.

When an economic crisis began to undermine the regional economy in the mid-1970s, a faction of this newly powerful bourgeoisie seized the initiative and began producing cocaine for an increasingly voracious international market. By building upon previously established military connections and their considerable wealth and influence in regional affairs, they mounted an international drug smuggling operation and amassed huge personal fortunes. The massive profits accrued through the cocaine traffic further strengthened the military-agro-industrial alliance and helped consolidate its power. With the 1980 coup d'etat of Luis Garcia Meza, they gained control of the state and subsequently utilized government institutions for nearly two years to promote their illegal activities and repress opposition to their rule.

NOTES

1. One quintal is the equivalent of 46 kilos.

2. As early as 1967, Che Guevara noted the concerns of a cruceno landlord who suspected Che and his guerillas of producing cocaine on a property purchased by the rebels in southern Santa Cruz. James, Daniel (ed.) 1969 The Complete Bolivian Diaries of Che Guevara and Other Captured Documents. Stein & Day: New York. p.80.

3. When not otherwise cited, information on Widen Razuk, his family and his associates was compiled from a number of sources. They included derechos reales in Santa Cruz, the Banco Agricola de Bolivia, El Diario: April 1, 1979 and El Comercio: Oct. 20, 1974.

4. Some of these individuals formed private

armies to protect the major drug traffickers, and several intimidated Santa Cruz residents when they congregated in a local bar and sang old German war songs from World War II. (see especially *Excelsior op. cit.* and *Narcotrafico y Politica*: 1982)

5. A list of prominent traffickers published by the Peruvian publication *Marka*, for example, lists a slightly different group of cocaine traffickers and categorizes them in a somewhat different manner than Bascope.

8
Economic Crisis and Social Change in the 1980s

Several days after taking power, Garcia Meza granted an interview to a Chilean magazine and told the reporter that he planned "to stay in power for twenty years, until Bolivia is reconstructed" [1]. But despite this claim, Garcia Meza lasted little more than one year. Almost immediately, his regime faced acute internal divisions and popular resistance, international isolation, and a mounting economic crisis for which the generals had no solution. These factors led to his downfall, and a series of three short-lived, caretaker regimes followed that were eventually obliged to return power to the popularly elected, civilian government of Hernan Siles Suazo in 1982.

The return of democratic government placed greater pressure on cocaine producers who were forced to move their operations to more remote locations in the Beni lowlands. The legitimate agro-industries also continued their precipitous decline, and the economic crisis in northern Santa Cruz reached dimensions rarely seen in the past. Because of these factors, many of the small-scale agriculturalists who had emerged in previous years found it increasingly difficult to consolidate their economic position and to ensure the financial security of the next generation. Poor peasants who had been marginalized by two decades of agricultural expansion, took to the offensive, as rampant inflation reduced their earnings and subsistence agriculture became more important. They reorganized syndicates and grassroots organizations, which became outspoken defenders of peasant rights as both agricultural producers and wage laborers. Before exploring the impact of the economic crisis on the rural population, however, we must first examine the fall of the military and the rise of civilian government.

THE FALL OF THE MILITARY AND THE RISE OF THE UDP

The military regime of Garcia Meza and those that followed had no coherent plan for running the government aside from their use of the state apparatus to operate the cocaine trade and enrich key members of the ruling clique. The generals faced serious difficulties in a number of areas from the very beginning. The regime encountered virtual international isolation. Although the Argentine military provided support for the coup and early financial backing, only sixteen states, which included Israel, South Africa, and other Latin American military dictatorships, recognized the government after one month.

The Carter administration, which was eager to see a civilian government come to power, strongly disapproved of the coup and the subsequent human rights abuses. The State Department recalled Ambassador Marvin Weissman, who had been the subject of anti-Semitic attacks, and then went a step further, suspending military assistance and cutting off economic aid. Garcia Meza initially hoped to weather the aid boycott until after the upcoming U.S. presidential elections when he expected a Reagan presidency to reverse this policy. Nevertheless, hopes of renewed aid under Reagan foundered on the drug issue, a topic that offended the moral sensibilities of the conservative, New Right coalition that swept Reagan into office. Consequently, the policy begun under Carter was continued by Reagan.

As foreign credit dried up and the country faced declining terms of trade for its traditional exports, the domestic economic crisis worsened. A large foreign debt, contracted primarily under the Banzer regime, needed servicing, production had to be reactivated, and ailing state-owned enterprises required assistance. Even though cocaine was generating more income than all other Bolivian exports combined, it could not offset the breakdown of the national economy [2]. Cocaine profits remained outside the fiscal control of the state and did little to replenish exhausted government coffers. Coca dollars filled the pockets of drug traffickers who did not reinvest in productive activities within Bolivia and kept much of their money in foreign bank accounts. Even though cocaine did spur the Santa Cruz economy and generated a short-term boom, the illegal nature of the cocaine traffic undermined confidence in legitimate businesses and made cocaine production itself a highly unstable industry.

As a result, working class opposition to the regime broadened to include other groups. The legitimate business interests in Bolivia became alienated from the regime, and sectors of the military not tied to the drug traffic, especially young officers, came to resent the way high ranking officers were corrupting the institution for their own personal profit. This discontent found expression in a series of attempted coups and protests that sought to oust Garcia Meza.

In Santa Cruz, one of the first signs of unrest appeared in early 1981. Sectors of the cruceno bourgeoisie, particularly those not connected with cocaine, had grown disillusioned with Garcia Meza, and this disillusionment turned to anger when the government announced that it would proceed with plans to build a new sugar mill at San Buenaventura in the department of La Paz. This mill would compete with the processing facilities in Santa Cruz that were already operating well below full capacity, and the prospect of the development of another growth center to rival Santa Cruz enraged regional oligarchs. Opposition to the project mounted among members of the Pro-Santa Cruz Committee despite the presence of a government-appointed controller, and in the face of this opposition, Minister of Interior Arce Gomez attempted to reorganize the departmental civic committees under closer supervision by the central government.

The Pro-Santa Cruz Committee responded by calling a 24-hour strike to protest the San Buenaventura mill and infringements upon its autonomy. The strike received popular backing by many crucenos motivated by strong regional sentiments, and the departmental police and military garrisons tacitly supported the strike as well. Consequently, the government was forced to back down on its threats to restructure the civic committees, and the construction of a new sugarmill was placed in greater doubt.

The regime was challenged again on May 5, 1981 when Carlos Valverde Barbery, a militant of the FSB, and a group of men occupied the Occidental Petroleum's Tita refinery on the southern outskirts of the city of Santa Cruz. Even though the Falangists had participated in a destabilization campaign prior to the 1980 coup, they were subsequently marginalized by the Garcia Meza regime and became angry as a result of their exclusion from governmental favors (Dunkerley: 1984: 330). Valverde Barbery threatened to blow up the Tita installation if Garcia Meza did not resign within 48 hours, and although he and his men were subsequently removed from the facility by the military, their action highlighted the rising discontent with the dictatorship.

During the weeks and months that followed, knowledge of the regime's corruption spread beyond the cocaine traffic and further undermined confidence in the government. News of a deal between a firm known as Rumy Ltda. and Generals Garcia Meza, Bernal and Terrazas to exploit semi-precious stones in the region of Lake Gaiba on the Brazilian border gave rise to a huge public scandal. According to the rightist Santa Cruz daily El Deber, the generals were to receive 50 percent of the income generated from sales, and although the deal was illegal for a number of reasons, it particularly outraged the military officers, because the land to be prospected belonged to the army development corporation (COFADENA) (El Deber: May 6, 1981). Garcia Meza also utilized the offices of the agrarian reform to grant family members 6,500 hectares of land in the province of Angel Sandoval, located in the eastern portion of Santa Cruz department. This property was situated fifteen kilometers north of the town of Santo Corazon and encompassed land previously settled by lowland Indian families [3].

New attacks on the regime soon surfaced from other quarters. Lieutenant Emilio Lanza led an aborted coup attempt in Cochabamba on May 13, 1981. Undaunted by his initial failure, Lanza tried again two weeks later, but again the uprising was put down. Another attempt by General Humberto Cayoja and Colonel Lucio Anez was preempted in June, but on August 4, 1981, Anez and General Alberto Natusch Busch took control of Santa Cruz, and naming their uprising the Movement of National Dignity, demanded the removal of Meza and the military election of a new president. This time, the coup leaders received support from six of the country's nine military garrisons as well as ex-presidents Hugo Banzer and Luis Adolfo Siles. Faced with this resistance and having no other choice, Garcia Meza resigned and handed power over to a junta of three commanders --Generals Bernal, Pammo, and Torrelio.

Over the next year, the brief presidencies of Generals Celso Torrelio and Guido Vildoso did little to stem rising discontent. The economy lay in shambles and renewed attempts by both business and labor leaders to oust the military forced the generals to return power to a civilian government. Exiled leaders began cautiously returning to the country, and huge public demonstrations expressed the anti-military sentiments of large sectors of the population. The COB mobilized some 100,000 people in La Paz on September 17, 1982 in a massive protest against the military and in favor of democratic rule. On the same day, nearly 10,000 people converged on the plaza in Santa Cruz for the same purpose. According to one businessman, who summed up the situation, "If God himself came down and you dressed him in an army uniform, the people would not accept him" (NYT: Aug. 9, 1982).

Finally on September 3, Hernan Siles Suazo returned from exile and on September 10, Siles and the UDP assumed control of the government. One of the first actions taken by President Siles was to authorize the capture of such notorious paramilitary leaders as Pier Luigi Pagliai, an Italian mercenary employed by Arce Gomez, to extradite Nazi war criminal Klaus Barbie, and to expel other Nazi sympathizers from Bolivia. The new government also set about restructuring the military high command, but fearing prosecution, Garcia Meza, Arce Gomez and others connected with the old regime quickly slipped across the border into Argentina where the ruling military junta granted them asylum.

Despite these initial efforts to dismantle the network of military officials and mercenaries involved in the cocaine traffic, the new government's problems were just beginning. Cocaine producers continued to do business much as before, even though they operated further underground and production centers were relocated to the Beni and the Chapare region of Cochabamba department. The military and economic power of some drug chiefs in conjunction with the economic crisis forced the Siles government to move slowly in surpressing the traffic. Furthermore, Siles vowed to protect the domestic production and consumption of coca leaves, which constituted the primary source of income for thousands of peasants.

The most brazen example of the power still wielded by these drug caudillos was provided by Roberto Suarez several months after Siles took office. Suarez had outmaneuvered many rural operators in the aftermath of the 1980 coup to become the leading cocaine trafficker in Bolivia, and with land in Santa Cruz and a base in the Beni, he controlled an enormous operation with many people on his payroll. In June 1983, Suarez stole U.S. $200,000 from the state bank in San Borja (Beni) and held two government employees hostage. He ostensibly took the money to pave the town's mud-covered airstrip after his plane was unable to land and promised to repay the entire amount within a few weeks. The government responded by sending 150 policemen to search for him, but could neither capture him while he had the runway paved nor interrupt his cocaine operations. Suarez eventually freed the hostages and repaid the money, and the entire incident proved to be an enormous embarrassment to the government (MH:June 27, 1983).

Meanwhile in Santa Cruz, the economic crisis and the freedom to organize under a democratic government led to the reversal of many of the trends that had developed over the past thirty years. The agro-industries were in retreat and many emerging small-scale agriculturalists encountered difficulty consolidating their gains. Peasant and worker groups began reorganizing and pressured the government for solutions to their ever more acute economic difficulties and participation in political decision making. Subsistence agriculture appeared more and more attractive as inflation wiped out the earnings of laborers and job opportunities decreased.

DEMOCRATIZATION AND ECONOMIC CRISIS

After the return of democratic rule, syndicate activity increased in northern Santa Cruz, and other grassroots organizations, which suffered intervention under the dictatorship, proceeded to rid their directorates of military-appointed controllers and to elect new leadership. The Federacion Nacional de Cooperativas Arroceras (FENCA) quickly convened a meeting to elect new officials. Delegates from all over northern Santa Cruz traveled to Montero to support local candidates, and when the meeting was convened, they jeered and hissed as the outgoing president--a military appointee--tried to bring the group to order. The Federacion de Colonizadores opened an office in Santa Cruz, and along with the conservative Federacion Especial de las Cuatro Provincias del Norte struggled to gain influence among settlers in the colonization zones north of Montero. Similarly, the sugarcane and cotton harvesters' unions began to operate once again. Migrant workers were eventually incorporated into the national labor laws, after the Confederacion Sindical Unica de Trabajadores Campesinos Bolivianos (CSUTCB), an independent, national-level, peasant confederation, pressured the government to sign a number of decrees favoring poor peasants and rural laborers.

As peasants revitalized local institutions, the disasterous climatic effects of El Nino seriously undermined agricultural production during 1982-83. Heavy rains caused flooding in the lowlands, and at the same time, a drought wreaked havoc in the highlands. In Nuevo Mundo and a neighboring community, Las Marotas, the Rio Hondo inundated several properties and ruined crops. One woman and her small child drowned. Many people abandoned the settlements and sought refuge with relatives in the towns or other settlements not affected by the water. Although such men as Juan Vega, Ignacio Betanzos and Julio Rodriguez sat out the disaster in their Mineros homes, they suffered extensive crop damage and saw much of their agricultural land ruined by the flooding. Further downstream, the residents of Paichanetu experienced a similar fate. The Rio Hondo itself changed course and grew to nearly twice its former width because of excessive run-off that was aggravated by years of deforestation.

Due to crop losses and the dislocations occasioned by the floods, many poor peasants were pushed further into wage labor, but unlike earlier years, salaried labor had become increasingly less remunerative in Santa Cruz. First, the demand for wage laborers among cotton and sugarcane producers dropped as cultivated acreage declined and the agro-industries contracted. Second, rising inflation surpassed 500 percent in 1982 and quickly wiped out the wages earned by salaried workers. Finally, the cocaine industry, which had provided a lucrative alternative to traditional wage labor, was moving to new production centers.

Although cocaine manufacture did not disappear completely from Santa Cruz, the political costs of doing business increased. As early as April 1982, pressure from the US embassy moved President General Celso Torrelio to permit a raid on cocaine factories in the Yapacani region of northern Santa Cruz. Although no major cocaine trafficker was taken prisoner, fifty peasants were killed. Approximately four tons of cocaine paste were captured and a herbicide known as 2-4-D, which contained dioxin, was sprayed over a ninety hectare area. This operation rekindled fears about the United State's desire to control the cocaine traffic at its source, and moved many producers to seek safer locations for their factories.

With the rise of Siles, major producers could no longer count on the military protection and assistance that they enjoyed under the former regime, even though corruption did not disappear. They also encountered greater difficulty monopolizing the production of base and the movement of coca leaves, as rising competition sprang up from below, and the manufacture of cocaine paste developed among colonizers in the coca-producing region of Chapare (MH: Aug. 6, 1983; LARR: June 24, 1983). Several major traffickers had already begun to manufacture pure cocaine, rather than shipping paste to Colombia for final processing as in the past, because they realized that cocaine hydrochloride brought a much higher price than unrefined paste (Dunkerley: 1982:314; LARR: July 29, 1983). In this way, it appears that some of the risk was transferred onto the shoulders of small producers.

While the political costs of producing cocaine increased, traffickers also encountered world market fluctuations in the price of cocaine by 1982. Prices for base peaked in 1981 at U.S. $5,000 per kilo, but because of over production the price subsequently declined to U.S. $1,000 per kilo in late 1982 and hit a new low of U.S. $700 in March, 1983 (LARR: June 24, 1983). In addition, fledgling coca crops in Colombia and Brazil began to compete with Bolivian coca, and the possibility arose that production could relocate outside the country (LARR: June 24, 1983; MH: Aug. 6, 1983) [4]. It seems that major cocaine producers, who continued to dominate the marketing system, informal credit, and the final stage of processing, benefited by the entry of small producers, because through the manipulation of such mechanisms they could shift losses to peasants.

The development of cocaine in Chapare and Beni represented one solution to the desperate situation faced by peasants all over Bolivia.

Even though cocaine prices had fallen from a 1981 peak, income generated through coca cultivation or from work as a <u>pisador</u> or courier was still more than that earned in any other sector of the economy. Not surprisingly, important internal migrations towards the new coca-processing centers gained momentum. Many of the new migrants to Chapare came from the altiplano, as they tried to escape the devastating consequences of the drought, but some peasants from Santa Cruz were also attracted to the zone.

Pablo Gutierrez is a case in point. At 21 years of age, he and his brother, Justino, are similar to other young men who earned money by stomping coca leaves. The Gutierrez brothers were born in the intermontane valleys of Chuquisaca department. They came to Santa Cruz in 1972 with their mother when they were still children. She had managed to put together a small savings by renting out the family land in Chuquisaca and then decided that the future looked brighter in Santa Cruz. When they arrived in the lowlands, the family lived with two elder brothers who had claimed land on the frontier after working as seasonal laborers for four years. The boys and their mother eventually settled in Mineros, where she supported her children by working as a maid and selling refreshments in the town plaza. When Pablo and Justino reached adulthood, they, too, began to work as agricultural day laborers and staked out claims to their own parcels of land in a newly opened frontier zone. They frequently returned to Mineros to visit their mother, purchase a range of basic necessities not available in the countryside, and enjoy the hustle and bustle of town life.

It was in Mineros that Pablo and his brother were recruited to work in clandestine cocaine factories, and on two separate occasions between 1982 and late 1984, they worked as <u>pisadores</u>, once in Santa Cruz and again in Chapare. They were recruited by acquaintances who needed workers and who offered them the equivalent of twenty dollars for a night's work. Both individuals lived in Mineros, and one man--Carlos Hurtado--owned a small, motorcycle repair shop on the outskirts of town. Carlos, who was in his late twenties, drove a shiny, new BMW around the dirt streets of Mineros that symbolized his new prosperity in the drug traffic. Pablo and Justino, along with some other young men, accompanied these individuals to makeshift camps erected in the jungle and were given a stipulated quantity of coca leaves to process. On both occasions, they worked for a week or two and then returned home with a sizeable income by local standards.

Stomping coca leaves provided a lucrative alternative to other forms of wage labor, but the economic importance of the cocaine industry for Pablo, his brother, and others like them in northern Santa Cruz ressembled other export-oriented agro-industries. Like wage labor on the sugarcane and cotton estates, processing cocaine offered one more way that peasants could supplement their meager returns from subsistence agriculture. By working for a day, a week, or two weeks at a time, they could earn the necessary cash to buy a range of items necessary for the maintainence and reproduction of their domestic units. Cocaine also provided some people with the opportunity to accumulate profits well above that required for sustaining a basically subsistence-oriented household economy.

The illegality of cocaine manufacture made it a highly unstable industry. When producers had to seek out new, safer locations for their activities, short-term local booms could go bust, and by 1984 signs of such a bust were already evident in northern Santa Cruz. Wage labor in cocaine factories was no longer available to the extent that it had been in the past, even though it continued to be an alternative for rural people in Santa Cruz. Economic conditions were steadily worsening. Inflation was spiralling upward at an uncontrolled rate that averaged 2,700 percent by the end of the year. This steady and rapid erosion of the Bolivian peso reduced earnings to nothing almost overnight, but it also allowed those with access to capital to engage in wild speculation and increase their wealth. Speculation--particularly with the U.S. dollar--rather than investment in productive activities proliferated. The economic crisis aggravated already existing economic inequalities, and in response to the ever more critical circumstances, rural people in northern Santa Cruz adopted a series of direct-action techniques to solve their problems [5].

For example, the cane workers' federation, under the new name of Federacion Sindical de Trabajadores Zafreros de Bolivia (FSTZB), lead a strike against growers at the beginning of the 1984 harvest, demanding pay increases for all sugarcane workers. The strike represented one of the first organized attempts by seasonal workers to articulate their demands not as subsistence cultivators, but as wage laborers. Due to previous decades of agro-industrial expansion and the recent disaster brought on by El Nino, a number of people had come to rely on harvest earnings as a major source of economic support for their families (Vilar and Samaniego: 1982), but they grew ever more frustrated as this income purchased less and less.

The strike grew out of these problems. It lasted for only one day, but during this time, 80 percent of the labor force, which numbered between 35,000 and 45,000 workers, refused to participate in the harvest until the growers agreed to a pay increase. Workers blockaded the entrances to the sugar mills. Several of the leaders received threats from sugarcane growers and truckers at the mill gates, but their cause was supported by some of the 3,500 mill laborers inside. While many of the strikers were migrants from the highland and valley regions of Bolivia, over 30 percent resided in the Santa Cruz lowlands and came primarily from the colonization zones and the southern province of Cordillera (Vilar and Samaniego: 1982). Not surprisingly, the small-scale agriculturalists did not support the work stoppage. In contrast to the large, capitalist producers, they generally paid higher wages in order to successfully compete for laborers. This was one reason why the main impetus for the strike did not originate with the workers on small properties but rather, with those concentrated on the large estates. Workers eventually received their requested increases and the strike ended in success.

The economic crisis and the contraction of the agro-industries also led to an increase in the number of land invasions in northern Santa Cruz. Many people in both urban and rural areas who had grown increasingly reliant on wage labor now turned their attention back to subsistence cultivation, as inflation reduced their purchasing power and consumer goods became more expensive. Unlike the land seizures organized by UCAPO, these more recent invasions grew out of the settlers' own initiative.

For example, in Las Marotas, a community adjacent to Nuevo Mundo and in the core of the commercial zone, poor peasants took over the properties of several small sugarcane planters, after flooding ruined their fields and forced them to move elsewhere. When the waters receded, however, the landowners did not immediately return to the land. Many remained in their homes in Mineros and turned their attention to cultivating land that they owned in different locations. Other poor peasants, who at one time worked as wage laborers on their properties, organized a syndicate, took control of the land, and began to plant crops. They argued that the property had reverted to the state because the former occupants were not using it productively, and therefore, the land was available for settlement by those willing to work it. The dispossessed settlers, however, charged that a few peasant leaders were exploiting the recent democratic opening to cause unnecessary strife in the settlement, and according to Ignacio Betanzos, such leaders were interpreting liberty to mean libertinism.

The local conflict quickly attracted attention from other groups. The Federacion de Colonizadores supported the new syndicate while the more rightist Federacion Especial de las Cuatro Provincias backed the original landowners. Commissions from both sides were sent to the community to review the situation, and feelings ran high. The house of one syndicate member was burned down and his crops were destroyed; others were jailed in Mineros. Although the issue was eventually resolved in favor of the former occupants, the underlying problems that gave rise to the conflict persisted.

Similar events occurred in the San Julian colonization zone. This newest of state-supported settlement projects in the province of Nuflo de Chavez was surrounded by large estates controlled by absentee landlords. As growing numbers of poor peasants arrived in search of land, unutilized portions of the estates became the target of invasions. In late 1984 conflicts also erupted in San Julian when repeated demands by poor peasants for potable water and land titles were ignored by the Instituto Nacional de Colonizacion. After several months of unsuccessful meetings between government authorities and local syndicate leaders, peasants erected three road blockades on the main highway between Santa Cruz and Trinidad, the capital of Beni. Challenging the peasants, a <u>cruceno</u> truck driver and known car smuggler attempted to pass one of the blockades, brandishing a pistol as he advanced. He fired shots that killed several of the protesters, and in response, those participating in the blockade stoned the individual and his driver to death (see Healy: 1985).

The blockade in San Julian, as well as the land invasions and the strike by seasonal wage laborers, demonstrate how the process of proletarianization, which started with the expansion of commercial agriculture, began to reverse itself. The economic crisis, the reappearance of democratic institutions, and the perseverance of the peasants themselves led to new attempts to reestablish subsistence agriculture and earn higher pay for their labor. Even though colonizers did not successfully achieve their goals in every instance, they regained the initiative and persisted in their demands.

Women in Nuevo Mundo from the poor peasant households--both "cambas" and "collas"-- also began seeking new solutions to their economic difficulties. Twenty women from this community organized a mother's club in 1984 with the intention of joining a regional woman's group headquartered in Mineros. They hoped to gain access to CARITAS food donations, which the central organization obtained from abroad and redistributed to local affiliates. They were soon told, however, that the central office could not accept any new groups, but the women were undaunted. They initiated rice and corn cultivation on a plot donated by one of the families. They intended to distribute the harvest among individual members in an effort to insure a basic subsistence livelihood to community residents faced by rising costs.

The economic crisis also highlighted how new and transitional the agrarian enterprises of the small-scale entrepreneurs still were. Although these entrepreneurs had overcome local pressure, personal doubts, and painstakingly built up their commercial operations over previous years, they now faced a serious threat to their economic well-being: one which tested the often shaky foundations of their family businesses and manifested itself in a number of different ways. For example, during most any day in 1984, a visitor entering the homes of Juan Vega, Segundino Villa, Julio Rodriguez or Ignacio Betanzos would have noticed an important change at mealtime. Meat no longer constituted an item on the family menu, even though it was considered a mealtime basic, and its consumption was a sign of prestige. The cost of meat had risen dramatically in the Mineros market, and the families could no longer afford to purchase it on a daily basis.

Income from sugarcane had also declined, and inflation consumed what remained. The cost of herbicides and other imported inputs rose in direct relation to the value of the U.S. dollar, and even with cooperative assistance, these items became increasingly difficult to purchase. These families had all suffered losses after the Rio Hondo flooded their fields. When the waters finally receded, the river was too wide to replace the old log bridge that had connected Nuevo Mundo and Rio Viejo to the paved highway and urban markets. In place of the bridge, a sugarcane grower from Montero installed a pontoon to ferry vehicles across the river. He charged high fees for this service which was the only one of its kind, and many small-scale agriculturalists were obliged to ship their crops to market via a longer route that passed through the town of Portachuelo. Although this alternative was cheaper than paying for the pontoon, it still represented an increase above their former transportation expenses.

In response to the crisis, Ignacio Betanzos sold a truck that he had only recently purchased. The cost of maintaining the vehicle, he explained, had become too much as imports were prohibitively expensive, and the truck, afterall, had been purchased second-hand and required constant attention and repair. He also began to contemplate moving his family back to Nuevo Mundo, where the cost of living was not nearly as high as in town, and rent out his Mineros home. Segundino Villa, for his part, began to downplay his agricultural operations, with the exception of subsistence crops such as rice, and devoted more time and energy to his commercial activities. By speculating with merchandise that he bought cheap and sold dear, Segundino found that he could maintain the value of his capital much more effectively than through agriculture. Nevertheless, he, too, was forced to tighten his belt and some of the outward symbols of his prosperity began to disappear. He sold a motorcycle that he had used to travel back and forth from Mineros to his property, and his telephone was disconnected, after his bills remained unpaid for several months.

The cooperative, which had long been dominated by the small-scale agriculturalists, grew more exclusive in response to the crisis. Sugarcane growers continued to dominate the major positions on the Central's board of directors, even though their hegemony was briefly interrupted in 1982, when partners from two remote, rice-growing communities elected a local candidate to the presidency of the Central. The sugarcane growers successfully established a separate section within the Central administrative structure to deal specifically with the problems of sugarcane production. To do this, they had to respond to numerous charges from other partners that they were trying to establish an independent power base to rival the administrative board. The cooperative advisor, for his part, withdrew from much of the day-to-day activities of the Central, spending more time organizing new cooperatives in the San Julian colonization zone.

In Nuevo Mundo, membership declined because several poor peasants withdrew from the organization, and no new people joined. According to Ignacio Betanzos, the community cooperative was finally operating well because only those individuals who really worked continued to participate in the organization, but Adan Aguilera viewed the situation quite differently. Don Adan withdrew from CCAM in 1983, after nine years as an active partner. He felt that the local leadership ran the cooperative solely for its own benefit and showed little concern for those partners who were not as prosperous.

The CCAM consumer store in Mineros closed, and in its place, the Central opened a new business that sold farm inputs such as herbicides. This shift represented part of a continuing trend away from supplying the rural population with low-cost, basic consumer goods and focusing, instead, upon provisioning more prosperous settlers and town dwellers. The CCAM consumer store had first opened in 1977 and began retailing a range of basic consumer items--flour, lard, sugar, matches, oil, and coffee--in Mineros, and wholesaling these same items to nine member stores located in rural communities. This system operated for three years and allowed community stores to buy large quantities of goods on credit before the rainy season. After continual losses due to bad bookkeeping practices and difficulties recovering credit, CCAM stopped the community wholesale operations and continued only with the retail store in Mineros. The Mineros store benefited the town population much more than rural people, whose communities could be cut off for days after heavy rains swelled rivers and made roads impassable.

Nevertheless, the store continued to enjoy a high reputation among those who used it. Prices were considered fair, and weights and measures were accurate, but when the store became unprofitable, the Central directorate decided in 1983 to sell farming inputs instead of basic subsistence goods. These manufactured items were well beyond the economic reach of most peasant families and especially under the inflationary conditions that existed at the time. As usual, the store was managed by one of the small-scale agriculturalists who lived in town. This man and his wife turned a small profit by speculating with the merchandise and exploiting differential price rises between Santa Cruz and Mineros. The cooperative store became ever more divorced from the needs of impoverished community dwellers and geared more to the needs of the small-scale agriculturalists who struggled to maintain their hard-earned economic gains.

The small-scale agriculturalists were threatened by the crisis and became more protective of their rights and positions with CCAM. But even if they had not been under pressure, their small capitalist enterprises still faced the problem of succession. The current generation will eventually be replaced by the next. Few of these men, however, could interest their children in a future in agriculture, nor did they actively encourage such a path for their off-spring. Many sent their children to Santa Cruz to be educated as professionals, because they did not want them to experience the same hardships that they had once endured. A professional career carried more prestige than farming a modest piece of land year after year.

Segundino Villa's two eldest daughters and their spouses, for example, were uninterested in a more active involvement in the family's agricultural activities. His brother-in-law, who is also a cane grower, watched his son leave for Santa Cruz almost immediately after completing high school. The young man hoped to study law and to one day become a lawyer. Given current conditions in Bolivia, however, it is improbable that most of these children will be able to successfully realize their professional aspirations, and continual downward pressure and the frustration of their ambitions could be the source of future social unrest.

But, it is still too early to predict the destiny of these families or the fate of their small-scale enterprises. They both remain extremely vulnerable. The small capitalist producers and entrepreneurs must not only confront a severe economic crisis and the problem of succession but also deal with renewed pressure from below. The rebirth of democratic organizations and the decline of the agro-industries curtailed the process of proletarianization that had been underway for some two decades. Poor peasants are now more aggressively seeking to reestablish their position as subsistence agriculturalists and are bringing such issues as land tenure, technical assistance and wages to the forefront of regional and national politics. Such demands will undoubtedly bring them into conflict with not only the small-scale agriculturalists, but particularly, the regional bourgeoisie that has utilized their land and labor to accumulate large profits and has tried to exclude both groups from important regional organizations and decision-making positions. The outcome of such future confrontations remains to be seen.

NOTES

1. Quoted in Dunkerley op. cit. p. 292.

2. The value of Bolivian exports at the time did not exceed U.S. $850 million.

3. On September 4, 1981 as I sat in a land records offices doing research, a man entered the office and approached the desk where I was working. He addressed the woman working at my side and handed her the land reform expediente pertaining to this grant, requesting that she duly register it in the office's files. After he departed, the head of the office and other officials gathered around. They read the details of the grant and proceeded to condemn Garcia Meza, venting their displeasure with corrupt highland bureaucrats who sought to usurp lowland resources.

4. This is what happened in the marijuana trade. Marijuana cultivation in the United States supplanted Jamaican and Colombian imports to a large extent and caused a slump in these countries.

5. See Healy (1985) for further discussion of these tactics in other parts of Bolivia as well.

Conclusion

My analysis has focused on capitalist development in northern Santa Cruz and the struggle to control land, labor, and capital--a process that generated profound divisions among settlers and large-scale, cash-crop producers. The expansion of the frontier and the growth of the regional economy actually created the conditions for the emergence of an entrepreneurial group of small-scale agriculturalists. Although they shared some of the concerns of the poor peasants, these families were primarily interested in expanding production for the market and strengthening their position as capitalist producers. Often of peasant origins, the timing of their arrival in Santa Cruz and past accumulations enabled them to make the transition from subsistence agriculture to small-scale capitalist production.

But the spread of capitalist production relations and the monopolization of resources by an emerging regional bourgeoisie limited accumulation among the small-scale agriculturalists and forced many poor peasants to work as wage laborers to satisfy their domestic needs. It may be tempting to construe the combination of wage-labor activities and subsistence agriculture that emerged as a precapitalist mode of production, but such a conclusion does not adequately take into account the special conditions of capitalist development in northern Santa Cruz.

Would the development of a completely landless proletariat similar to that which appeared, for example, in Great Britain (Thompson: 1966) have served the interests of the large, cash-crop growers? The answer is most likely no. The sugarcane and cotton growers needed a labor force with very specific characteristics. First, labor demand was highly seasonal, and although some permanent employees did exist, most were employed a maximum of only six months. Second, workers had to be available en masse to begin the harvest since delays caused profit losses.

Under these circumstances a landless proletariat would not necessarily have been the best solution. How would such a labor force sustain itself during the nonharvest months? There would always be the very real possibility that workers would leave the area for other employment opportunities and not return for the next harvest. Naturally, growers could have paid higher wages to maintain laborers throughout the year and offered better working conditions, but another less expensive alternative was open to them. By appropriating the best land for themselves and monopolizing the flow of credit and technological assistance, they were assured that poor peasants could do no more than eke out a subsistence living on remote, under-capitalized plots.

During periods of expansion, commercial agriculture threatened the very basis of subsistence agriculture, which was so crucial to the survival of capitalist production, and constant tension colored relations between settlers and the bourgeoisie. The poor peasants and the small-scale agriculturalists did not always respond similarly; in fact their interests often conflicted. While the small-scale agriculturalists struggled to defend their position first and foremost as sugarcane growers, the response of the poor peasants during large-scale commercial agriculture expansion involved their diverse strategies of being both wage laborers and subsistence cultivators, which they chose as needed in order to survive. This behavior reflected neither a purely "peasant" nor a strictly "proletarian" consciousness, but was the result of the changing political climate in

Bolivia and the outcome of the structural conditions that shaped settlement and commercial agriculture development in northern Santa Cruz. The regional dynamics of this process are summarized below.

THE AGRARIAN REFORM IN NORTHERN SANTA CRUZ

While the Bolivian agrarian reform instituted major changes in the countryside, it failed to alter fundamentally class relationships in Santa Cruz and it modified the land-tenure system only superficially by creating new categories for agricultural properties. As a compromise between the conflicting demands of different interest groups, the agrarian reform was a reformist rather than a revolutionary approach to social change and was used to promote the development of capitalism in Bolivian agriculture.

Changes in production relationships between pre-1952 Bolivia and the postreform period entailed a deeper integration of cruceno agriculture into national and international markets and altered the form and degree of coercion that affected peasants. Whereas servile labor obligations were used to maintain a permanently unfree labor force, particularly in the highlands, the labor relationships that developed after the revolution were based much more on choice. But, although the agrarian reform abolished forced labor, the resources available to the peasantry did not substantially increase. As a result, rapid migration to the cities and the lowland provinces of Santa Cruz department began, because the former colono population had to seek other economic opportunities to satisfy its subsistence needs.

Meanwhile, lowland landlords converted their properties into agricultural enterprises and embarked on large-scale, cash crop production. State-sponsored and internationally financed settlement programs were a further effort to dilute the political demands of highland and valley peasants. These projects centered on the development of nominally uninhabited lands in the oriente and diverted attention from the fragmented parcels of the highlands and valleys. Among their goals was the creation of a class of independent small farmers capable of supplying cheap food to the cities and relieving population pressure in other parts of the country. They were not an attempt to alter the basic relationship of the peasantry to other classes: funds earmarked for settlement schemes were minimal compared with the amounts directed to the sugar industry. The settlement programs dealt only with a relatively small, carefully selected group of beneficiaries and did not involve the vast majority of the peasantry. Most families settled in the colonization zones through the formation of their own organizations, and many moved to the frontier after initially coming to the region as seasonal laborers.

Economic investment by both the state and international development organizations during the postreform period concentrated on those areas less affected by the land redistribution, such as southern Chuquisaca, Beni, and northern Santa Cruz, where peasant organizations were weak and landlords more effectively coopted the agrarian-reform movement (Heyduck 1974; Healy 1982; Heath 1959; and McEwen 1975). Santa Cruz received special emphasis because the demands of a vocal minority coincided with the recommendations for economic development proposed by the United States. By permitting former latifundists to keep large extensions of land and channeling assistance to them, the state and international development organizations laid the basis for the emergence of a powerful bourgeoisie in subsequent years.

CAPITALIST DEVELOPMENT AND SOCIAL DIFFERENTIATION

The development strategy pursued by state and international organizations did not alter the existing power relationships in Santa Cruz, and their vigorous support of capitalist development enormously strengthened an emergent lowland bourgeoisie composed of both traditional cruceno families and new investors. This particular modernization plan was designed to increase agricultural exports and food production to satisfy the foreign-exchange requirements for industrial development, but almost all the assistance--credit, guaranteed prices, sudsidized machinery, agricultural extension and research--benefited large-scale producers of export crops. Aside from rice, food production received very little emphasis; settlers obtained only minimal support, and many saw their resources siphoned off by more dominant groups.

Through the control of local institutions and their growing power in government, the traditional lowland elite and a new group of beneficiaries maintained almost total control over the economic resources that flowed to Santa Cruz after the agrarian reform. They forged a number of powerful common interests as they became involved in cash-crop cultivation, urban-based commercial activities, and the industrial aspects of agriculture. Military rule further strengthened this class and stronger ties developed between lowland capitalists and military officers--particularly during the 1970s. Lowland entrepreneurs provided the military with political support and were rewarded with credit, land, and favorable marketing policies. Also, powerful generals and colonels took advantage of their control of the state apparatus and the lucrative investment possibilities in Santa Cruz to increase their own personal wealth.

Despite their close collaboration, lowland capitalists and military commanders could not effectively transform labor relations and reorganize production; the structure of capitalist accumulation proved to be extremely fragile. Growing problems with labor and indebtedness motivated the lowlanders to make technological improvements to reduce their need for wage laborers and raise labor productivity. These measures served only to further indebt producers to international banks, and a world recession aggravated their problems. Some then turned to the cocaine trade, which developed out of the social relations of production established in previous decades and confirmed the military and agro-industrial alliance.

Meanwhile, capitalist development and the spread of market relations created a large group of marginalized peasants who were increasingly pushed into wage labor during the 1960s and 1970s as the agro-industries expanded. The charter members of the frontier communities established in the Mineros region during the late 1950s and 1960s enhanced the productive potential of jungle land by investing labor in forest clearing, cultivation, and cutting access roads. Through their syndicates they distributed frontier land to individual families, defended their rights, and organized social life in the new communities. Nevertheless, many settlers were not able to establish viable farming operations because of a constant lack of capital, the distance from market centers, the poor roads, the problems with tropical agriculture, and the constant domination and exploitation by middlemen.

Large-scale commercial growers and a second wave of settlers, primarily from the highlands and valleys, purchased the land and took advantage of the improvements without having to suffer the same hardships. Communal solidarity dissolved, and ethnic conflict between highland migrants and lowland peasants reflected the process of social differentiation that was reshaping the communities. As settlers grew more divided, the syndicates broke down, and the rise of military rule and the signing of the Pacto Militar-Campesino dealt the organizations an additional blow.

With no organization to defend their interests and faced with the steady contraction of their subsistence base, many households devised new strategies to meet their basic subsistence needs. These strategies were extremely flexible and made it possible for households to combine resources from a wide range of activities. The exact combination of wage labor and subsistence agriculture depended on both changes in the composition of the domestic unit, long-term and seasonal fluctuations in the regional economy, and political conditions in Bolivia. The expansion of the agro-industries in the 1960s and 1970s pushed peasants further into wage labor, but they successfully resisted this tendency by intensifying domestic labor, manipulating patron-client relationships, and collaborating with other impoverished households. They also organized politically despite almost continual military repression. The formation of the Federacion de Colonizadores and the land invasions directed by UCAPO were the most concrete manifestations of their discontent.

Although the expansion of the regional economy marginalized large numbers of settlers, it also created the conditions for the emergence of an entrepreneurial group of small-scale agriculturalists who came primarily form the highlands and valleys. They prospered in Santa Cruz by investing in sugarcane production and commerce during the 1960s and early 1970s; thus, some families extended their small-scale capitalist operations to the Santa Cruz lowlands while others made the transition from peasant production to capitalist farming.

These men and their families often benefited from previous savings from economic activities in other parts of Bolivia or northern Argentina. The original lowland settlers had enjoyed fewer opportunities to accumulate small savings, as Santa Cruz, prior to the growth of the agro-industries, was a stagnant, commercial backwater. Second, the small-scale agriculturalists often enjoyed better connections in both the urban commercial sector and the colonization zones. The timing of their arrival was also of crucial importance. They established themselves in the communities after the initial wave of settlement had already taken place. The impoverishment of the original settlers provided them with a source of labor, and the previous improvements to the land were of great benefit to them. Finally, they had access to a resource that had been unavailable to previous generations of lowland peasants: bank credit. By the mid-1970s regional banks and foreign development agencies were making credit available to settlers through rural cooperatives, and these individuals were in the best position to take advantage of the opportunities offered by these organizations.

The organization of the CCAM cooperative in Nuevo Mundo, Rio Viejo, and Paichanetu strengthened a small group of settlers making the transition to capitalist production and took the place of the original community syndicates as the most important and influential local-level organizations. The CCAM, like similar organizations in northern Santa Cruz, emerged when military rule precluded independent syndicate activity. It concentrated instead on narrowly defined technological matters. But the cooperative's services--credit, transportation, a sugarcane quota, a rice mill, and heavy, land clearing machinery--enabled the small-scale agriculturalists to enlarge their commercial and agricultural operations and gain control of the institutions.

The cooperative also provided them with an ideological justification for their activities. Its doctrine stressed that cooperating with one's neighbor was the best way to achieve the economic advancement and betterment of everyone. This was consistent with peasant concepts of reciprocity and redistribution and did not encourage the sole pursuit of individual profit. The failure of poorer families to improve their situation could then be blamed on incompetence and laziness.

But, settlers did not let the rich forget their responsibilities to the poor; they defended the right to a subsistence living by constantly reminding the better-off families of their civic duties. These families were obliged to spend their hard-earned cash on a range of activities to maintain their moral claim to peasants' labor power, even though such expenses often constituted a drain on their own resources. Thus, notions of cooperation, reciprocity, and redistribution were manipulated by both groups, as they struggled to create a new lifestyle in northern Santa Cruz

The concerns and demands of the large numbers of poor, wage-earning peasants in northern Santa Cruz became the focus of attention in Santa Cruz after the military fell in 1982 and the economic crisis intensified. Cocaine producers were put on the defensive, and the Chapare region of Cochabamba department came to rival Santa Cruz as the center of cocaine production. The legitimate agro-industries continued to decline, and a severe economic crisis brought on by years of the military's fiscal mismanagement engulfed Santa Cruz.

In response to the worsening conditions and the new freedom to organize under a democratic government, many peasants who had been pushed into wage labor by two decades of agro-industrial expansion aggressively reasserted their right to cultivate land and earn higher wages, and the process of proletarianization began to reverse itself. Syndicates and grassroots organizations reemerged, and land invasions and demands for financial support from the state increased. The agro-industries posed less of a threat to rural people, and subsistence agriculture appeared extremely attractive given the debilitating effects of rampant inflation.

The protests of peasants as subsistence cultivators and wage laborers reflect the process of class formation in the region. As in the past, the political consciousness and organization of these people will determine the direction of social change in the region. Future agrarian reform must be directed at the large-scale capitalist enterprises, and the many channels to extract surplus from the peasantry must be altered.

The crisis also has undermined the still unsteady foundations of the small-scale capitalist enterprises built up by the new generation of small-scale agriculturalists. Faced by a decline in prices for their principle crops and the rampant inflation that aggravated urban-living costs and rapidly consumed their earnings, the families tightened their control over the cooperative, began selling off their possessions, and in some cases, even contemplated a return to the countryside. The future of their small businesses will depend on those political and economic factors that shape the contours of social relationships and condition the class struggle in northern Santa Cruz.

Bibliography

NEWSPAPER SOURCES

Aqui. #4 (published clandestinely) 1980.
El Deber. Feb. 7, 1969; May 5, 1969.
El Diario. Jan. 4, 1979.
El Comercio. Oct. 20, 1974.
El Mundo. Jan. 19, 1982.
Excelsior. April 7, 1981; April 8, 1981; April 9, 1981.
FT (Financial Times). Aug. 15, 1980.
Ideas. Sept. 15, 1930.
LARR (Latin American Regional Report). June 24, 1983; July 29, 1983.
LAT (Los Angeles Times). Aug. 31, 1980; Sept. 11, 1980.
Marka. March 5, 1981.
MH (Miami Herald). June 27, 1983; Aug. 6, 1983.
NYT (New York Times). June 5, 1980; June 19, 1980; Aug. 7, 1980; Aug. 11, 1980; Aug. 30, 1980; Aug. 9, 1982; Aug. 31, 1982.
Presencia. March 29, 1973; May 9, 1973; June 8, 1972.
Progresso. Aug. 6, 1962.

BOOKS, ARTICLES AND REPORTS

Adams, R.
    "Rural Labor," in J.J.Johnson (ed.) Continuity and Change in Latin America. Stanford: Stanford University Press, 1964 (pp. 49-78).

ADEPA - Asociacion de Productores de Algodon.
   Memoria 1971-72. Santa Cruz, Bolivia, 1972.
Albo, J.
   Bodas de plata o requiem para una reforma
   agraria. Cuadernos de Investigacion 17. La
   Paz: CIPCA, 1979.
Alcoreza, C. and J. Albo
   1978: El nuevo campesino ante el fraude.
   Cuadernos de Investigacion 18. La Paz:
   CIPCA, 1979.
Bascope A., R.
   La Veta Blanca: coca y cocaina en Bolivia.
   La Paz: Ediciones Aqui, 1982.
Birdsall, N. and W. McGreevy
   "Women, Poverty and Development," in
   M. Buvinic, et al (eds.) Women and Poverty
   in the Third World. Baltimore: Johns Hopkins
   University Press, 1983.
Boletin de la Sociedad Geografica e Historica de
Santa Cruz
   "El porvenir de Bolivia esta en el oriente,"
   vol. 3, nos. 8 & 9 (1906).
Bonacich, E.
   "A Theory of Ethnic Antagonism: The Split
   Labor Market," American Sociological
   Review, no. 5 (1972):533-547.
Brocheux, P.
   "Moral Economy or Political Economy? The
   Peasants are Always Rational," Journal of
   Asian Studies, vol. 42, no. 4 (1983):791-
   804.
Cardoso, F. H. and E. Falletto
   Dependencia y desarrollo an America Latina.
   Mexico: Siglo XXI Editores, 1971.
CIDCRUZ (Centro de Investigacion y Documentacion-
Santa Cruz)
   Santa Cruz: La Reforma Agraria. La Paz,
   Bolivia, 1983.
Clark, R. J.
   "Land Holding Structure and Land Conflicts
   in Bolivia's Lowland Cattle Region,"
   Inter-American Economic Affairs, vol, 28,
   no. 2 (1974):15-38.
Crist, R.E. and C.M. Nissly
   East from the Andes: Pioneer Settlement in
   the South American Heartland. Gainesville:

University of Florida Press, 1973.
Dandler, J.
"Peasant Sindicatos and the Process of Cooptation in Bolivian Politics," in J. Nash, J. Dandler, and N. Hopkins (eds.) *Popular Participation in Social Change*. The Hague: Mouton, 1976 (pp. 341-352).
Davis, S.
Victims of the Miracle. Cambridge: Cambridge University Press, 1977.
Deere, C. D.
"The Differentiation of the Peasant Family and Family Structure: A Peruvian Case Study," *Journal of Family History*, vol. 3, no. 4 (1978):422- 438.
deJanvry, A.
The Agrarian Question and Reformism in Latin America. Baltimore: Johns Hopkins University Press, 1981.
deJanvry, A. and C. Garromon
"The Dynamics of Rural Poverty in Latin America," *Journal of Peasant Studies*, vol. 3, no. 4 (1977):206-216.
Dos Santos, T.
"The Crisis of Development Theory and the Problem of Dependency in Latin America," in H. Bernstein (ed.) *Underdevelopment and Development*. London: Penguin Harmondsworth, 1973.
Duncan, K. and I. Rutledge (eds.)
Land and Labor in Latin America. London: Cambridge University Press, 1977.
Duncan Baretta, S.R. and J. Markoff
"Civilization and Barbarism: Cattle Frontiers in Latin America," *Comparative Studies in Society and History*, vol. 25, no. 4 (1978):587-628.
Dunkerley, J.
Rebellion in the Veins: Political Struggle in Bolivia: 1952-1982. London: Verso, 1984.
Eckstein, S.
"Transformation of a 'Revolution from Below' - Bolivia and International Capital," *Comparative Studies in Society and History*, vol. 25, no. 1 (1983):105-135.
Eder, G. J.
Inflation and Development in Latin America:

A Case History of Inflation and Stabilization in Bolivia. Ann Arbor: University of Michigan Press, 1968.

Erasmus, C.
"Community Development and the Encogido Syndrome," Human Organization, vol. 27, no.1 (1968):65-73

FAO - Food and Agriculture Organization
Report of the Agricultural Credit Identification Mission to Bolivia. Rome: FAO, 1972.

Feder, E.
"The New World Bank Program for the Self-Liquidation of the Third World Peasantry," Journal of Peasant Studies, vol. 3, no. 3 (1976):343-354.

―――. "Campesinistas y descampesinistas: tres enfoques divergentes (no incompatibles) sobre la destruccion del campesinado," Comercio Exterior, vol.27, no.12 (1977):1439-1446 and vol. 28, no.1 (1977):42-51.

Fifer, J. V.
"Bolivia's Pioneer Fringe," The Geographical Review, vol. 57, no. 1 (1967):1-23.

―――. "The Search for a Series of Small Successes: Frontiers of Settlement in Eastern Bolivia," Journal of Latin American Studies, vol. 14, no. 2 (1982):407-432.

Fletcher, G. R.
"Santa Cruz: A Study of Economic Growth in Eastern Bolivia," Inter-American Economic Affairs, vol. 29, no. 2 (1975):23-41.

Foster, G.
"Peasant Society and the Image of Limited Good," American Anthropologist, vol. 67 (1965):293-315.

Foweraker, Joe
The Struggle for Land. Canbridge: Cambridge University Press, 1982.

Frank, A. G.
Latin America: Underdevelopment or Revolution. New York: Monthly Review Press, 1969.

Furtado, C.
　　Economic Development of Latin America: A Survey from Colonial Times to the Cuban Revolution. Cambridge: Cambridge University Press, 1970.

Geertz, C.
　　Agricultural Involution: The Process of Ecological Change in Indonesia. Berkeley: University of California Press, 1963.

Gonzales, M.
　　Plantation Labor and Social Control in Northern Peru, 1875-1933. Institute of Latin American Studies Monograph # 62. Austin: University of Texas Press, 1985.

Graber, K.
　　Comparacion de gastos entre distintos tipos de mecanizacion en la zona de Santa Cruz, Bolivia. Asociacion de Desarrollo Economico Menonita. Santa Cruz, Bolivia, 1977.

Green, M.
　　The Development of the Bolivian Oriente since 1950 and the 'Junkers' Transition to Capitalism in Bolivian Agriculture, 1979 (mimeo).

　　Capitalist Penetration and Social Relations of Production Among Sugarcane and Rice Producers in Santa Cruz, Bolivia, 1977 (mimeo).

Grupo de Estudios Andres Ibanez
　　Tierra, estructura productiva, y poder en Santa Cruz. La Paz, Bolivia, 1983.

Gudeman, S.
　　The Demise of the Rural Economy: From Subsistence to Capitalism in a Latin American Village. London: Routledge and Kegan Paul, 1978.

Healy, K.
　　Caciques y Patrones. Cochabamba: El Buitre, 1982.

　　"The Rural Development Role of Bolivian Peasant Sindicatos in the New Democratic Order," Paper presented to the XII International Congress of the Latin American Studies Association in Albuquerque, New Mexico, 1985.

Heath, D.
"Land Reform in Bolivia," *Inter-American Economic Affairs*, vol. 12, no. 4 (1959a): 3-27.

―――― Commercial Agriculture and Land Reform in the Bolivian Oriente," *Inter-American Economic Affairs*, vol. 13, no. 2, (1959b): 35-45.

Heath, D., C.J. Erasmus and H.C. Buechler
Land Reform and Social Revolution in Bolivia
New York: Praeger Publishers, 1969.

Henkel, R.
"The Move to the Oriente: Colonization and Environmental Impact," in Jerry R. Ladman (ed.) *Modern-Day Bolivia: Legacy of the Revolution and Prospects for the Future.* Centre for Latin American Studies, Arizona State University, 1984 (pp.277-299).

Hermosa Virreira, W.
Los pueblos guarayos. La Paz: Academia Nacional de Ciencias de Bolivia, 1972.

Heyduck, D.
"Bolivia's Land Reform Hacendados," *Inter-American Economic Affairs*, vol. 27, no. 1, (1973):87-96.

Hindness, B. and P. Hirst
Pre-capitalist Modes of Production. London: Routledge and Kegan Paul, 1975.

Holmberg, A.
Nomads of the Long Bow: The Siriono of Eastern Bolivia. Washington: Interdepartmental Committee on Scientific and Cultural Cooperation. Department of State, 1950.

Ibarnegaray Ponce, R.
"El desarrollo agrario en Santa Cruz (1900-1952)," *Avances de Investigacion* 2. Museo Nacional de Etnografia y Folklore, 1982 (pp. 17-30).

INE - Instituto Nacional de Estadistica
Censo Nacional de Poblacion y Vivienda: Resultados Provisionales. La Paz: Ministerio de Planeamiento y Coordinacion, 1977.

―――― Bolivia: migraciones internas recientes segun el censo nacional de 1976. La Paz: Ministerio de Planeamiento y Coordinacion, 1976.

Iriarte, G. y equipo CIPCA
  Sindicalismo campesino: ayer, hoy, y manana.
  Centro de Investigacion y Promocion del
  Campesinado 21. La Paz, Bolivia, 1980.

James, D.
  *The Complete Bolivian Diaries of Che Guevara
  and Other Captured Documents.* New York:
  Stein and Day, 1967.

Klein, H.
  *Parties and Political Change in Bolivia:
  1880-1952.* London: Cambridge University
  Press, 1969.
  *Narcotrafico y politica: Militarismo y mafia en
  en Bolivia.* Madrid: Iepala, 1982.

Ladman, J. and R.L. Tinnermeier
  "A Model of the Political Economy of
  Agricultural Credit: The Case of Bolivia,"
  Economics and Sociology, Occasional Paper
  No. 632, 1980.

Leeds, A.
  "Mythos and Pathos: Some Unpleasantries on
  Peasantries," in R. Halperin and J. Dow
  (eds.) *Peasant Livelihood: Studies in
  Economic Anthropology and Cultural Ecology.*
  New York: St. Martin's Press, 1977.

LeGrand, C.
  "Colombian Transformations: Peasants and
  Wage-Labourers in the Santa Marta Banana
  Zone," *Journal of Peasant Studies*, vol. 11,
  no. 4 (1984):178-200.

Lenin, V.I.
  The Development of Capitalism in Russia.
  Moscow: Progress Publishers, 1977.

Lewis, O.
  *La Vida: A Puerta Rican Family in the
  Culture of Poverty.* New York: Random House,
  1966.

Mallon, F.
  *The Defense of Community in Peru's Central
  Highlands.* Princeton: Princeton University
  Press, 1983

Marx, K.
  Capital, Vol. 1. New York: International
  Publishers, 1977.

Maxwell, S.
  "Differentiation in the Colonies of Santa
  Cruz: Causes and Effects," Working Paper No.

13. Santa Cruz: Centro de Investigacion de Agricultura Tropical, 1980.

McEwen, W.J.
Changing Rural Society: A Study of Communities in Bolivia. New York: Oxford University Press, 1975.

Mitchell, C.
The Legacy of Populism in Bolivia: From the MNR to Military Rule. New York: Praeger Publishers, 1977.

Mintz, S. W.
"Canamelar: The Subculture of a Rural Sugar Plantation Proletariat," in J. Steward, et. al. The People of Puerto Rico. Urbana: University of Illinois Press, 1959 (pp. 314-417).

——— "The Folk-Urban Continuum and the Rural Proletarian Community," American Journal of Sociology, no. 59 (1958):136-143.

Nations, J. and R.B. Nigh
"The Evolutionary Potential of Lacandon Maya Sustained-Yield Tropical Forest Agriculture," Journal of Anthropological Research, vol. 1, no. 36 (1980):1-30.

Ortiz, M.S.
Estudio socio-economico o estudio de la realidad de 94 comunidades rurales de la provincia O. Santiesteban y 2 communidades de la provincia de Warnes. Santa Cruz: CIAT, 1979.

Painter, M.
Ethnicity and Social Class Formation in the Bolivian Lowlands. Institute of Development Anthropology. Binghamton, New York, 1985.

Platt, T.
Estado boliviano y ayllu andino: tierra y tributo en el norte de Potosi. Lima: Instituto de Estudios Peruanos, 1982.

Polachik, J.
"The Moral Economy of the Kiangsi Soviet, 1928-1934," Journal of Asian Studies, vol. 42, no. 4 (1983): 805-829.

Rappaport, R.
Pigs for the Ancestors: Ritual in the Ecology of a New Guinea People. New Haven: Yale University Press, 1968.

Redfield, R.
　　"The Folk Society," *American Journal of Sociology*, vol. 52 (1947):293-308.

──── *The Folk Culture of Yucatan*. Chicago: University of Chicago Press, 1941.

Reye, U.
　　"Aspectos sociales de la colonizacion del oriente boliviano," *Aportes*, no. 17 (1970):51-79.

Riester, J.
　　En busca de la loma santa. La Paz: Los Amigos del Libro, 1977.

Riester, B., J. Riester, B. Simon and B. Schuchard
　　Me vendi me compraron: analisis socio-economico en base de testimonios de la zafra de cana en Santa Cruz de la Sierra. Santa Cruz, Bolivia, 1979.

Riviere d'Arc, H.
　　"Public and Private Agricultural Policies in Santa Cruz, Bolivia," in F. Barbira-Scazzocchio (ed.) *Land, People and Planning in Contemporary Amazonia*. Cambridge Centre for Latin American Studies, Occasional Publication No. 3, 1980.

Roca, J. L.
　　Fisonomia del regionalismo boliviano. La Paz: Los Amigos del Libro, 1980.

Roseberry, W.
　　"The People of Puerto Rico", *Revista/Review Interamericana*, vol. 8, no.1 (1978):26-36.

──── *Coffee and Capitalism in the Venezuelan Andes*. Austin: University of Texas Press, 1983.

Royden, T. C. and E. Boyd Wennergren
　　El impacto de las carreteras de acceso en la colonizacion espontanea Chanc/Piray. La Paz: MACA, 1973.

Sanabria Hernandez, H.
　　Breve historia de Santa Cruz. La Paz: Editorial Juventud, 1979.

──── "Apuntes para una historia economica de Santa Cruz," *Revista de la Universidad Gabriel Rene Moreno*, no. 25 and 26 (1962).

Schmink, M.
"Household Economic Strategies: Review and Research Agenda," Latin American Research Review, vol. 19, no. 3 (1984):87-101.

―――― "Land Conflicts in Amazonia," American Ethnologist, vol.9, no.2 (1982): 341-357.

Schmink, M. and C. Wood
"Blaming the Victim: Small Farmer Production in the Amazon Colonization Project," Studies in Third World Societies, no.7 (1979):77-93.

Shoemaker, R.
The Peasants of El Dorado: Conflict and Contradiction in a Peruvian Frontier Settlement. Ithaca, NY: Cornell University Press, 1981.

Silverman, S.
"The Peasant Concept in Anthropology," Journal of Peasant Studies, vol. 7, no. 1 (1979):49-69.

Spalding, K.
Huarochiri: An Andean Society Under Inca and Spanish Rule. Stanford: Stanford University Press, 1984.

Stearman, Allyn MacLean
Camba and Colla. University of Central Florida Press: Gainesville, 1985.

Steward, J.
Theory of Culture Change: the Methodology of Multilinear Evolution. Urbana: University of Illinois Press, 1985.

Tax, S.
"World View and Social Relations in Guatemala", American Anthropologist, vol. 43 (1941):27-42.

Thompson, E.P.
The Making of the English Working Class. Vintage: New York, 1966.

―――― "The Moral Economy of the English Crowd in the 18th Century," Past and Present, vol. 50 (1971): 76-136.

Thorn, R.
"The Economic Transformation", in J. Malloy and R. Thorn (eds.) Beyond the Revolution: Bolivia since 1952. Pittsburgh: University of Pittsburgh Press, 1971 (pp.157-215).

USAID - United States Agency for International Development
    Bolivian Rural Financial Sector. La Paz: Ohio State University Report, 1979.

Wallerstein, I.
    The Modern World System: Capitalist Agriculture and the Origins of the European World Economy in the Sixteenth Century. New York: Academic Press, 1974.

Warman, A.
    Ensayos sobre el campesinado en Mexico. Mexico: Editorial Nueva Imagen, 1980.

Wasserstrom, R.
    Class and Society in Central Chiapas. Berkeley: University of California Press, 1983.

Weeks, D.
    "Bolivia's Agricultural Frontier," Geographical Review, vol. 36, (1946):546-567.

Weil, J.
    The Organization of Work in a Quechua Pioneer Settlement. Ph.D. Dissertation. Columbia University, New York, NY, 1980.

Weinstien, B.
    The Amazon Rubber Boom. Stanford: Stanford University Press, 1983.

Wesel, K.
    An Economic Assessment of Pioneer Settlement in the Bolivian Lowlands. Ph.D. Dissertation. Cornell University, Ithaca, NY, 1968.

White, S.
    Contributions of the Alliance for Progress: USAID and the Development of Santa Cruz, 1968 (mimeo).

Whitehead, L.
    "National Power and Local Power: The Case of Santa Cruz de la Sierra, Bolivia", in F. Rabinovitz and and F. M. Trueblood (eds.) Latin American Urban Research, Vol. 3 (1973):23-46.

Whitten, N. E. (ed.)
    Cultural Transformations and Ethnicity in Modern Ecuador. Urbana, Ill.: University of Illinois Press, 1981.

Wiggens, S.
 Colonizacion en Bolivia. Sucre: ACLO, 1976.

Wolf, E. R.
 Europe and the People Without History. Berkeley: University of California Press, 1982.

――― "Remarks on the People of Puerto Rico", Revista/ Review Latinoamericana, vol. 8, no. 1 (1978):17-25.

――― Peasants. Englewood Cliffs: Prentice-Hall, 1966.

――― "Aspects of Group Relations in Complex Society", American Anthropologist, vol. 58, no. 6 (1956):1065-78.

Zeballos Hurtado, Hernan
 From the Uplands to the Lowlands: An Economic Analysis of Bolivian Rural-Rural Migration. Ph.D. Dissertation, University of Wisconsin, Madison, Wisconsin, 1975.

Index

Acculturation, 6
ADEPA. See Asociacion de Productores de Algodon
Agrarian reform, 31-35, 42, 47, 57, 58, 59(table), 61, 62, 75, 90, 175, 198, 215, 217-218
  as capitalist enterprise, 217
  future, 223
  under MNR, 78
  production process and, 99
  urban poor and, 43-44
Agricultores, 34
"Agricultural enterprises," 32
Agriculture
  commercialization, 11, 12, 35, 43, 47, 48-51, 53, 57, 61-63, 65-71, 73-74, 81, 88-90, 91, 93, 95, 97-98, 99 104, 119, 121, 171, 180, 216
  expansion, 29, 35, 47, 48-51, 61-63, 64(table), 65-71, 73-74, 76-81, 83, 88-90, 91, 93-94, 95, 96-98, 104-119, 121, 180, 208, 215
  export-oriented, 46, 50, 51, 53, 65, 93, 124, 180, 219
  large-scale, 4-5, 11, 48, 50, 52, 53, 58, 59 (table), 61-63, 70, 71, 93, 100, 220, 223
  slash-and-burn, 156-157
  small-scale, 140, 147-148, 155-157, 158, 161-162, 164-165, 168-171, 195, 201, 206, 209, 212, 213, 215, 216, 221, 222, 223
  subsistence, 4, 9, 11, 13, 27, 64, 66, 73, 83-84, 85-86, 87, 99, 102, 109, 110, 113, 118, 162, 170, 207, 208, 209, 216, 223
  swidden, 79-81
Aguilera, Adan, 211
AID. See United States, Agency for International Development
Albo, J., 3
Alliance for Progress, 139
Anez, Lucio, 199
Apatronados, 35. See also Labor
Arce Gomez, Luis, 186, 189, 191, 197, 200
Argentina, 30, 131, 175, 196
Arredondo, Hernan, 64(table), 178
Asentados, 35. See also Labor
Asociacion de Caneros de

237

Cuatro Ojitos, 95
Asociacion de Productores de Algodon, 191
Assimilation, 6
Ayni, 80. See also Labor, exchange

BAB. See Bolivian Agricultural Bank
Badini Merlin, Lina, 186
Banana production, 102, 127-128
Banco Agricola, 152(figure), 153(table)
Banco Hipotecario, 152(figure), 153(table)
BankAmerica, 48, 52
Banking system, 52
Bank of Boston, 48
Bank of Brazil, 40, 52
Banzer, Hugo, 50, 51, 53, 57, 58, 97, 141, 161, 177, 178, 184, 185, 186, 188, 196, 199
Barbie, Klaus, 189, 200
Barrientos, Rene, 45-46, 92, 96
Bascope, A., 191
Beef production, 3, 23, 49, 50-51, 53, 56(table), 61, 141, 153(table), 164-165, 182, 183
Beni, 26, 32, 53, 55(table), 218
Bernal, Waldo, 198, 199
Betanzos, Ignacio, 148, 149, 151, 155, 165, 166, 202, 207, 209, 210, 211
Bleyer, Pedro, 190
Bohan Plan, 37-38, 39-41 (table)
Bolivian Agricultural Bank (BAB), 52, 53, 56 (table), 57, 140
Bolivian Communist Party (PCB), 189
Bolivian Land and Cattle Co., 61
Bolivian Land and Forestry Co., 61
Bourgeoisie, 144-145, 173-194, 213, 218-219
cocaine and, 184
cultural responsibilities, 222
unrest among, 197
See also Agriculture, small-scale; Class, formation; Merchants
Brazil, 27, 30, 38, 42, 175, 183, 192
Bread for the World, 152 (figure), 153(table), 164, 170
Brigadas Agrarias Moviles, 57
Busch, German, 30

Cacao, 54(table)
Camara Agropecuaria del Oriente (CAO), 49-50, 141, 175
Campesinos, 34
Canadian International Development Agency, 152 (figure), 153(table)
Candia, Rigoberto, 175
CAO. See Camara Agropecuaria del Oriente
Capital accumulation, 11, 124, 125, 131-132, 135, 138, 174-179
Capitalism, 74, 217. See also Agriculture, commercialization
CARITAS, 208-209
Carter, Jimmy, 188, 196
Casa Bernardo, 34
Casa Elsner, 27, 28, 34
Casa Schweitzer, 27, 28, 34
Casa Zeller, 27-28, 34
Cash crops. See Agriculture
Cassava production, 102, 127-128

Cattle ranching, 3, 23, 49, 50-51, 53, 56(table), 61, 141, 153(table), 164-165, 182, 183
Cayoja, Humberto, 199
CCAM. See Central de Cooperativas Agropecuarias Mineros
Central de Cooperativas Agropecuarias Mineros (CCAM), 147-148, 150-154, 157-158, 159, 161, 165, 166, 167, 169-171, 210-212, 221-222
Central Obrera Boliviana (COB), 31, 96, 199
Chaco War, 29-30
Chagas disease, 155
Chamber of Commerce and Industry, 179, 190
Chane, 24
Chapare, 3
Chavez, Lorgio, 40(table)
Children, 10, 102, 115, 212
Chile, 25, 29, 38
China, 27
Chiquitano Indians, 78
Chiriguano Indians, 66, 85
Chuquisaca, 55(table), 218
Citibank, 48, 52, 53, 57
Citrus fruits, 102
Civil unrest, 96-97, 197-199, 206-208, 219, 223
Clark, R. J., 3
Class
  conflict, 116-117, 119, 179-180, 216
  formation, 5, 17, 85, 91-92, 94, 115, 119, 158, 173, 177-178, 179, 218, 219, 223
  mobility, 163, 169. See also Agriculture, small-scale
  transformation, 148
Climate, 19, 202
COB. See Central Obrera Boliviana
Cocaine, 4, 13, 17, 24, 114, 168, 173, 183-193, 193-194(n4), 194(n5), 197, 200, 202-205, 219, 222
Cochabamba, 55(table), 85
Coffee, 25
Colombia, 186, 192, 203, 214(n4)
Colonization, 2-5, 24-25, 36, 38, 40(table), 42, 62, 65, 68-69, 70-71, 73, 75-87, 91-94, 95-98, 104-106, 109-119, 131-145, 173, 217-218
Comite Ad-Hoc de Trabajadores de Cana, 168
Commerce, 1, 25-26, 123-124, 129-131, 138
Commodification, 94, 124-125, 130. See also Agriculture, commercialization
Community, 6-7, 90-92, 98, 220
  institutions. See Cooperatives; Peasantry, organizations; Syndicates
  stores, 211
  structure, 10, 158-160, 162-163, 167, 169, 171-172(n2)
Compadrazgo, 79, 127
Confederacion Sindical Unica de Trabajadores Campesinos Bolivianos (CSUTCB), 201
Consolidaciones, 58
Contraband, 175, 176
Contratistas, 27, 35, 67-68, 69, 106, 110, 180
Cooperatives, 16-17, 139, 140, 141, 147-172, 210-211
  community structure and, 158-160, 162-163, 167, 169, 171-172(n2)

formation of, 148-155
leadership, 161-162, 168
services, 154, 155, 160, 163, 170, 171, 222
structure of, 151, 152 (figure), 163, 168
See also Central de Cooperativas Agropecuarias Mineros
CORDECRUZ. See Corporacion Regional de Desarrollo de Santa Cruz
Corn, 53, 54(table), 56 (table), 100, 101(table), 102, 122, 123
Corporacion Regional de Desarrollo de Santa Cruz (CORDECRUZ), 45, 152 (figure), 153(table)
Corregidores, 85, 160
Cotton, 3, 23, 48, 50, 51, 53, 56(table), 61, 66, 69, 122, 141, 181, 216
Cotton Import and Export Corporation, 181
Credit, 48, 51-57, 83, 84, 138, 139-140, 153(table), 154, 157-158, 163-164, 180, 181, 216, 221
Crisis, 181-183, 193, 195, 201, 205-209, 212-213, 222-223
Cruz 6 de Agosto, La, 76, 93, 104, 111
CSUTCB. See Confederacion Sindical Unica de Trabajadores Campesinos Bolivianos
Cuba, 27
Culture, defined, 6

Dairy farms, 54(table)
Debt, 68, 102, 106, 107, 108, 125-126, 157-158, 219
Democracy, 195, 201, 213, 223
Departmental Federation of Private Entrepreneurs, 179
Dependency theory, 7-8
Development organizations, 52, 95, 138-139, 147, 149, 164, 166, 218
Dotaciones, 57, 58
Drug trafficking. See Cocaine; Marijuana

Education, 153(table), 170
Empresa Nacional de Arroz (ENA), 126-127
ENA. See Empresa Nacional de Arroz
Entrepreneurs. See Agriculture, small-scale; Bourgeoisie; Merchants
Environment, 156
Ethnicity, 85. See also Indians
Ethnic relations, 44, 115-117, 119
Extension services, 40(table)

Falange Socialista Boliviana (FSB), 179, 189, 198
Families, 111, 113. See also Compadrazgo; Households; Kinship
Federacion de Campesinos Caneros y Productores Agricolas, 123
Federacion de Caneros de Santa Cruz, 49
Federacion de Colonizadores, 96, 188, 201, 207, 221
Federacion Especial de las Cuatro Provincias del Norte, 95-96, 201, 207
Federacion Nacional de Colonizadores. See Federacion de Colonizadores
Federacion Nacional de Cooperativas Arroceras (FENCA), 141, 201

Federacion Sindical de Cosechadores de Algodon, 168
Federacion Sindical de Trabajadores Zafreros de Bolivia (FSTZB), 206
FENCA. See Federacion Nacional de Cooperativas Arroceras
Food imports, 31
Foreign aid. See Development organizations; United States, aid from
Foreign capital, 36-43, 47. See also United States, aid from
Foreign colonies, 42-43
Franciscans, 46(n1)
Frank, A. G., 8
Frontier settlement. See Colonization
FSB. See Falange Socialista Boliviana
FSTZB. See Federacion Sindical de Trabajadores Zafreros de Bolivia

Garcia Meza, Luis, 24, 185, 186, 189, 190, 191, 193, 195, 196, 197, 198, 199, 200, 213(n3)
"Geneva Agreement," 182
Godoy, Juan, 174
Government policies. See Agrarian reform; Import-substitution
Great Britain, 150, 216
Green, M., 3
Green peppers, 54(table)
Growth, 174-180
Guabira sugarmill, 23, 37, 39(table)
Guarani, 24
Guarayo Indians, 78, 85
Guarayo mission, 46(n1)
Gueiler, Lidia, 188
Guevara, Che, 139, 193(n2)

Guevara Arce, Walter, 185

Hacendados, 48
Hansa organization, 34
Hansen, Gene, 175
Holmberg, A., 75
Households, 17-18(n1)
  economy of, 103-104, 118, 119, 158
  subsistence requirements, 126, 162-163, 169-170

IAS. See Inter-American Agricultural Service
Import-export houses, 27-29, 33-34, 75
Import-substitution, 31, 58
INC. See Instituto Nacional de Colonizacion
Indebtedness, 68, 102, 106, 107, 108, 125-126, 157-158, 219
Indians, 34, 44, 66, 71(n1), 78, 85. See also individual groups
Industrial sector, 38
Inflation, 202, 205, 209, 223
Infrastructure, 22(figure), 23, 25, 27, 28, 29, 30, 37, 41(table), 47, 49, 74, 84-85, 94, 124, 220
Inheritance claims, 112, 113
Instituto Nacional de Colonizacion (INC), 58, 95, 97, 208
Inter-American Agricultural Service (IAS), 33
Inter-American Development Bank, 45, 52, 152(figure), 153(table)
Inter-American Foundation, 152(figure), 153(table)
Intermediaries, 83, 92, 94, 99, 106, 124-125, 126, 127-128, 131, 154. See also Merchants
International aid. See

Development organizations; United States, aid from Israel, 196

Jamaica, 214(n4)
Jesuits, 25
Junta Rural del Norte, 29, 175-176

Kinship, 75, 80, 89, 110, 113, 115, 162, 192. See also Compadrazgo; Families

La Belgica sugarmill, 39 (table), 49
Labor, 1, 3, 9-10, 16, 34-35, 48-49, 61, 65-68, 70, 71(n3), 80, 81
  commodification of, 125. See also Proletarianization
  contractors, 27, 35, 67-68, 69, 106, 110, 180
  costs, 100-104
  domestic, 9-10, 78, 102, 113. See also Kinship
  exchange, 80, 81, 110
  migrant, 2, 3, 47, 66-68, 73-74, 84, 121, 182, 201, 216. See also Migrants
  organization, 8-9, 30. See also Cooperatives; Peasantry, organizations; Syndicates
  productivity, 180
  shortages, 34, 48, 65-66, 68, 69, 128, 180
  wage, 4-5, 9, 10, 11, 12, 35, 47, 64, 65, 66, 69, 81, 83-84, 87-89, 102-103, 104-110, 113, 116, 118, 119, 132, 154, 158, 167-168, 169, 202, 205, 215, 220. See also

Proletarianization
La Esperanza sugarmill, 39 (table), 49
Laguna, Hector, 40(table)
Land
  acquisition, 74, 76, 78, 86, 175
  as commodity, 94
  disputes, 57, 62-63, 75-76, 78, 111, 113
  distribution, 57-58, 96
  grants, 3, 12, 42-43, 57, 60(table), 61, 78, 177
  invasions, 207, 208, 221, 223
  syndicate, 112(figure)
  tenure, 33
  See also Tenancy agriculture
Landivar, Felix, 161
Lanza, Emilio, 199
La Paz, 55(table), 66
Latifundists, 32, 75, 76, 175, 218. See also Agriculture, large-scale
Lenin, V. I., 4
Ley de Tierras Baldias, 26
Limpias, Orlando, 64(table)
Livestock. See Beef production; Dairy farms; Pigs; Poultry
Lumbering, 33, 40(table), 74, 75, 78, 106

Mahogany. See Lumbering
Malky Salomon, Julio, 186
Mamani, Eusebio, 149-150, 159
Mamani, Pedro, 149-150, 159
Marijuana, 214(n4)
Marketing, 54(table), 126, 130, 181
Marriage, 111, 113, 119(n1)
Marx, Karl, 9, 14
Mechanization, 40(table), 54(table), 100, 155-158, 171(n1), 180. See also Technology

Mendoza, Manuel Jesus, 176
Mennonites, 171(n1)
Merchants, 122, 124-125, 129-130, 131, 211-212. See also Bourgeoisie; Intermediaries
Middlemen. See Intermediaries; Merchants
Migrants, 2, 3, 47, 66-68, 73-74, 84, 85-87, 89, 91, 95, 113-119, 122, 124, 131-145 See also Labor, migrant
Military rule, 16, 45-46, 50, 51, 220, 222
  class formation and, 177-178, 179, 219
  cocaine traffic and, 173, 184, 188, 190-193, 198, 200
  corruption of, 198
  development under, 71
  fall of, 196-199, 222
  peasants and, 90, 92-93
  repression under, 189
Mining sector, 25, 26, 30, 31, 117
Ministry of Agriculture, 140
Minka, 80. See also Labor, exchange
Mintz, S. W., 6, 7
MIR. See Movement of the Revolutionary Left
Misin and Company, 181
Mitsubishi Corporation, 181
MNR. See Movimiento Nacional Revolucionario
MNRI. See National Revolutionary Movement of the Left
Modernization, 218-219. See also Technology
Modernization theory, 6
Monetization, 81, 91. See also Commodification
Moneylenders, 83, 92, 125. See also Credit

Monopolization, 215. See also Agriculture, large-scale
Movement of National Dignity, 199
Movement of the Revolutionary Left (MIR), 189
Movimiento Nacional Revolucionario (MNR), 31-35, 70, 76, 91, 92, 190
  bourgeoisie and, 173
  development programs, 37-42, 45
  factionalism of, 45
  import-substitution program, 31, 58
  support for, 34
  U.S. relations, 37, 43
Muyurina Agricultural School, 40(table)

National revolution, 1, 24, 30-31, 48, 51, 52, 65, 76, 179
National Revolutionary Movement of the Left (MNRI), 189
National Sugar Commission, 39(table)
Natusch Busch, Alberto, 199
Nino, El, 202, 206
Nuflo de Chavez, 24
Nunez brothers, 176

Ocampo, Aldo, 178
Ocampo family, 177-178
Occidental Petroleum, 198
Oil
  crisis, 180
  prices, 51
  production, 24
OPEC. See Organization of Petroleum Exporting Countries
Organization of Petroleum Exporting Countries (OPEC), 51

Oriente, 32, 33, 37, 43, 218
Oruro, 55(table), 66

Pacific War, 25, 38
Pacto Militar-Campesino, 92-93, 149, 188, 220
Paglial, Pier Luigi, 200
Panama, 175
Pando, 55(table)
Paraguay, 29-30, 42
Patrons, 162-163. See also Tenancy agriculture
Paz Hermanos, 33
Paz, Jose, 190
Paz, Roberto, 33
Paz, Rosendo, 33
PCB. See Bolivian Communist Party
Peanuts, 54(table)
Peasantry, 9-13
  agricultural expansion and, 61-71, 74, 76-81, 83, 88-89, 96-98, 104-119
  defined, 9
  income strategies, 10, 11, 81-89, 90, 102, 114-115, 118, 125, 158, 167, 215, 216, 220. See also Labor, wage
  MNR and, 38, 42, 76, 91, 92
  organizations, 16, 17, 96, 139, 140-141, 168-169, 188-189, 195-196, 201, 206, 213, 218, 220, 223. See also Cooperatives; Syndicates
  resettlement of, 38, 40(table), 217-218. See also Colonization; Migrants
  work relations, 34-35
  See also Agriculture, subsistence; Labor
Pereda Asbun, Juan, 188
Perseverancia, 184

Peru, 26, 29
Pessoa, Hugo, 179
Petroleum. See Oil
Pigs, 54(table)
Pineapples, 54(table)
Planning, 181
Point Four program, 37-38, 177
Population, 23, 24
Portugal, Martha, 64(table)
Potatoes, 54(table)
Potosi, 55(table), 66
Poultry, 54(table)
Presencia, 69
Pricing, 100, 126, 127, 223
Private property, 90-91
Privatization, 173
Producers' associations, 140-141, 179, 191
Production, 156
  costs, 100-104, 122-123, 181
  quotas, 123. See also Sugarcane, quotas
  social relationships of, 8-9
Proletarianization, 5, 11-12, 13, 65, 81, 83-89, 96, 99-119, 158-160, 180, 208, 213, 215-216, 217, 220-221, 223. See also Labor, wage
PROMIGRA, 73, 69-70, 180
Pro-Santa Cruz Committee, 44-45, 116, 179, 197, 198

Racism, 44. See also Ethnic relations
Railroads. See Infrastructure
Ralli Brothers and Company, 181
Razuk, Miguel, 186
Razuk, Widen, 184-185, 186
Reagan, Ronald, 196
Reciprocity, 162, 163, 169, 222
Redfield, R., 6

Redistribution, 162, 163, 169, 179-180, 218, 222
Reducciones, 25
Rescatistas de cana, 130
Revolution. See National revolution
Rice, 23, 25, 26, 48, 50, 53, 54(table), 56(table), 81, 100, 102, 122-123, 125-127, 130, 131
  marketing, 126, 130, 153 (table)
  pricing, 126, 127
  producers' associations, 141
  U.S. aid and, 39-40(table)
Riester, B., 3
Riviere d'Arc, H., 3
Rodriguez, Julio, 148, 202, 209
Roseberry, W., 7
Rubber, 26-27, 75
Rumy Ltda., 198

Saavedra Experimental Station, 40(table)
San Aurelio sugarmill, 39(table), 49
Sanchez, Jose, 174
Sanchez, Ltda., 174-175
Sandoval Moron, Luis, 43-44
Santa Cruz, 4, 5, 21(figure), 218
  climate, 19
  demographics, 117-118
  geography, 19, 23
Schweitzer, Erwin, 176-177, 190
Schweitzer, Roberto, 190
Schweitzer family, 27, 28, 34, 176-177, 190
Settlement programs. See Colonization
Siles, Luis Adolfo, 199
Siles Suazo, Hernan, 189, 190, 195, 199-200, 203
Siriono Indians, 75

Social change, 5-8
Social differentiation, 220. See also Class, formation; Community, structure
Sociedad Agricola Ganadera Perseverancia, 185
Sociedad de Estudios Geograficos e Historicos de Santa Cruz, 29
Soleto, Lorenzo, 63, 64 (table), 106, 107, 109, 110
Soleto family, 176
South Africa, 196
Soy beans, 23, 50, 53, 54 (table), 56(table), 182
Spaniards, 24-25
Special Fund for Economic Development, 52-53
Speculation, 205
Steffan, Jack, 39(table)
Steward, J., 6
Suarez, Abelardo, 179
Suarez, Roberto, 200
Suarez Gomez, Roberto, 191
Sugarcane, 23, 48, 49, 50, 51, 53, 56(table), 61, 66, 89-90, 91, 95, 107-109, 122-123, 131, 216
  crisis and, 181-182
  introduction of, 1, 3, 24, 94
  marketing, 130
  prices, 182
  producers' associations, 140-141
  production costs, 123
  quotas, 128-129, 130, 154, 182
  small producers, 123
  U.S. aid and, 39(table)
Surazos, 19
Syndicates, 76-79, 85, 86, 90-94, 97, 98, 147, 148-149, 160-161, 170, 188, 195, 207, 222, 223. See

245

also Peasantry, organizations

Tarija, 55(table)
Technology, 180, 212, 216. See also Mechanization
Telchi, Abraham, 179
Tenancy agriculture, 86, 94, 103, 110, 118, 168
Third World, 5-6
Timber. See Lumbering
Tin, 25, 30, 31. See also Mining sector
Tomatoes, 54(table)
Torrelio, Celso, 199, 202
Trade. See Agriculture, export-oriented; Commerce
Transportation, 41(table), 128-129, 154, 155, 209-210. See also Infrastructure

UCAPO. See Union de Campesinos Pobres
UDP. See Unidad Democratica Popular
UNAGRO. See Union Agroindustrial de Caneros
UNAGRO mill, 153(table)
Unidad Democratica Popular (UDP), 189, 190, 199
Union Agroindustrial de Caneros (UNAGRO), 23, 63, 153(table)
Union de Campesinos Pobres (UCAPO), 96, 186, 207, 221
United States, 192, 214(n4)
  Agency for International Development (USAID), 37, 45, 52, 95, 139
  aid from, 36-38, 39-41 (table), 43, 52, 70, 175, 177, 185, 218
  aid suspension, 196
  cocaine industry and, 202-203
  cocaine traffic to, 187
  coups and, 45
  development programs, 173
  Drug Enforcement Agency, 190
  economic expansion, 5, 7
Upward mobility, 163, 169
Urbanization, 44, 47, 102, 114, 217
USAID. See United States, Agency for International Development
Usufruct rights. See Tenancy agriculture

Vaca Diez, Mario Quintela, 185-186
Valverde, Juan Carlos, 179
Valverde Barbery, Carlos, 198
Vega, Juan, 132-135, 141-143, 148, 149, 164, 202, 209
Vegetables, 54(table), 102
Venezuela, 192
Vietnam War, 139
Vildoso, Guido, 199
Villa, Segundino, 135-138, 141, 143-144, 150, 209, 210, 212

Wallerstein, I., 8
War of the Pacific, 25, 38
Weissman, Marvin, 189, 196
West Germany, 45
Wheat, 54(table)
Wiggens, S., 3
Wolf, E. R., 6, 7, 8-9
Women, 9, 10, 78, 85, 102, 105, 113, 208-209
Working conditions, 104-110, 167-168
World Bank, 52